The Authentic Voice

The
Authentic
Voice

The Best Reporting on Race and Ethnicity

EDITED BY

Arlene Notoro Morgan,

Alice Irene Pifer,

and Keith Woods

Columbia University Press / New York

Columbia University Press
Publishers Since 1893
New York   Chichester, West Sussex

Funded by the Ford Foundation, the W. K. Kellogg Foundation, and
the McCormick-Tribune Foundation

Sponsored by the Columbia University Graduate School of Journalism

Library of Congress Cataloging-in-Publication Data

The authentic voice : the best reporting on race and ethnicity / edited by
Arlene Notoro Morgan, Alice Irene Pifer, and Keith Woods.
p. cm.
Outgrowth of the "Let's do it better!" workshop series, held at Columbia
University Graduate School of Journalism since 1999.
Includes bibliographical references and index.
ISBN 0–231–13288–3 (cloth : alk. paper)—ISBN 0–231–13289-1 (pbk. : alk. paper)
1. Race relations—Press coverage—United States.   2. Ethnic relations
—Press coverage—United States.   3. Minorities—Press coverage
—United States.   I. Morgan, Arlene Notoro.   II. Pifer, Alice Irene.   III. Woods,
Keith, 1958– .
PN4888.R3A98 2006
070.4′493058—dc22
2005036398

Printed in the United States of America

c 10 9 8 7 6 5 4 3 2 1
p 10 9 8 7 6 5 4 3 2 1

Arlene Notoro Morgan

> *To David Morgan, my life partner, helpmate, and best friend. To my daughters, Elizabeth and Lauren, for teaching me about life. To my life-long friend and mentor, Acel Moore, for leading the way. Above all, to my mother Mary Notoro, for her inspiration and support.*

Alice Irene Pifer

> *To Mike Talley and Lisa Redd, who helped change forever the way I see race. To Barb Gilin, who has been with me confronting the lies of racism since the very early days. To Sister Serena and Sister Corrine, who were the first to show me another way of being a white person. And to the members of my family, who have loved me as I've changed.*

Keith Woods

> *To my wife, Denise, and our family: Danielle, Keith Jr., Andrea, Matthew, and Noah. They deserve a world where we get race right. And to my late parents, Verdun P. Woods Sr. and Bernice Q. Woods, who raised me to make such a claim.*

CONTENTS

PART I: THE SEARCH FOR IDENTITY

CHAPTER 1

CHAPTER 2

CHAPTER 3

PART IV: CULTURAL COMPETENCE

FOREWORD

"See me, feel me, touch me . . ." This touching plea, from The Who's rock opera *Tommy*, rings with the universal longing to be understood, appreciated, and respected. It's a common denominator that cuts across age, culture, race, and gender.

Think about yourself. What do you want from others? To be seen for who you are? To be acknowledged? To be valued? In some cases, even to be loved? Inspiring those responses gives people a sense of self-worth, both as individuals and as groups.

Not coincidentally, these responses are the key to building bridges between journalists and their readers or viewers.

As the United States becomes more diverse, being able to see, feel, and touch its changing communities will require new skills and sensibilities from journalists. They'll need to be able to see the world through the lenses of cultures that may be foreign to them. They'll be called on to interpret news events not only from the standpoint of their worldviews but through the perspectives of others. And they'll be expected to understand that, in a changing America, there are no "others" anymore. These new ways of thinking should challenge and change our storytelling—because if they don't, we will drift away in a haze of irrelevance. Multicultural flexibility must become the new norm.

Fortunately, these skills are learnable—and teachable. That's why this book matters so much. It gathers an unprecedented set of stories with real-life lessons for journalists in training.

The lessons—about journalism and about reporters and editors—are real, personal journeys. So you will not only learn about the reporting; you'll go behind the scenes to understand what fallible, earnest people learned on the path to understanding. Those lessons can make journalists more capable and competent in their craft.

At *The Mercury News*, we underwent a transformation over the past decade, learning to diversify our staff and to change our content to see our community true and whole. We went a long way—and there's a long way to go.

We came to understand why it's important to have a voice that authentically reflects readers or viewers: It's a question of accuracy. All journalists want their work to be viewed as accurate. There's little argument there. Just in terms of common sense, this premise holds tremendous power. And in order for our news reports to be fundamentally accurate, we must reflect the entire community. Because if, over time, our news pages or broadcasts represent only narrow segments of the community, how can we consider our work to be an accurate depiction of the places where we live? When, for example, we visit certain communities only to report about crime and violence, we end up presenting a distorted picture and not a reflection of reality.

In the early nineties, a group of Latino leaders angrily denounced a series we ran on wannabe gangbangers. They complained that we only saw their community when trouble was brewing. And you know what? They were right. We hadn't reported regularly on that community's deep religious faith, on its steamy cuisine, on its mostly rotten schools and its devoted teachers, on its issues with a white-dominated immigration bureaucracy, or on its role models, many of whom had overcome poverty and were now showing others the path to success. In other words, we hadn't developed a context for our criticism. Without it, we were presenting a skewed view of their world. Moreover, we were causing them pain and undermining our reputation.

There's another reason for creating the biggest tent possible, so that everyone in our communities can fit inside. The Bill of Rights charges us with watching over the powerful on behalf of everyday people. That mandate to pursue social justice applies to all, not some, of our community. We're here to serve—and see—broadly.

When people see their lives or people like themselves in our journalism, they're more likely to believe we're credible or, in other words, authentic. The best test of that claim is a simple gut check. I once joked with a mostly middle-aged male, mostly white group of Rotarians while explaining the importance of diversity: "Imagine we deliver a newspaper to your home every day. It has no sports section, no business news, nothing about prostate cancer or the Republican Party: why would you want to read that paper?" Now, imagine parts of your community that you don't see often in your hometown newspaper or local television broadcasts. Why should those folks invest the time or energy to read or watch, let alone to view the media as authentic storytellers?

On the occasions when we do see the influence of cultural perspectives, we can open windows of truth. An Asian American developer recently broke off settlement negotiations with the city of San Jose after winning a lawsuit, a move that ultimately cost the city millions of dollars. I asked him if it was because the city treated him badly, causing him to "lose face." "Absolutely," he said.

Another instance: a sportswriter discovered that a high school in a largely Asian community near San Jose could no longer field a varsity football team because that's just not a sport that many Asian American students play. But the tennis and badminton teams were hell on wheels. Those revelations captured a changing America in a powerful way.

Sometimes cultural understanding is important in keeping stories out of the paper or off the air. When the number of homicides in nearby Oakland reached triple digits for the first time in several years, editors gathered to talk about how to approach a story on the rising violence. The discussion quickly turned to what several editors called "black-on-black crime" because, they pointed out, many of the victims and assailants were African American. A Latina assistant city editor objected, along with an African American photo editor. They argued that the real story was not about race. It was about people killing people. Had this rising violence happened in an affluent, predominantly white city, would we be calling it "white-on-white" crime? The answer was a resounding no. The story that ultimately made it into the paper explored how young Oakland residents who live in the toughest neighborhoods were coping with the rising violence.

This book has stories about people living side by side and worlds apart. It offers tips about how to work a beat in 360 degrees—developing sources up and down the power ladder and deep into communities.

What this book won't do is preach political correctness. In fact, it'll urge you to take on the difficult perceptions and differences that define people. But it will help you take on those issues with an understanding of the complexity of race and the rich mix of backgrounds that make up America today.

When you finish this book, you'll just be starting, because learning to report on the new America will provide revelation after revelation. As you grow in your sophistication and multicultural understanding, your audience will validate your work as you draw them into your storytelling.

David Yarnold
former editor, *The Mercury News* (San Jose, Calif.)
and founder of the APME/ASNE Time Out for Diversity Program

PREFACE

A discerning journalist might wonder what's so different about reporting on race and ethnicity that someone would dedicate a book, DVD and a website to the subject. To earn the mark of excellence, after all, stories have to meet the same high standards, no matter what the topic. They should offer a compelling tale that flows from deep reporting. They should be packed with relevance, rich in detail, flush with meaningful facts.

The stories in this book easily meet those demands. They also have in common three other traits of first-class journalism: They provide the sort of context that enhances understanding and increases accuracy. They come alive with the three-dimensional voices of ordinary people. Finally, they embrace the complexity that makes human relations interesting.

These traits emerged as vital a few years ago when we set out to determine what was unique about this kind of reporting. And while all journalism should aspire to the combined completeness described above, we learned something by studying the best stories about race and ethnicity entered in the *Let's Do It Better!* workshop at the Columbia University Graduate School of Journalism. We found that the most successful reporting about race and ethnicity delivered solid, fundamental journalism and fused voice, context, and complexity into one authentic piece.

To do that, the journalists honored through the years at Columbia and featured in this book had to surmount the ignorance, fear, and rampant clichés that uniquely sabotage reporting about race relations and cultural difference. They demonstrate that, done well, these stories can transform fear and ignorance into curiosity; turn cliché-laden frames into opportunities for surprise and discovery.

Journalism students and professionals alike can use these case studies to figure out how to access unfamiliar cultures or get people to talk about one of society's most taboo topics. In interviews and essays, reporters, producers, and editors explain how to fine-tune language, substituting precision for euphemism. They educate, provoke, and validate old reporting techniques and introduce new ones. In fact, the stories, interviews, and Web links are themselves a collective history lesson that will benefit readers of this text whether or not they aspire to a career in journalism.

Since the attacks of September 11, 2001, journalists have been doubly challenged to forge reports that are honest and clear about the obstacles faced by new immigrants as well as under-covered groups that have been here for generations. This project represents a compilation of work that we believe will foster important conversations in the classroom and newsroom, enrich the learning experience, and inform professional development. Waiting in these pages, for example, is a look at the shifting demographics of the Midwest, which saw a huge influx of Somalis in Minnesota, and the unfolding stories of Latino and Asian immigration in New Jersey, Washington, D.C., and Atlanta. And while there are stunning history lessons to be found in stories about land stolen from black people or the federal government's gross mismanagement of money in Indian Country, those stories are also strong examples of investigative reporting.

We've divided the work into four categories—identity, equality, untold stories, and cultural competence—that reflect the way news organizations tend to frame coverage. Each section offers three or four stories, along with a how-to essay by the producers, reporters, or editors who presented the work at the Columbia workshop. We've added a list of discussion points for each chapter, along with research links and suggested readings. The DVD offers the entire broadcast piece, interviews with the journalists that expand their essays, and additional discussion questions pitched to those interviews. A detailed DVD index directs the user to discussions of specific topics such as ethics and handling stereotypes. The accompanying Website—*www.theauthenticvoice.org*— provides additional material, such as the remaining parts of series that begin in the book, links to other pertinent Websites, a teacher's guide, an assortment of other honored stories that supplement the DVD and text, and blog space to continue the conversation beyond the formal classroom discussion. From time to time, we will update the Website with new stories to create a living resource for teachers and students interested in finding fresh material that celebrates the profession's best work.

Anyone who's ever offered a story up for praise knows that the act invariably invites criticism. Pulitzer Prizes administrator Sig Gissler, who founded the *Let's Do It Better!* workshop, once summed up the challenge of honoring good work this way: "If you want to paint a bull's eye on any piece of journalism, just call it excellent." Prizes do not guarantee perfection. The beauty of the stories chosen for this book is that each can teach powerfully through excellence as well as through the occasional flaw. Use the stories, then, not just to provide guidance on craft but also to promote critical thinking. That, after all, may be the greatest skill journalists can learn as they take on what is certainly one of society's toughest topics, borrowing from the wisdom of those who did it better.

How to Use This Book/DVD/Website

The Authentic Voice package works equally well in a traditional classroom setting, with small discussion groups, or for individual, self-directed learning. Each section is designed to provide a number of entry points to stories. The textbook chapters mimic a newspaper layout, with photographs, sidebars, graphic elements, and icons that point you to the connecting parts in the DVD and the project's Website, *www.theauthenticvoice.org.* Series, such as *Torn from the Land* or *Rim of the New World,* start in the text and continue on the Website. The best way to explain how to use the package is to take you through two chapters: *Tug of War* and *The Color Line and the Bus Line.*

The *Tug of War* chapter in this volume contains the story and photographs that appeared in the *Star Tribune* of Minneapolis. The text also includes a deconstruction essay, written by reporter Allie Shah on how she and photographer Rita Reed created the piece. The chapter concludes with discussion points, suggested readings, and references to Websites for enhancing learning about Somali culture and the Islamic faith. On the DVD, you'll find an interview with Shah that explores further this journalist's thinking and decision-making processes, followed by more discussion questions.

As with every chapter in the book, journalists, educators, diversity trainers, and even community leaders can use the story to explore everything from storytelling structures—Shah uses narrative to great effect—to strategies for respecting and reporting through cultural roadblocks. In *Tug of War,* for example, matters of modesty were so significant for the two Somali girls that Shah and Reed had to negotiate for facts and photographs. Their decisions should both inform and provoke users of the book, DVD, and Website. Discussion leaders can click on the discussion points on the DVD to return quickly to critical sections of the interview.

The story of *The Color Line and the Bus Line* appears on the DVD, while the book reprints the script and presents background essays. The deconstruction, written by ABC *Nightline* producer/editor Eric Wray, discusses how heavily race factored in the story's development from start to finish. Tom Bettag, *Nightline*'s former executive producer, adds an explanation on the goals of the *America, in Black and White* series.

The DVD interview features former *Nightline* anchor Ted Koppel and Wray. Users of the DVD can move in a click of the mouse or remote control to the broadcast or the interview that's up for discussion. One of the critical issues of that story, for example, is how Wray, a black man, convinced Koppel, a white man and Wray's boss, to see the value of reporting on the incident, which initially seemed like a routine accident to Koppel.

Relevant to all the chapters is the index section on the DVD that, with a click, links users to discussions of a number of issues that consistently come up when reporting on matters of race and ethnicity. Those issues include:

- How to get people to talk frankly about race and ethnicity
- How to handle racial and ethnic identification
- How to write stories about racial and ethnic perceptions that illuminate and inform
- The role a journalist's race and ethnicity plays in decision making

Users of *The Authentic Voice* can discuss the stories individually, deal with topical issues like those listed above, or do both.

We developed the DVD interviews and discussion points to animate, celebrate, and scrutinize the ideas, sources, and word choices of the journalists. At times, we challenged those choices and revealed holes in the logic or knowledge of the journalists we interviewed. Mostly, though, we were awed by the beauty of their craft, the breadth of their understanding, and the depth of their conviction. As you use this project, ask the questions we asked: Are the stories authentic? Do they communicate voice, context, and complexity, the essential elements of strong storytelling about race and ethnicity? Do they tackle the complicated issues that stories about race and ethnicity so often neglect to cover?

One educator described our project as "showing ourselves to ourselves." We've worked hard to place before you strong stories and interviews that suggest new ways of thinking about powerful storytelling. But we've avoided telling you what to think. That's your job. That's your journey. We hope you'll find it as fascinating as we did.

Many of the newspapers from which we reprint stories follow Associated Press style or use other style guidelines. Columbia University Press follows The Chicago Manual of Style. *The result is that there are some unavoidable inconsistencies both among the newspaper stories and between the stories and the material that is original to this book.*

SYMBOLS USED IN THIS BOOK

 DVD: This symbol indicates a reference to the companion DVD.

 WEB PAGE: This symbol indicates a reference to the web address www.theauthenticvoice.org

 DISCUSSION POINT: This symbol indicates a discussion point related to the story.

 RESEARCH: This symbol indicates a research source.

The Authentic Voice

PART I

The Search for Identity

- *Tug of War, Star Tribune, Minneapolis*

- *About Race Series, KRON-TV, San Francisco*

- *Best of Friends, Worlds Apart, The New York Times*

- *The Family Secret, ABC News, 20/20*

CHAPTER 1

STORY

TUG OF WAR

ALLIE SHAH, *STAR TRIBUNE*

ALLIE SHAH

Allie Shah is a reporter at the *Star Tribune,* Minnesota's largest newspaper. Before joining the newspaper in 1997, she worked as a correspondent for *The Philadelphia Inquirer* and as an intern for The *Chicago Tribune*.

Shah is a native of Des Moines, Iowa and a graduate of the University of Minnesota's School of Journalism and Mass Communications. She is passionate about writing, traveling and finding good Indian food.

Tug of War

Reporter Allie Shah and photographer Rita Reed of the *Star Tribune* in Minneapolis had to win a tug-of-war of their own to tell the story of cultures in conflict that bore that title. For them, the struggle was between telling a more traditional, often voyeuristic story of newcomers, and recounting the universal and complex story of fitting in, the challenge faced by the piece's main characters.

The team told a tale of Somali teenage girls beset with all the challenges of their age—boys, parents, makeup—while they try to reconcile their conservative cultural and religious mores with the more permissive society they found in the United States. The story that emerges, told gracefully in words and pictures, gives readers a chance to discover parts of themselves and their own stories in the lives of Nimco and Fartun. It is steeped in the respect and knowledge the *Star Tribune* team brings to bear on the reporting and writing as their sources unveil their lives in front of a newspaper audience. It also puts on display the collaborative skills that a writer and photographer must employ to create a unified piece that showcases their individual voices.

Readers of this chapter also can gain insight into the question of how much a reporter's background—Shah is Muslim—influences and informs the reporting process. In this chapter, Shah shows journalists how to write *from* a community rather than just *about* it, deftly educating readers about a culture and religion while giving other readers a fresh perspective on the challenges of assimilation.

Tug of War offers lessons in accurately framing a story, choosing strong characters to illustrate and drive the story, and using details not just to bring a story to life but, here, to show the difference between the universal struggle to fit in and the specific challenges of growing up Muslim and Somali in the United States.

SOMALI GIRLS COMING OF AGE ARE CAUGHT IN CULTURAL TUG OF WAR

By Allie Shah
Star Tribune Staff Writer
Published June 25, 2000

At gym time, teenage girls in the locker room strip off T-shirts and jeans and squeeze into tank tops and spandex shorts. But Fartun Nur, 17, peels off layers of shiny fabric that shield her from the outside world.

First goes the floor-length skirt. Then the long-sleeved shirt. She keeps the hijaab on, adjusting it to make sure it still hides her hair. Next, she slips on a knee-length tunic and billowy trousers and hustles to the "girls-only" gym class.

Nimco Ahmed, 18, strolls into the locker room, her headphones completing her western look. She trades her boot-cut jeans for track pants, not caring, as other Somali girls do, if they're too revealing. With one last look in the mirror, she trots to the co-ed gym class.

For Fartun (pronounced far-TOON) and Nimco, life is a daily test. Far from the civil war in their homeland, Somali girls confront a cultural war in a country so unlike their own.

America, with its melting pot, equal rights, and obsession with sex and youth, beckons them at every turn. These new values collide with traditional Somali values that call for clear roles for men and women, respect for authority and an identity based on family, not self.

Nowhere is this clash more visible than at Roosevelt High School in Minneapolis. Far from the days when Gov. Jesse Ventura and other working-class whites dominated the hallways, today's Roosevelt boasts the largest Somali student population in the city—and perhaps the nation.

Nearly a third of the 1,550 students enrolled at the start of the school year were Somali, in part because Roosevelt offers special language services.

Roosevelt, with its clangy school bell and yesteryear feel, is a haven for Somali girls. School is about the only place where they can roam free of their families' scrutiny.

Somali families expect the females to carry the culture and maintain the family honor. So while Fartun's brother can blend in with male classmates who wear the same baggy jeans and T-shirts, she stands out in her Somali clothes.

Sons may visit restaurants or hang out on the basketball courts, but daughters are expected to stay home, out of public view, protecting their modesty.

It's at school, in the hallways, classrooms and cafeteria, where Fartun and Nimco confront America. Mingling with kids from Iran, Vietnam, Mexico, Somalia and the United States, they navigate the currents of the American mainstream.

Nimco: Life in Two Worlds

Like a turtle, Nimco has learned how to live both in water and on land. At home and at Roosevelt.

In her mother's clothing and perfume store in Minneapolis' Phillips neighborhood, she speaks rapid-fire Somali, laughing and joking with her relatives. "Galab Wanaagsan. Seetahay?" (Good afternoon. How are you?) At school, she expertly shouts, "Whassup?" to friends from all nations. "I'm kinda international," she explains.

Rita Reed/Star Tribune/Minneapolis–St. Paul 2005
Nimco Ahmed takes advantage of some extra time to study for a test.

Armed with a cell phone and a Discman, she weaves through the halls, waving and smiling at people who call her by name. "I like this guy. He is funny as hell," she says, passing an Asian boy with frosted hair.

Spotting some Somali girls, she playfully charges into them. They push back and laugh, and she walks away, grinning. All the while walking and talking, she fishes a piece of gum from her purse and places it in a friend's outstretched hand.

But for the transparent scarf wrapped snugly around her hair, Nimco looks like other American students. Same Mudd jeans and platform shoes. Multiple earrings on each lobe. A giant blue hair claw to keep loose strands in place beneath her scarf. She loves American fashions.

When she first got to Roosevelt in 1998, after spending eight years in Germany, Nimco didn't wear the hijaab (pronounced HEE-job)— the Arabic word for "cover" used to describe the scarf Muslim women wear over their hair for modesty. The other kids saw her bare head and assumed she was Ethiopian.

"I started feeling bad," she said.

These days, she wears the hijaab, when she feels like it. She does it to let everyone know she's Somali, and so she can get used to the feel of the fabric tugging at her hairline, reminding her who she is, what she is. Somali. Muslim. Woman.

Someday, when she's married with children, she'll add another layer to her modesty, she says. She'll wear the jalaabiib (pronounced Jawl-a-beeb), the larger head covering that resembles a nun's habit. It's the one her mother and Fartun wear. By then, Nimco will stop wearing pants, too, she vows.

These changes she will make to set a good example for her kids and to raise them right in Islam, the Muslim religion. "I have a lot of respect for the religion," she says solemnly.

Which Rules to Follow?

Sitting in her bedroom, a pile of colorful scarves resting on her dresser next to a purple Minnesota Vikings cap, Nimco reflects on the challenge of living in two cultures. At school, she sidesteps the fistfights and verbal taunts that are common between Somali and American kids. "Some of them say, 'You smell bad,'" Nimco said. Some kids don't understand or flat out don't like Somali customs, such as washing hands and feet in the school bathrooms before praying.

To visit the Roosevelt cafeteria is to witness the cultural apartheid. Somali girls gather on one side of the room, apart from the Somali boys, the Asian kids, the whites and the African-Americans.

Immanuel Huggins, an African-American friend of Nimco's, counts Somali girls among his friends. "A lot of them are pretty," he said.

Rita Reed/Star Tribune/Minneapolis–St. Paul 2005
Nimco, far right, with her pants rolled stylishly into capris, joins other Somali girls at lunch.

Most of the tension between Somalis and other kids stems from misunderstandings about the Muslim religion and Somali culture, he said.

"When you see a girl who wears the scarf, and she might speak another language, and then they think you're speaking about them, it starts making divisions.

"Their culture is probably the farthest thing from our culture."

At home, Nimco sometimes suppresses her outgoing nature to respect the reserved Somali tradition in which she was nurtured. She avoids eating at Somali restaurants and coffee shops, knowing that such behavior by a girl can set tongues wagging.

After all, a girl's reputation is all she has, and it doesn't take long in this cozy Twin Cities Somali community before your business is everybody's business. "If I do something bad outside the house, it's going to be inside the house. Somebody's going to tell," Nimco explains. "My mom—she's not going to hurt me or anything—but she's going to feel bad. I don't want her to feel bad. I want my mom to be happy about what I'm doing."

Therein lies Nimco's dilemma. How to live by American rules at school without upsetting her people? Sometimes, she finds, she must lie.

A member of the Roosevelt track team, she runs in shorts, exposing her legs in public. The instant the race is over, she pulls on her warm-up pants. But if her mother knew she wore shorts, she'd disapprove. So would others in the Somali community.

Once during track practice, a group of Somali men approached her, and panic swept over her and other girls at school. "What were those Somali guys doing here? Did they see her running in shorts?" they asked each other. Turns out the men just wanted to talk to Nimco about a summer athletic team they were forming.

The Dating Dilemma

In the perfect Somali world, boys and girls don't date. They marry. At school, Somali girls may disappear for a few days and return married to men twice their age.

Dates and school dances are tricky in a culture that prohibits unmarried males and females from even touching one another. Some of the girls at Nimco's school have boyfriends who walk them to class and call them on the phone, but they do it on the sly. Some girls dance with partners, but only a few dare tell their parents.

This year's prom proved to be more trouble than it was worth for Nimco. She'd planned to go with a friend, a Somali boy. It wasn't a date, she insists.

A week before the dance, her friends warned her that it might not look good to have her picture taken, all dressed up, with this Somali guy. She didn't want people talking about them like they were a serious couple, so she backed out.

On the day of the dance, Nimco stood barefoot with a curling iron in one hand and hair spray in the other, holding court before a small crowd of girls in the school locker room. Instead of going to the prom, she did hair for girls who were going.

Nimco's friend, Ifrah (pronounced EE-fra) Mohamed, a very westernized girl who doesn't "cover" like other Somali girls, squirmed in the chair and eyed the hijaab-clad crowd watching her. "I can't believe your parents are letting you guys go," Ifrah said to them. "Every place I go, I'm the only Somali girl."

Even Ifrah used to lie to get out of the house.

> In the perfect Somali world, boys and girls don't date. They marry. At school, Somali girls may disappear for a few days and return married to men twice their age.

"Last year I had to throw so many fits," she said. At last she told her father: "Dad, this is America. Just let me have one night."

Nimco smiled understandingly as she twisted the curling iron. "Sometimes it's hard to follow the right thing," she said later. "We are different. We want to do everything that people our age here do. Most of them [Somali elders], they really don't get it."

Fartun: Decidedly Somali

For Fartun, the tug comes from another direction, from Africa. In Kenya, where she grew up, she made a conscious decision to hide her dark brown locks from public gaze. She was 14, the age when many Somali girls start wearing the hijaab.

It was Eid, an important Muslim holiday, and her mother spread out an assortment of pretty scarves from which Fartun chose one. Admiring her new look in the mirror, she decided to make the hijaab a part of her permanent identity. Only at home among relatives or among women does she take it off.

At Roosevelt, she wears the full jalaabiib in a rainbow of colors: turquoise, eggplant, mint green, lemon. There's an elegance about her that must have followed her from Kenya. Her family moved there before the Somali civil war broke out in the early 1990s. There, she had a nanny and a spacious house. She never lived in the refugee camps that housed so many Somalis.

Her mother, Geni (pronounced GEH-nee) Nur, may speak of Somalia, but Fartun's memories of the country they left when she was a child are fuzzy at best.

Her home and life in Kenya are what she misses, and she plans to go back there one day. In her poetry book, she records her longings, writing about "the country I'll never forget."

"Kenya's where I grew up. . . . It's just not the same when you start another different life."

"Things Got Changed"

In the bustling hallways at school, Fartun's no social butterfly. Backpack in tow, she heads straight to class, her face expressionless. She takes her schoolwork seriously, following directions, working diligently whether she's solving a problem in math class or lifting weights in gym class. In history class, when other students debate a point with their teacher, Fartun listens silently.

She wasn't always shy.

Back home, she was a real "little devil." She loved to torment the nanny and play practical jokes on her friends. Everyone knew her then.

Recently, one of her uncles said to her: "Is that you, Fartun? You're so quiet. What happened to the old Fartun?"

"Things got changed," she replied.

Rita Reed/Star Tribune/Minneapolis–St. Paul 2005

Fartun's shyness appears during lunch in the Roosevelt cafeteria, where she reads a book rather than socialize with the other Somali girls.

There are times, however, when she is laughing with her school friends or hanging out at the Mall of America when she feels American, Fartun concedes. But when she is home with her brother and sisters, playing a game of "Remember when . . ." she feels a gulf between herself and her classmates that's wider than the continent she left behind.

"I lost my life, where could it be?" she writes in one poem that describes her painful "thunderous silence."

When the bell signals the end of the school day, she threads her way through the throngs of students running and hollering outside the building. Not until she walks through the front doors of the Somali mall off Lake Street, where she is surrounded by other Somalis, does she start to relax.

"When I'm here, I kind of talk a lot. I don't know why," she says, smiling.

Fartun and her mother trade shifts at the 10-by-12-foot store where they sell scarves, long skirts, fabrics, shoes, international phone cards and other items. Inside the stall, Fartun greets customers and arranges the inventory. When it's slow, she does her homework or talks to friends who drop by.

When her mother is working at the store, Fartun's at home in charge of seven of her eight siblings, ranging in age from 16 to three years old. "I'm like the supervisor. She's the manager," Fartun says. She puts the younger ones down for naps, cleans the house and whips up whatever's available for dinner. One day it was egg noodles and meatballs.

The decor of the third-floor apartment across the street from Abbott Northwestern Hospital in Minneapolis breathes Somali culture. Large Persian rugs on the floor. Rich maroon curtains from floor to ceiling. The sweet, musky smell of spices and incense. Bunches of silk flowers hanging high on the walls.

Even so, American culture infiltrates. The children sit in the living room, crowded around the TV set. They are captivated by *Passions*, a daytime soap opera offering the typical fare of sex and violence. But when a Victoria's Secret commercial comes on showing leggy lingerie models, Fartun immediately changes the channel. With one eye on the TV, she plops on the couch, cradling her cousin. "We call her Maggie, like Maggie Simpson" of "The Simpsons" TV show, she says, grinning at the pacifier-sucking infant.

The phone rings and Fartun shifts the baby and picks up the phone. "It's Daddy!" she announces happily, now talking in Swahili. She's one of the lucky ones. Many Somali teens are here without either parent, their families blown apart by famine or war. When Fartun's family immigrated to Minneapolis to join other family members, her father stayed behind with her baby sister. Fartun says he couldn't leave his truck delivery business, and he wanted his youngest child to stay in Africa, so that she would know where she belongs.

Not since October 1998 has she seen her father, but she plans to visit him this summer.

Both: Trying to Hold On

What will Nimco's future be like?

Her mom doesn't know.

But she is worried.

Mohobo Hashi, 51, sits behind the counter of her clothing and perfume shop in Minneapolis' Phillips neighborhood and studies her feisty daughter. Nimco, clad in a flannel shirt, plaid pants and hijaab, squats beside her and translates her thoughts:

"Here in America, to raise the girls, it's kinda hard. Back in Somalia, you can tell them what to do. . . . Here in America, the girls tell you what to do!" At this, she throws her hands up and shrugs helplessly.

Earlier this year, a Somali man said he wanted to marry her daughter. Hashi laughed. Nimco has ideas of her own, she told him.

In many ways, Hashi resembles Nimco. She has the same high cheekbones and cheerful smile. They both wear sandals that reveal lacquered toenails. Hashi's are ebony, the color traditionally worn by Somali women; Nimco's are a metallic pink, the shade worn by many American teens.

As a teenager, Hashi's life was nothing like her daughter's. By the time she was Nimco's age, she already had two children. Her only education came in an Arabic school, where she studied the Qur'an, the Muslim holy book. There was no prom. No shopping at the mall. And certainly no dating. Islam prohibits it.

> "Here in America, to raise the girls, it's kinda hard. Back in Somalia, you can tell them what to do .... Here in America, girls tell you what to do!"
> —Mohobo Hashi

Sometimes she wonders if coming to America was the best thing for her family.

"I'm really worried about that—that our kids will change," she said. "They're really young, and they're around other [non-Somali] people all the time. They're not seeing every day their culture," she says.

Wrestling with Change

There is some good coming out of the changes in the Somali girls, some say. At Roosevelt, the girls are working hard at their education, harder than the boys, said Abdirahman (pronounced Ab-di-rah-MON) Mukhtar, another friend of Nimco's. "Back in Somalia, most girls didn't go to universities; they were ex-

Ritu Reed/Star Tribune/Minneapolis–St. Paul 2005

Fartun, in white, is in her element at a family party for women and children. She, the other women and the kids dance to the beat of Somali music until well after midnight.

pected to marry," he said. "Right now, once they get the opportunity, they want to work hard. They want to develop new paths for Somali women."

All the same, he and others share Hashi's concern that some girls and boys are changing too quickly, copying another culture and discarding their own.

"Girls who are so quick to change on the outside are probably not very strong on the inside," observed Muse (pronounced MOO-sah) Mohamed, past president of the Roosevelt Somali Student Association. He didn't interact much with the girls because he didn't think it was appropriate, but he noticed some were starting to wear pants.

"It is hard for Somali immigrants to swim against the current," Mohamed said. "It's like spilling a glass of water in the ocean."

Hashi wants Nimco to have a good education and to be a good person, a Muslim, and a mother. For a woman, education is good, but, "the most important thing for a girl is to have children of your own blood," she says.

Will her daughter make good on her vow to wear the jalaabiib, marry a Somali man, and raise her children properly in Islam?

"Allah knows," Hashi says, pointing to the ceiling.

Nimco knows the elder Somalis worry that the girls will forget their culture and take up the new one, but she insists that won't happen to her.

"I don't want to have a problem with my family. I don't want it to be different," she said.

When it's time to marry, and that time is drawing near, she says she'll choose a husband of her own, a Somali man who appreciates her independent spirit.

Talk of marriage makes Fartun blush. She declines to discuss it. Like Nimco, she shares a passion for knowledge. Both plan to go to college after they finish high school in a year or two.

Where they'll be, who they'll be in the future, neither one knows. "It's confusing," Fartun says.

Just before school let out for the year, Fartun and Nimco joined other Roosevelt students of African descent in celebrating their heritage. With African

Rita Reed/Star Tribune/Minneapolis–St. Paul 2005

Nimco's classmate playfully bumps into her during gym class.

drums beating, they stepped onto the stage in the school auditorium. For once, they were hard to tell apart, not only from each other but from their American-born peers.

A long white gown and hijaab covered Nimco. Fartun stood nearby, wearing a new bold grin. The drums picked up. The emcee introduced them by name.

And just for a moment, Fartun and Nimco were the same. Somalis and Americans, too. Somali-Americans.

THE MAKING OF

TUG OF WAR

By Allie Shah
Star Tribune Staff Writer

The whole thing started out as a fishing expedition, albeit one with a little focus.

Veteran photographer Rita Reed approached me about doing a story on Somali women, a very visible and growing ethnic group in Minneapolis. We gravitated to the teenagers in part because we knew language wouldn't be much of a problem.

I covered schools at the time, and I knew of a high school teeming with Somalis. For the better part of a school year, we immersed ourselves in the world of young Somali girls and came out with a complex, coming-of-age tale.

Developing Cultural Expertise

I had a head start on some of the cultural background because I am a Muslim, as are most Somalis. I was considered a Muslim "sister," which helped me gain the confidence and trust of the people we met. But I don't speak Somali, and I don't wear the hijaab, so I wasn't exactly an insider.

I approached the story the same way I would a new beat. I started a source list, identifying different layers of people and organizations. The first layer included the people who worked with Somalis, such as the school principal, teachers, youth workers, and nonprofit groups. The next layer covered a wide array of students and families. Finally, the principal subjects emerged: Nimco, Fartun, and their mothers.

Before sitting down with my sources, I did a fair amount of reading to get a better understanding of Somali culture. I read books and articles about Somali history, culture, and religious and gender issues. I attended a conference designed to give teachers a crash course in "Understanding Somali Culture and Islamic Values." When a prominent Somali author came to town, I went to his book reading. When a famous Somali singer performed live, I showed up for the concert. The more you know about a subject, the easier it is to establish rapport with your sources and put into context the events in their lives.

Most important, I found people who took me by the hand and got me into the community. These "angels" were knowledgeable and respected people who introduced me to parents and students. This was extremely important because the language barrier sometimes prevented me from effectively communicating with parents about my motives. Some Somalis are suspicious of people who ask a lot of questions. Stories circulate in the community about child protection workers and immigration officials coming to people's homes to investigate alleged abuses. One angel, a high school science teacher, was truly a godsend! She allowed Rita and me to hang out in her classroom and introduced us to both Nimco and Fartun.

Using Immersion

I'm a big believer in immersion, especially when it comes to reporting on race and ethnic matters. It's like learning a foreign language. The quickest way to become fluent is to live in the world and soak up as much as you can. I spent months with Nimco and Fartun. I went to school with them, becoming a familiar face in the hallways and the lunchroom. I

> The quickest way to become fluent is to live in the world and soak up as much as you can.

hung out with them at their friends' houses, at the library, at the mall. I tagged along when Fartun tutored children or worked in her mother's clothing store at the "Somali mall," a major gathering place. I shadowed Nimco at track practice and meets. I went to their homes, met their mothers, and exchanged small gifts in accordance with custom. I showed them photos of my family and friends and asked to see their albums. I got used to listening to the radio stations the girls liked, and that helped keep me in their world even when I was back in my own world for a few days.

By immersing myself, I also earned the trust of many in the local Somali community. People got used to seeing me. They began to approach me and open up about their lives, their hopes and fears. Having so many different sources allowed me to give Nimco and Fartun some space when they needed it. It's hard work being the ambassador for your community, and there were days when the girls didn't want us around or were tired of answering my questions.

Immersion also helped me later in the writing process to speak in an authoritative and authentic voice.

Negotiating Information

Sometimes we had to make deals to get information.

I needed to write about Nimco's track meets and the dilemma she faced over the required uniform: a tank top and shorts, not exactly a modest outfit, by

Somali standards. The anecdote illustrated the daily judgment calls girls like Nimco must make as they try to navigate their two worlds. She did not want any photos published showing her in shorts, in part because she didn't want her mother to see them and get flack from other Somalis. She also argued that baring her legs for a few minutes while she ran a race in front of a sparse crowd was not as bad as showing her legs in the newspaper for thousands of readers to see. Rita promised to crop the pictures so that Nimco's legs weren't showing, so long as I could describe in words what the photos didn't show.

Since the girls were under eighteen, we asked their parents for written consent to have their names and photos published. We didn't stop there. We felt it was necessary, given the language barrier, to show them samples of our work so that they could grasp more fully what we were doing. That would help avoid any misunderstandings after the story appeared in the paper.

Rita and I also did a small daily story on a school event organized by the Somali students so that the girls would have a clear idea of what all this photo taking and interviewing led to. This was especially important, given the community we were covering. Some Somali women and girls believe that it is immodest to have their photographs taken, let alone publicly displayed.

Adding Context and Complexity

Fartun and Nimco's struggle to bridge the generation gap with their parents and the cultural gap with their peers had all the elements of a heart-wrenching drama. It became, however, even more powerful and relevant as part of a larger, universal story of teenagers navigating the bumpy road of high school, where fitting in and finding one's identity are the twin peaks teens climb every day.

Compounding their struggle was their experience as new immigrants from a country ravaged by war. Having survived Somalia's civil war, these girls now found themselves at the center of another battle: a cultural clash. I tried to capture that battle by showing how, every day, the girls had to make choices that reflected this quiet, cultural war. For example, the gym class scene illustrated not only the contrast in values about appropriate clothing and exercise activities but also the range of choices the Somali girls make in order to negotiate both worlds. Both Nimco and Fartun covered their bodies and their hair in gym class. But while Fartun avoids the co-ed class and chooses to drape herself in long, baggy clothing, Nimco opts for clothing that covers but still allows her to blend in with her peers. She also joins the co-ed gym class.

Another example is the scene in which Nimco forgoes the prom and helps the other Somali girls get ready instead. I used dialogue between Ifrah, the very Americanized teenager, and the other Somali girls waiting to get their hair done by Nimco to show readers how the prom is a particular source of tension for Somali teenagers.

It would have been simple but essentially inaccurate to portray the differences between Nimco and Fartun as a good girl/bad girl dichotomy. In reality, the contrast between the two was subtler. They may very well end up in the same place culturally years from now, but Nimco's path to traditional Somali wifehood is less direct than Fartun's.

I got to the heart of that distinction by not giving in to knee-jerk assumptions. Particularly when covering a community that I'm not from, I'm very careful about drawing conclusions. I constantly search my notes for examples and quotes to back up my assertions. During the months I trailed Fartun and Nimco, I kept a diary of my visits. In it, I recorded not only key quotes and observations but also my impressions about what I had seen and heard. Often I shared my conclusions with the girls to check for accuracy. By now, I was planning to write their story as a narrative, and I wanted the voice to be true to their experiences.

Rita Reed/Star Tribune/Minneapolis–St. Paul 2005
Fartun makes Samboza, a Somalian delicacy.

This is how I crafted the part of the story that explains Nimco's decision to start wearing the hijaab regularly. I had seen her wearing it off and on. I asked her about that, and she told me that when she first came to Minneapolis she never wore it, but then she started feeling bad because her classmates didn't know that she was Somali. She also said she plans to wear the full hijaab like her mother someday so that she can set a good example for her kids. In a separate conversation, she talked about the scarf pulling on her hairline. Another time she told me she wants to get used to wearing it. That's how I came up with this passage: "These days, she wears the hijaab, when she feels like it. She does it to let everyone know she's Somali, and so she can get used to the feel of the fabric tugging at her hairline, reminding her who she is, what she is. Somali. Muslim. Woman."

These lines also serve another purpose. They show the serious side of Nimco. When telling a story through characters, there's always a danger that they'll come off as caricatures rather than multidimensional people. Daily newspapers often run the risk of painting situations as more polarized than they really are, because of time and space constraints. With this story, I included anecdotes and descriptions that fleshed out Nimco and Fartun's many sides, even if they seemed to be contradictory.

For instance, Nimco's fun-loving, flirtatious side was well documented in the photos and descriptions of her interacting with her peers. She also had a deep reverence for her religion and her mother, and she was proud of her Somali heritage. The on-again, off-again hijaab was a sign that she was a work in progress, as most of us are at that age. It also served as a reminder that although Nimco planned to wear it all the time when she's a wife and mother, she viewed that day with a typical young person's perspective of the future: it's far off.

> Daily newspapers often run the risk of painting situations as more polarized than they really are, because of time and space constraints.

In Fartun's case, her quiet and conservative demeanor tells part of her story. Equally important, however, is her very playful and even mischievous side, revealed among close friends and family. By including the nickname she chose for her little sister—"Maggie," after the satirical cartoon *The Simpsons*— and Fartun's reputation as a prankster, I sought to fully reveal her as a character.

Showing and Telling

All writers know it's much more powerful to show readers the truth than just to tell them about it. In this story, often the most revealing way to explain the tension and adaptation going on in the lives of these girls was to paint a scene.

The difference between the Somali mothers and their daughters' coming-of-age stories is told by Nimco's mother, Mohobo Hashi, who says she already had two children by the time she was Nimco's age. While I listened to Hashi talk, I was struck by how similar and yet different this mother and daughter looked.

Nimco's features resembled her mother's, but their clothing was completely different. Nimco looked like any American teenager, while her mother's clothes told the story of a new immigrant.

My time immersed in both the traditional Somali world and the teenage world had taught me two things: older Somali women and those who are newest to the country tend to favor a particularly dark shade of nail polish. I had noticed it at the Somali mall. At the high school, the girls preferred shiny, pale hues.

That piece of information was the inspiration for this passage: "In many ways, Hashi resembles Nimco. She has the same high cheekbones and cheerful smile. They both wear sandals that reveal lacquered toenails. Hashi's are ebony, the color traditionally worn by Somali women; Nimco's are a metallic pink, the shade worn by many American teens."

I used another scene to demonstrate the tension Fartun faces as she chooses which American culture to keep and which one to throw out. In Fartun's home, Somali culture is alive as evidenced by the decor, which includes large Persian floor rugs, rich maroon curtains that stretch from floor to ceiling, and the sweet, musky smell of spices and incense. But the television set beams in American culture, and some of it runs counter to Fartun's cultural and religious values. *Passions*, a daytime soap opera offering the typical fare of sex and violence, captivates her attention. But when a Victoria's Secret commercial comes on, showing leggy lingerie models, Fartun immediately changes the channel.

Doing the *Tug of War* story reminded me how rich the story vein is in under-covered communities. Getting those stories requires the same thorough and thoughtful reporting and writing skills that are the hallmark of all good journalists.

To screen the Allie Shah interview, select IDENTITY on the DVD Main Menu then "Tug of War."

A Primer on Somali Culture

Religion

Almost all Somalis are Muslim, or followers of the religion of Islam. That shapes many of the customs, values and personal conduct in Somali culture.

While some observe the religion more strictly than others, Somalis believe in the five pillars of Islam:

- Belief in Allah, one God.
- Regular prayer (five times a day).
- Fasting from food and water from dawn to dusk every day during the holy month of Ramadan.
- Giving to charity.
- Spiritual pilgrimage to the holy city of Mecca, Saudi Arabia, at least once in a lifetime.

Family structure

- The family is the prime source of personal identity. "Genealogy is to Somalis what an address is to Americans," one historian observed. "When Somalis meet each other they don't ask, 'Where are you from?' Rather, they ask, 'Whom are you from?'"
- Families are large and interdependent. Aunts, uncles, grandparents, parents and children often live under one roof.
- Polygamy is not uncommon. Muslim men may marry up to four wives under certain conditions.
- Men are the heads of the families. Women run the home.

Gender relations

- Islam requires men and women to dress modestly. For many Somali girls, that means covering every part of their bodies except their faces, hands and feet. Pants are considered too revealing.
- After puberty, contact between unrelated men and women is limited. Physical touch—even a handshake—may be considered inappropriate.
- Women typically don't go out to restaurants or coffee shops, because it is considered immodest. The public arena is the man's domain.
- Dating in the Western sense is prohibited, although it's common for young men and women to participate in traditional dances at social events. Marriages traditionally were arranged by families, but that is changing.

DISCUSSION POINTS

DISCUSS

- One challenge in detailing the differences of cultures is keeping judgment out of the journalism. Where does the writer do this especially well? Where do you think she could have done it better?
- Allie Shah uses fine details to show readers the "Westernized" culture and the Somali culture at the heart of this story's conflict. Which of the details best show those two cultures?
- The reporter uses a few Arabic words in the story, defining them and providing pronunciation, even for the names of the two main characters and their families. What does that add to your understanding of this story? Could you argue for leaving out the definitions and pronunciations?
- In her essay, Shah talks about checking her assumptions to keep them from blindly guiding the story. What assumptions do you make about Fartun and Nimco after reading the story? How might you check those assumptions before writing a story?
- What other tug-of-war stories—tales of people living in dual cultures—can you identify in your community?

SUGGESTED READINGS AND WEBSITES

RESEARCH

Books

Abdullahi, Mohamed Diriye. *Culture and Customs of Somalia*. Westport, Conn.: Greenwood Press, 2001.

A look at the culture and history of Somalis of the Horn of Africa across Somaliland, Somalia, Djibouti, Ethiopia, and Kenya.

Gardner, Judith, and Judy El Bushra, eds. *Somalia—The Untold Story: The War Through the Eyes of Somali Women*. London: Pluto Press, 2004.

The book details the effect of the Somali war of the nineties on that country's women, including the opportunities it opened up for them, the changing family structure, how women coped with sexual violence, and their role as peacemakers.

Hussein, Ikram. *Teenage Refugees from Somalia Speak Out (In Their Own Voices)*. New York: Rosen Publishing Group, 1997.

Geared to young adults, this book is the first-person account of seven Somali teenage refugees and their flight from civil war–torn Somalia. The book also provides a historical survey of the country from ancient times to the present.

Websites

www.freep.com/100questions

The Detroit Free Press *guide to the one hundred most commonly asked questions about Arab Americans. The guide offers answers to help reporters write accurately about the culture, language, and religion of this ethnic group.*

CHAPTER 2

STORIES
ABOUT RACE SERIES

**CRAIG FRANKLIN, KARYNE HOLMES,
PAM MOORE, AND PETE WILSON
KRON-TV, SAN FRANCISCO**

CRAIG FRANKLIN

Craig Franklin is a three-time winner of the prestigious George Foster Peabody Award for excellence in television news, once for the 1999 *About Race* series, which also won the first three of Columbia University's *Let's Do It Better!* awards.

KARYNE HOLMES

Karyne Holmes, an Emmy-winning editor at KRON-TV, was the principal editor on the *About Race* project and shared in the station's George Foster Peabody Award for Best Documentary, and the Northern California Society of Professional Journalists Award.

PAM MOORE

Pam Moore is an anchor at *KRON 4 News*. Moore's work on the *About Race* series garnered a number of awards. Moore also received the Associated Press Television-Radio Association award for Best Investigative Reporting in 2001.

PETE WILSON

Pete Wilson is an anchor of *ABC7 News at 6* in San Francisco. Wilson, who joined *ABC7* News in January 2002, has been a top-rated anchorman in the Bay Area for twenty-three years and a major market anchor and radio talk show host for over thirty years.

About Race

In the summer of 1997, when then-president Bill Clinton called for a national conversation on race relations, the staff at KRON-TV in San Francisco launched *About Race*, a two-year series examining the way people handled one of the country's most explosive social issues.

Two of those stories—*What Is Race?* and *News and Race*—used geneticists, ordinary citizens, and KRON's own staff to explore the science of race, to debunk racial myths, and to probe workplace tensions that often lie beneath the surface.

Producer Craig Franklin, anchors Pete Wilson and Pam Moore, and tape editor Karyne Holmes, formed the nucleus of the KRON team. Dan Rosenheim, the news director at the time, was the behind-the-scenes force who drove the project.

The team's internal deliberations, journalistic skills, and personal growth all contributed to stories that defied two major television mantras: that the public won't watch long stories and that people don't want to talk about matters of race. The team also had to deal with Rosenheim's goal for the work to be carried out without "blowing up" the newsroom.

In this chapter, journalists will learn more about the debate that continues to rage over the significance of biological differences rooted in race. They'll get an up-close look at how individual beliefs, the makeup of a news organization, and the divisions in society all contribute to the way the story of race relations is told. The KRON team shows how strong, honest communication across race can strengthen and broaden reporting and how a diverse group of journalists with the courage to take on their fears can find fresh angles from which to view a timeless problem and locate sources who are both thoughtful about the subject and willing to talk about it on camera.

The essay and DVD interviews ask journalists to consider provocative notions of fairness, balance, accuracy, and truth. Should journalists give voice to every view of race relations, no matter how bigoted, outdated, or unproven? Should journalists consider how the audience will react to the race or ethnicity of the sources placed before them? Does the race or ethnicity of the reporter or producer matter in the field? Finally, what role does leadership play in providing coverage that could "blow up" not only a newsroom but a community as diverse as San Francisco?

Those who worked on the *About Race* series show in this chapter how the pursuit of intriguing, inspiring, and often belief-busting stories about race relations can bring rewards far beyond the prizes their reporters may envision.

"WHAT IS RACE?" (TRANSCRIPT)

KRON-TV, *About Race* Series
Airdate: February 24, 1997
Reporter: Pam Moore / Producer: Craig Franklin / Editor: Karyne Holmes

Susan Shaw:
[studio intro]

America is arguably the most diverse country in the world, but after generations of being called a melting pot it seems at times we're no closer to getting along.

Pete Wilson:
[studio intro]

It's been said we're all experts on race, at least we all know what we believe. So this week and through the coming year we will be reporting extensively about race. We will be exploring what we feel and why, looking at and looking beyond our anger and anxiety to clarify the confusion that swirls around a very hot button issue. We begin tonight with the help of Pam Moore.

Pam Moore:
[studio intro]

Well, you know if you're not a politician, if you're not a civil rights leader, you might sometimes wonder what can I do about race? It's too big, too complicated, too scary an issue. So this week we look at the basics: race in the schools, at work, how to talk about race and ways that you can make a difference. Tonight we start with the most basic question of all: what is race?

[voice-over]

We begin our story with a pop quiz on genetic science.
　　Here we have a group of four men.
　　If you were able to look just at their genetic code—their DNA—the question is which of these men have the most genetic differences?
　　The answer comes from Dr. Sylvia Spengler, a geneticist at U.C. Berkeley.

Dr. Sylvia Spengler:

I have no question, given what I know about human genetics, that the tall person and the short person are significantly more different than the two men of similar height—one black, one white.

Pam Moore:

Sylvia Spengler is part of the human genome project—scientists around the world trying to map a location and function of every gene in the human body.
　　She represents the viewpoint of most geneticists today that "race" has no real meaning in science.

Dr. Spengler:	Trying to mix genetics with race, to my mind, is inappropriate. Cannot be done. The one take-home lesson is genetic basis of race isn't [*sic*]. Race is something we do to each other. It has nothing to do with what our DNA does to us.
Pam Moore: [voice-over]	No such thing as race? Has science suddenly gone mad? Can't they see the difference between Al Gore . . . Michael Jordan . . . Jackie Chan? And don't those differences come from our DNA?
[interview]	We do see differences . . .
Dr. Spengler:	That's right . . .
Pam Moore:	. . . when we see race—when we see maybe body shapes and nose shapes or hair texture differences—isn't that based genetically?
Dr. Spengler:	It's based genetically, but it's a very small part of us.

Pam Moore: [voice-over]	Take skin color, for example.
	    This is the stuff that often divides us.
	    It's called melanin—the substance that colors our skin and helps protect us from sunlight.

About Race

Pam Moore, anchoring *"What Is Race?"*

Courtesy of KRON-TV

"No such thing as race? Has science suddenly gone mad? Can't they see the difference between Al Gore . . . Michael Jordan . . . Jackie Chan? And don't those differences come from our DNA?"

—Pam Moore

Pure melanin is the color and texture of charcoal dust. But our bodies can also produce it in shades of brown, yellow, and red.

The mix of melanin we show to the world is controlled by our genes, but it is indeed a very small part of us.

How small?

While each cell in the human body has 100,000 genes, only about 6 genes control skin color—6 out of 100,000!

[on camera] What's more—everybody watching this program shares the same 6 genes—including the genes for dark skin! Now what that means may shock some people—that each of us has the potential to produce skin as dark as an African native.

How could that be?

Well, according to science, we are all descendants of Africa.

[voice-over] Professor Luigi Luca Cavalli-Sforza of Stanford University has studied the genes of people all around the world, and believes that he has found our genetic ancestors.

Dr. Luigi Luca Cavalli-Sforza: It's likely that the bushmen are the people who have contributed most to the origin of modern humans . . . therefore, to the people who went out from Africa to colonize the rest of the world.

Karyne Holmes was the principal editor of the *About Race* series, a groundbreaking local news project to examine race in the San Francisco Bay area.

Pam Moore: [voice-over]	About 40,000 years ago, some Africans moved north, where their skin needed less protection against the sun, and eventually grew lighter.
	Some moved to Siberia, where their eyelids grew narrow to protect against driving cold and bright snow.
	Europeans and Asians may look different from Africans, but they never lost their genes for dark skin—genes that can still be partly activated by a trip to the beach.
	Which is why geneticists say race—like beauty—is only skin deep.
Dr. Cavalli-Sforza:	If you expect that there exist pure races, that is totally absurd.
Dr. Spengler:	I tell people, think of what they would look like without skin. When you do that, you see we're all alike—we're primates.
Pam Moore:	Which brings us back to our pop quiz:
	Why are the tall and short man more genetically different than the black and white man? Because remember: only 6 genes control skin color.
	A person's height, on the other hand, is affected by dozens of genes.
Rob: [white]	My first response was: oh there's way more difference between Reggie and I.
Matt: [white]	I mean I can't look, look into Reggie and Rob and say: your DNA is close.
Pam Moore:	We wondered how the men who posed for our pop quiz would react to this genetic news. They are classmates at the University of San Francisco.
Matt:	Now that this information is out, people might accept it, people might not but you can't erase what, what you've learned throughout your whole life.
Reggie: [black]	You know, even if I could erase that, I think that I would still be troubled by society, because I don't think society will allow things to be that way.
Pam Moore:	But this group still has questions, like what about racial differences in sports? Isn't that genetic?
	One old stereotype is about blacks in sports.
	For example: 80 percent of players in the NBA are African American. And some people say black athletes have a genetic trait called "fast-twitch muscles"—which allow them to run, jump and shoot better than whites.

But science tells us that lots of athletes have fast-twitch muscles—while not all black people are good at sports.

In this group, Ryan is the best basketball player, while Reggie says he's not so hot.

Reggie: It's nothing but a stereotype really. I've always believed that, you know—whoever you are, whatever color you are, if you work really hard at doing something, you most likely will become good. Whether it be basketball, football, baseball—whatever it is.

Pam Moore:
[voice-over] Why are Latinos good at soccer? Do we ever talk about their "soccer" genes?

Is there a "martial arts" gene for Asians?

A "golf" gene for whites?

What about Tiger Woods? Did he get his abilities from his black father or his Asian mother?

And that's exactly the problem with trying to define people by race—there are no clear scientific categories that truly separate humans by the color of their skin.

But that doesn't mean some people don't try.

The 1994 book *The Bell Curve* provoked a huge controversy by comparing race with intelligence—using IQ tests to show that Asians and whites are generally smarter than blacks.

The authors concluded that part of the difference is probably genetic.

Courtesy of KRON-TV

Sylvia Spengler knows genetic experts all over the world who read *The Bell Curve* and were astounded by that conclusion.

She says the small number of genes that control racial characteristics like skin color or curly hair have no connection with genes affecting intelligence—just as a man's height has nothing to do with how smart he is.

[on camera]

So, if race isn't based on science, then what is it?

Well, the best evidence is that race is not in our genes, it's in our heads—something we made up a long time ago.

In the days when humans could see that the earth was flat, they could also see that people looked different.

And while we now accept that our eyes deceived us about the globe, our belief in racial differences has been tough to change.

Copyright © 1997 KRON-TV San Francisco
All interview photographs by Russ Katsumoto and Gary Mercer.

"NEWS AND RACE" (TRANSCRIPT)

KRON-TV, *About Race* Series
Airdate: October 22, 1999
Reporter: Pete Wilson / Producer: Craig Franklin / Editor: Jim Joy

Wendy Tokuda: [studio intro]	You might think of journalists as thick-skinned people who cover all sorts of controversial topics.
Pete Wilson: [studio intro]	But when it comes to race, like lots of folks, we tend to shy away from even talking about it. It's confusing, it's explosive, too personal. Tonight we point the camera at ourselves—and the struggle to report—about race.
[voice-over]	Reporter Greg Lyon and cameraman Rick Villaroman get along well together.
Greg Lyon: [dialogue]	*It was the smoke that attracted photographer Ken Schwartz . . . I blew it. Let me try it again.*
Rick Villaroman:	*Try it again [cross talk].*
Greg Lyon:	*Yeah.*
Pete Wilson:	But behind the harmony is a gap they've never talked about.
Rick Villaroman:	How do I explain not being white to a person who's white?
Greg Lyon:	We do well on stories together. But there's another level at which we apparently don't communicate. And that came as a surprise to me.
Pete Wilson: [voice-over]	The surprise came when Greg and Rick joined Channel 4's Race Committee—15 people assigned to look at race in our own news operation. Newscenter 4 has been doing in-depth stories about race for the last two years—after President Clinton's call for a national conversation about race.
President Bill Clinton:	It's high time we all began talking with each other.
Pete Wilson:	We've looked at race in the workplace, in churches, at school . . .
Teacher:	What's different about them, and what's the same about them?
Pete Wilson:	We've looked at interracial marriages and frictions between the Chinese and Japanese American communities.

A common theme has been how people are trying to deal with race relations in their own lives.

Dan Rosenheim is news director of Channel 4.

Dan Rosenheim: And one of our goals as a news organization is to go out and look at the issue and get people to talk to the issue, so that the public has a better understanding and the public can engage in a better conversation.

Pete Wilson: But Rosenheim wanted to look at our own understanding too.

How well do we get along in the newsroom?

How diverse is our news coverage?

To help answer those questions, he created the KRON Race Committee.

Greg Lyon remembers the first meeting last year.

Greg Lyon: If you'd asked me before that meeting, do people at Channel 4 get along over racial boundaries, I would have said absolutely, without a doubt. Coming out of that meeting I had to say—I guess not.

Pete Wilson: There were no cameras at that first meeting, but here's what happened.

"We all know what can happen. People either 'blow up' in anger or 'shut up' in fear—fear of being blamed for having the wrong point of view."

—Pete Wilson

Courtesy of KRON-TV

Pete Wilson anchors the *About Race* series.

In a quiet voice, Rick Villaroman told the group that he felt Channel 4 was a socially segregated workplace, based on skin color.

Rick Villaroman: There were definite cliques of people—and not cliques of people who had certain likes and interests. Cliques of people who were white, cliques of people who were Hispanic, cliques of people who were black.

Greg Lyon: Rick Villaroman was the one who expressed what apparently a lot of people were feeling. Which was that, if you're a minority, a racial minority, you are to some degree isolated here at Channel 4. And I had no idea that was true.

Pam Moore: For all of us it was an eye opener. It helped you look around the room a little differently.

Pete Wilson: Anchor/reporter Pam Moore and news producer Kevin McCormack are co-chairs of the Race Committee.

Pam Moore: Everybody wants to go to work, do your job, and go home. You know, you want to go in, let's not be hassled, let's get it over with, let's go home. And if you think you're doing a good job, then what's the problem? Don't fix it if it's not broke. But the

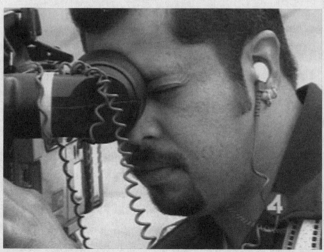

Courtesy of KRON-TV

Cameraman Rick Villaroman framing up a shot.

"There were definite cliques of people—and not cliques of people who had certain likes and interests. Cliques of people who were white, cliques of people who were Hispanic, cliques of people who were black."

—Rick Villaroman

	problem is, there are some undercurrents that are going on that are often not on the radar, but are still relevant.
Pete Wilson: [on camera]	Relevant to journalists because our job is to cover the people, events and issues of an especially diverse Bay Area—a tricky task says Rosenheim, because we already have trouble even talking about race.
Dan Rosenheim:	I think journalists, like everyone else, have to have their feet held to the fire for there to be progress. Have to learn to talk about it comfortably if possible, in a civil and reasonable way, even if not a comfortable way, for certain.
Pete Wilson:	But Rosenheim knew when he started the Race Committee, it was like playing with dynamite.
Dan Rosenheim:	I was beginning a process—authorizing, encouraging, setting off a process that once it begins, there's no way that I or any one individual can control it.
Pete Wilson:	We all know what can happen. People either "blow up" in anger, or "shut up" in fear—fear of being blamed for having the wrong point of view.
Rick Villaroman:	There were people in the room who got sensitive at the suggestion that you don't understand what it's like not to be white. And oh! Well! I think I'm well-rounded, and you know—the response! The defensiveness that I got.
Greg Lyon:	When you talk about issues of race in America today, I do think that whites are, are—whites feel themselves to be, ah, perceived as the bad guys. Yeah. But I don't think the folks on the other side of the fence are necessarily pointing the finger at Greg Lyon and saying you're the culprit here, even though I may feel that way. And so I need to step back and say, okay, we can have this dialogue. But yeah, you do feel defensive. Yeah.
Pete Wilson:	One reason journalists may feel defensive is we're supposed to be objective about the issues we report on, including race.
Kevin McCormack:	With something like race, the issues aren't always clear—where the biases are, where your prejudices are—where people are even aware that they may have prejudices.
Pam Moore:	I think objectivity in journalism is a goal that we all strive for. But the reality is that all of us bring to the table our own issues, views, biases, concerns, attitudes about everything.

Pete Wilson:	KRON is not the only news operation confronting racial issues.
	More and more journalists are trying to deal with race after continued criticism that mainstream news does not adequately cover the diversity of the Bay Area.
	One of the jobs of the Race Committee was to study ethnic diversity in our own news.
	It's August 1998. During marathon sessions, they watch three days of tapes—from daybreak to nightbeat.
	No one is sure exactly how to measure diversity on the news.
KRON employee 1: *[dialogue]*	*Let's say we want . . . I mean, I don't know. . .*
KRON employee 2:	*Let's discuss it with her later.*
KRON employee 3:	*We'll discuss it with her later.*
Pete Wilson:	But with help from the Public Research Institute at San Francisco State University, the committee has devised a kind of "score card" to count the race of people as they appear on the screen—as well as what roles they play in the stories.
KRON employee 4: *[dialogue]*	*Occupation of speaker. You have an elec . . . you have a public official.*
Kevin McCormack:	It definitely wasn't a quota system. We weren't trying to say that these are numbers that we have to have. But we wanted to try and identify areas where we really weren't reflecting the diversity of the Bay Area.
KRON employees (various): [dialogue]	*Central involvement is white.* *All the speakers were white.* *Speakers are white.* *Central involvement white.* *Two African Americans.* *So we have a white, white, white.* *Okay, yeah.*
Pete Wilson:	Producer Teri Aitkins was on the committee.
Teri Aitkins:	In my group anyway, we felt wow! Lot of white people on TV. We're putting a lot of white people on TV—very rarely people of color.
Pete Wilson:	But here's what makes diversity such a complicated subject to pin down.

The fact is, even in the diverse Bay Area, whites make up a majority of the population. When the score cards were sent to San Francisco State for independent analysis, the raw numbers showed that whites were actually under-represented on our news compared to population figures. Blacks were over-represented. Hispanics were slightly under-represented and Asians were substantially under-represented.

Teri Aitkins: And then when statistics came back, it showed that we were reflecting the diversity of our community fairly well. Not the best, and there could be improvements, but we were reflecting the diversity of our community on a pretty decent basis. And that was a surprise to us.

Pete Wilson: But the committee still expressed concern that most experts interviewed on the news were white.

And a lopsided 21 out of 23 "human interest" stories were about white people.

Kevin McCormack: Television is perception. If you have 15 stories and most of the experts in these stories are white, it doesn't matter how many people of color you have in the background. But still the story's dominated by people who are white. And, unless you

Courtesy of KRON-TV

A meeting of the Diversity Committee.

"If you'd asked me before that meeting, do people at Channel 4 get along over racial boundaries, I would have said absolutely, without a doubt. Coming out of that meeting I had to say—I guess not."

—Greg Lyon

can redress that balance somehow, I don't think you're reflecting the communities you're trying to serve.

Pete Wilson:
[on camera]

So how much has changed in the years since the Race Committee first met? Well, obviously the newsroom didn't blow up. But we do often argue about just exactly how to cover issues of diversity, ethnicity, and race—and exactly what our goals should be.

Dan Rosenheim:

It's not the revolution. This is not a dramatically, qualitatively different newsroom today than it was a year ago. So I hope there's been some progress. But I think it's a, it's a very slow, painstaking, one step at a time thing. And we've got a long way to go.

Pete Wilson:

And as we said at the start, Greg and Rick get along well together. But they still find it hard to talk about race.

Greg Lyon:

I don't think there's been any great sea change. But—I don't think social change happens that way. Except once in a great while. I mean, I think it is made up of subtle movements. And, um—maybe the fact that people are thinking about it is having an effect.

Rick Villaroman:

For us to even venture to look at the issue says a lot about the place that I work. We're in the business of communication. Let's be honest about it. Let's really talk about what the issues are, and let's not make stuff up. Let's not say that it's all okay. Because it's not all okay. There's a lot of work that still needs to be done. Let's do it!

Pete Wilson:

[studio close] Now, we want to emphasize that the Race Committee's work was not a truly scientific study. But rather more of a snapshot of our news.

However, KRON is now a part of a national study looking at diversity in a dozen newspapers and TV stations all around the country.

Results of that study will be released late next year, and of course we'll share them with you.

Copyright © 1999 KRON-TV, San Francisco

THE MAKING OF

THE *ABOUT RACE* SERIES

By Craig Franklin

When I was assigned as lead producer on KRON-TV's *About Race* project in 1997, several reporters warned me to steer clear. "It's a no-win subject," they said. "You'll just make viewers mad. It's bad for your career."

I was also hearing whispers that some African American staff members at the station wanted me off the project because of a notorious blowup I'd had four years earlier with a black colleague. I'll come back to that later.

About Race was our station's response to President Clinton's call in June 1997 for what he termed a "national conversation about race." KRON-TV, the *San Francisco Chronicle,* and KQED-FM public radio had teamed up with the idea of giving people information that might help them talk about race.

The problem was, we had trouble dealing with race in our own newsroom, and now the white management was assigning a white producer to make sense of it all. My assignment was to search out stories that would serve as

"In working together on About Race, Karyne and I ended up living the very subject we were reporting on. Through fighting, talking, and listening, we reshaped our pain and differences into an unlikely friendship . . ."

—Craig Franklin

Editor Karyne Holmes and producer Craig Franklin

"models of race relations" while avoiding preaching, finger-pointing, sensationalism, and unnecessary conflict.

In the beginning, I found the subject so intimidating that it gave me bad dreams. In one dream I remember vividly, I was assigned to clean up the vast parking lot at the end of the runway at San Francisco International airport. Armed with a Eureka upright vacuum cleaner, I earnestly pushed back and forth across the oil-spotted pavement while people and planes came and went, paying me no attention. To make matters worse, no one had told me how clean the parking lot was supposed to be or when I would be done. Finally, after vacuuming one huge section, I looked back to see that the power cord was dragging behind me, unplugged. At the end of the dream I was standing there, plug in hand, with no power in sight.

When I told an older black reporter about this dream the next day, she said, "Welcome to race."

Allies and Introspection

Here's what my bosses did early in the *About Race* project: They gathered an advisory panel of eight experts on race relations, comprising educators, outside journalists, and community leaders. These expert "allies" helped narrow our focus on what kinds of information people might need in order to talk

KRON anchor Pam Moore

"While each cell in the human body has 100,000 genes only about 6 genes control skin color—6 out of 100,000. What's more—everybody watching this program shares the same 6 genes—including the genes for dark skin."

—Pam Moore

about race. As a result, we decided our first stories would deal with basic questions: What is race? What is the nature of prejudice? What can we do to get
along better?

My bosses also sent me to a weekend workshop called "Unlearning
Racism," in which a diverse group of fifty people and facilitators talked, and
occasionally cried, about the day-to-day realities of race in their lives. I found
it unpleasant, confusing, and discouraging, feelings I would encounter often
on the race beat. But it was an important first step for me in becoming comfortable with being uncomfortable when talking to people about race.

Newsroom leaders gave me time to develop the stories. How often have
you seen a TV reporter stick a microphone in a victim's face and ask, "How
do you feel?" Good luck getting past people's racial armor with that kind of
deadline-driven daily news approach, what one colleague calls "drive-by journalism." I needed time to explore the four roads that would lead to getting
something worthwhile on the air. Those four roads were research, source development, story production, and personal growth.

From "Aha!" to a Story

By the fall of 1997, I was reading piles of books and articles and having hundreds of conversations about race, trying to understand the complexities and
searching for ways to frame those complexities into stories that would make
sense to viewers.

At first, the lazy part of me dreaded the reading and the white part of me
dreaded the talking. I worried about saying the wrong thing, especially to people of color. So the approach I used was to admit my ignorance up front and
then simply listen. That approach turned out to work surprisingly well. People,
regardless of their race, were eager to talk about race with a journalist. But
most didn't want to talk in front of a TV camera. Many people of color said they
don't trust what they perceive as a white media, and many white people told
me that they felt as though they couldn't talk about race honestly for fear they
would be seen as politically incorrect or racist.

As I listened, I paid special attention to my own feelings, those "aha!" moments that revealed truths that moved me, surprised me, informed me, and
stayed with me. I remember two particular examples.

I took a black ally out to lunch to pick his brain about the race project, and
he said, "You know, there's really no such thing as race." Say what? I thought he
was joking or in denial. "Ask a geneticist," he said. So I did. I'll never forget the
excitement when I got on the phone with Sylvia Spengler, a white geneticist at
U.C. Berkeley, who laughed and said, "Your friend is absolutely right." Sud-

denly I felt like I had a breaking news story: "NO SUCH THING AS RACE!" blared the headline in my head. It turns out a lot of people in our audience shared my ignorance, and the genetics segment, "What Is Race?" became perhaps the most memorable.

Another time I was talking with a black neighbor about race when he pointed out the difference between our everyday realities. "When you wake up in the morning," he said, "you don't have to say to yourself, 'I wonder what's going to happen to me today because I'm white.'" That statement challenged my egalitarian beliefs. I didn't want to believe that he and I could be living in the same neighborhood but different worlds. Still, I couldn't shake the feeling that my neighbor had said something truer than my own beliefs. I just needed to figure out how to turn this idea of different realities into a television story.

The "Racial Rorschach Test"

The *About Race* project needed people who could articulate their racial insights on camera, what I called "honest voices." Our production team tried interviewing diversity trainers, political activists, and other so-called race experts. They were honest enough but often sounded unspontaneous or tied to an agenda. Even more insidious, the race of the expert literally colored their credibility in the eyes of viewers. Let me explain that. Our production team was made up of black and white people. When we interviewed black experts, they tended to be more credible in the eyes of black team members than in the eyes of white members; the opposite was true when we interviewed white experts. We began referring to this phenomenon as the "racial Rorschach test." I had already seen it in action when I trusted the information about genetics from the white scientist while doubting the black ally who had told me about the myth of racial genetics in the first place.

Our *About Race* team addressed this problem in two ways. First, we admitted it was an issue and began openly talking about it. Second, we started looking for everyday folks willing to share their thoughts about race on camera. We felt that these folks would pass the racial Rorschach test with our viewers more readily than the experts would. To find these voices, we went to offices and hair salons, schools and private homes, often without a camera until we could build enough trust to come back with the gear.

To make people more comfortable on camera, we often tried to match the race of the interviewer with the interviewee. That's not to say all people in a group think alike. But we found that a racial connection helped bring out those honest voices. Having said that, it was also good to have someone in the room who was not the same race as the interviewee, a backseat interviewer who could ask the perhaps stupid but enlightening question from across the racial divide: How do Asians feel being the "model minority"? How do black people feel when they work in a mostly white workplace? Why does the subject of race make some white men angry?

I think the key to getting people to go on camera was simply treating them and their viewpoints with respect.

First, Engage the Viewer

Race is such a volatile subject that we were afraid of viewers zapping us with their remotes at the first hint of preaching or finger-pointing. So from the start we wanted to engage them with fresh information before challenging them with deeper issues.

We framed the first few stories as a pop quiz. The idea was to get people at home thinking about their own beliefs and then provide them with some solid information.

For example, I wanted to do a story representing my neighbor's viewpoint that people live in different realities based on race. I broke the subject down into three elements: (1) pop quiz questions; (2) facts from studies and government statistics; and (3) comments about race relations from our honest voices.

The first pop quiz question was: "How important is race in your daily life?" The result was dramatic. Most white people answered that they don't think about race very much (many said they consider themselves "colorblind"), while most people of color answered that they think about race every day. To me, that segment was revelatory. No wonder we have trouble talking about race!

The second element—studies and statistics—added context and factual oomph to the story, showing racial inequities in education, employment, health care, and family wealth. And our third element, honest voices, showed people talking about their different realities. Specifically, we showed black workers and customers in a hair salon, and a white couple in their suburban home.

The hair salon was the idea of a black colleague, who personally vouched for me to the salon's owner. That allowed me to hang out for a couple of afternoons without a camera. When the owner finally agreed to let the camera in, I brought along Fred Blankenship, a personable black intern who got the discussion going.

Once people got used to the camera, they wouldn't stop talking, although I got nervous phone calls afterward from two people worried that they had said the wrong thing. I told them I would go over the script with them before editing, something I had never done before. I did this because I had gained their honest voices through trust, and I felt a responsibility to maintain that relationship and not suddenly bully people once I had my sound bites. One lady in the salon changed her mind about being on camera but still allowed us to use her voice. We made no other changes.

Finding a white person to go on camera was tougher. There were many apologies and broken appointments. Finally I found a woman who had just survived cancer treatment and told me, "What the hell, this can't be worse than facing death." Once she agreed, her husband reluctantly followed. And again, once the camera was rolling, they had a lot to say. Since I had set the precedent of going over the script with people from the hair salon, I offered the same opportunity to the white couple. They felt they were treated fairly in the script, and we made no changes.

Race Is Personal

As journalists, we are supposed to be accurate, fair, and balanced. But race is more personal than any subject I've ever covered, and examining my own biases became part of my essential research.

I suppose that my research had actually been sparked four years earlier when I was teamed with Karyne Holmes, a black video editor, to produce a documentary about the history of black baseball players. At the time, I consid-

The KRON-TV team during its interview with Keith Woods

"Race is such a volatile subject that we were afraid of viewers zapping us with their remotes at the first hint of preaching or finger-pointing. So from the start we wanted to engage them with fresh information before challenging them with deeper issues."

—Craig Franklin

ered myself a well-intentioned, racially sophisticated, sensitive guy. So it shocked me when our increasing disagreements led to a blowup: Karyne accused me of being racist, and I called her incompetent. At this point, a little counseling might have helped, but we really didn't know how to talk about race at our TV station. Management simply removed Karyne from the documentary, and I finished without her. That incident left me with a bad reputation among many of my African American colleagues, and it also made me start thinking about race, albeit with some resentment.

Karyne and I didn't speak again until the *About Race* project started four years later, and Karyne was assigned as my tape editor. The two people with probably the worst personal race relations in the building were going to be reunited for a lengthy, high-pressure project on race relations.

At Karyne's suggestion, we took a long, long walk and decided we didn't have to like each other, but we had to learn how to talk about our differences more honestly. In working together on *About Race,* Karyne and I ended up living the very subject we were reporting on. Through fighting, talking, and listening, we reshaped our pain and differences into an unlikely friendship that has grown through several more years of collaboration.

About Race forced me to question my own biases and the rules of journalism. Who was I to decide what was fair or balanced? Was my white reality more objective than Karyne's black reality?

As a result of these questions, *About Race* became highly collaborative. Karyne and I, along with black reporter Pam Moore and white reporter Pete Wilson, became the core team, analyzing every fact, picture, and sound bite from various perspectives, trying to anticipate and narrow the racial Rorschach messages we might be sending to our audience.

Our bosses formed the next layer of analysis. And as I mentioned earlier, I began reading draft scripts to several of our key sources. That was tricky, because we risked watering down the stories to accommodate everybody's point of view. Instead, I think we managed to bolster fairness and balance in our stories, challenge or confirm the honest voices, and add context and nuance in ways that no single person's vision could have accomplished.

To this day, I still read draft scripts, or parts of scripts, to key sources as a way of improving my stories, whether or not they are about race.

It Made a Difference

Judging from the hundreds of e-mails we received, I think we succeeded in engaging viewers with the *About Race* project. Even the criticisms were usually wrapped in appreciation. Also, some five hundred teachers requested copies of

About Race, which KRON-TV provided free of charge. Many of my colleagues said that it was our proudest moment as a news station.

Over the years, we continued reporting on race, from stories about mixed-race marriages and biracial people to cutting-edge science on how the brain reacts to racial differences. We even did a two-part series about how TV news affects race relations. But perhaps even more important, we steadily integrated race and ethnicity into our total news coverage, pulling in people and issues that might previously have been ignored.

That's not to say everyone agreed with our more inclusive news philosophy. A new white manager once complained to me, "We're supposed to be journalists, not social workers." But in a way, we've always been both. Like it or not, our journalism affects the social fabric when we focus on crime and sensationalism, showing people of color in predominantly antisocial roles. And our journalism also affects the social fabric when we pay attention to developing better tools for covering the most diverse nation in the history of the world.

All interview photographs by Russ Katsumoto and Gary Mercer.

To screen the KRON-TV team interviews, select IDENTITY on the DVD Main Menu then *About Race* Series.

DISCUSSION POINTS

- How important do you think it is to have racial and ethnic diversity among journalists when telling stories like "What Is Race?" in the *About Race* series?
- Why, in the arena of local broadcast television, do you think the KRON series on race was so groundbreaking?
- What insights, myths, and stereotypes do you think these pieces revealed?
- What do these stories and Craig Franklin's essay say about how comfortable the mainstream media is with exploring this subject?
- Relying on your own experience, discuss how using the racial Rorschach test described by Franklin can affect the way stories about race relations are reported.
- In handling a race assignment, how would you deal with the comment by the KRON news manager who said, "We're supposed to be journalists, not social workers"? Do journalists have a social responsibility to delve into these topics even when they are not breaking news?

SUGGESTED READINGS AND WEBSITES

Books

Broussard, Albert S. Black *San Francisco: The Struggle for Racial Equality in the West, 1900–1954.* Lawrence: University Press of Kansas, 1993.

This study explores the Black Panther Party's origins in the tumultuous history of race relations in the San Francisco Bay Area after the Second World War and documents the role that this new radical view played in transforming the nature of African American protest.

Lind, Rebecca Ann. *Race/Gender/Media: Considering Diversity Across Audience, Content, and Producers.* New York: Allyn and Bacon, 2004.

This University of Illinois at Chicago professor's compilation of forty-four essays addresses a variety of issues—from production to content to audience—to help students think more critically about creating stories on race and gender.

Websites

www.pbs.org/kqed/fillmore/learning/people/broussard.html

More of Professor Broussard's extensive writings are available on this site.

www.ciij.org

"News Watch" is a diversity-oriented Website, housed at San Francisco State University's Department of Journalism.

www.spj.org/diversity_search.asp

The Rainbow Sourcebook Search engine of the Society of Professional Journalists Diversity site.

CHAPTER 3

STORY

BEST OF FRIENDS, WORLDS APART

MIRTA OJITO, *THE NEW YORK TIMES*

MIRTA OJITO

Mirta Ojito, an author and freelance journalist, teaches immigration reporting at the Columbia Graduate School of Journalism, where she was the outstanding Mid-Career Program graduate in 2001. She left *The New York Times* in 2002 to write her widely acclaimed memoir *Finding Mañana: A Memoir of a Cuban Exodus,* the story of her journey from Cuba to Miami during the Mariel boat lift. "Best of Friends, Worlds Apart," which defines the racial and economic landscape of Miami through the friendship of two Cuban immigrants, was part of *The Times*'s 2001 Pulitzer Prize–winning series *How Race Is Lived in America.*

WORLDS APART

Reporter Mirta Ojito's story of two Cuban friends who floated across the sea in rafts and then drifted apart in Miami is a study in how racial identity inexorably rises to the surface in relationships. The story, part of *The New York Times*'s Pulitzer Prize–winning series *How Race Is Lived in America,* pushes readers to see the complex realities of race that often reside outside the dichotomous frames of right and wrong.

This story vividly depicts how race defines the American lifestyle and at the same time offers a dual lesson about how to write humanely about the way demographic change impacts a city. In telling the story of Achmed and Joel, Ojito captures the cultural landscape that has evolved in Miami since 1959, when Fidel Castro rose to power in Cuba.

Ojito's own experience as a sixteen-year-old immigrant to Miami during the Mariel boat lift provides a depth of understanding about Cubans that few reporters possess. Still, she confesses that the black Cuban experience came as a surprise to her, just as it would to any reporter exploring a story outside of his or her racial or ethnic group.

Ojito's work demonstrates how a reporter's attention to small details, revealing anecdotes, and telling quotes can turn fragmented insights into a coherent image of how racial attitudes perpetuate segregation. The reporting that went into this tale was painstaking and at times tedious. Ojito took nothing for granted. When she was unsure about what Achmed or Joel thought, she retraced important questions to ensure that she was capturing the racial feelings that surfaced with both of her characters. When she wanted to know about the current racial climate in Cuba, she sought out the research she needed to answer those questions.

This eloquent narrative about how two childhood friends ended up occupying different worlds offers a broader portrait of how Miami treats its white and black citizens.

BEST OF FRIENDS, WORLDS APART

Joel Ruiz Is Black. Achmed Valdés Is White.
In America They Discovered It Matters

By Mirta Ojito
New York Times Staff Writer
Published June 5, 2000

MIAMI—Havana, sometime before 1994: As dusk descends on the quaint sea-side village of Guanabo, two young men kick a soccer ball back and forth and back and forth across the sand. The tall one, Joel Ruiz, is black. The short, wiry one, Achmed Valdés, is white.

They are the best of friends.

Miami, January 2000: Mr. Valdés is playing soccer, as he does every Saturday, with a group of light-skinned Latinos in a park near his apartment. Mr. Ruiz surprises him with a visit, and Mr. Valdés, flushed and sweating, runs to greet him. They shake hands warmly.

But when Mr. Valdés darts back to the game, Mr. Ruiz stands off to the side, arms crossed, looking on as his childhood friend plays the game that was once their shared joy. Mr. Ruiz no longer plays soccer. He prefers basketball with black Latinos and African-Americans from his neighborhood.

The two men live only four miles apart, not even 15 minutes by car. Yet they are separated by a far greater distance, one they say they never envisioned back in Cuba.

In ways that are obvious to the black man but far less so to the white one, they have grown apart in the United States because of race. For the first time, they inhabit a place where the color of their skin defines the outlines of their lives—where they live, the friends they make, how they speak, what they wear, even what they eat.

"It's like I am here and he is over there," Mr. Ruiz said. "And we can't cross over to the other's world."

It is not that, growing up in Cuba's mix of black and white, they were unaware of their difference in color. Fidel Castro may have decreed an end to racism in Cuba, but that does not mean racism has simply gone away. Still, color was not what defined them. Nationality, they had been taught, meant far more than race. They felt, above all, Cuban.

Here in America, Mr. Ruiz still feels Cuban. But above all he feels black. His world is a black world, and to live there is to be constantly conscious of

Joel Ruiz, left, and Achmed Valdés, remain as good friends as ever, yet they both know there is little that binds them anymore but their memories.

race. He works in a black-owned bar, dates black women, goes to an African-American barber. White barbers, he says, "don't understand black hair." He generally avoids white neighborhoods, and when his world and the white world intersect, he feels always watched, and he is always watchful.

Mr. Valdés, who is 29, a year younger than his childhood friend, is simply, comfortably Cuban, an upwardly mobile citizen of the Miami mainstream. He lives in an all-white neighborhood, hangs out with white Cuban friends and goes to black neighborhoods only when his job, as a deliveryman for Restonic mattresses, forces him to. When he thinks about race, which is not very often, it is in terms learned from other white Cubans: American blacks, he now believes, are to be avoided because they are delinquent and dangerous and resentful of whites. The only blacks he trusts, he says, are those he knows from Cuba.

Since leaving Havana on separate rafts in 1994, the two friends have seen each other just a handful of times in Miami—at a funeral, a baby shower, a birthday party and that soccer game, a meeting arranged for a newspaper photographer. They have visited each other's homes only once.

They say they remain as good friends as ever, yet they both know there is little that binds them anymore but their memories. Had they not become best friends in another country, in another time, they would not be friends at all today.

Two Boys on a Bus

They met on a bus, No. 262, the one that took Joel from his home in the racially mixed neighborhood of Peñas Altas to middle school, 35 minutes away. Achmed got on in Guanabo, and they sat together talking, as boys do, about everything and nothing.

Both grew up in orderly homes, with hard-working parents who supported the Castro government. Their fathers worked for the state oil company. Their mothers—Joel's was a nurse, Achmed's an administrator in stores for tourists—knew each other and sometimes met for coffee.

The boys' friendship was cemented through school and sport. They stood up for each other against troublemakers. "Just to know we were there for each other was good," Mr. Ruiz recalls. When his girlfriend got pregnant in high school, Achmed was the first person he told. They played soccer and baseball and ran track. Joel often stayed for dinner at Achmed's, where there was a color television and an antenna powerful enough to pick up American channels.

Because of her job, Achmed's mother had access to some of Havana's best restaurants. Every year she would take him out for a birthday dinner, and every year he would invite his best friend, Joel. "I couldn't think of anybody I would rather spend my time with," Mr. Valdés recalled.

But as they grew older, each became restless with the limitations of life in Cuba.

Achmed was in sixth grade when an aunt who had fled to Venezuela gave him a pair of white sneakers. He loved them so, he immediately wore them to school. Almost as immediately, the principal visited him at home to warn him about the troubling political implications of those foreign sneakers. At the university, too, his professors wondered why he wore foreign clothes and rode a nice bicycle. He wondered right back why he could not wear and ride whatever he wanted. When he was expelled for failing two classes, he saw it as punishment for being politically incorrect.

Before long, he found work at sea, trapping lobsters and selling them for $4 each. In a country where most people earn less than $10 a month, it was a living, though not a life. When the government allowed thousands of Cubans to leave in small boats and rafts in 1994, he was ready.

His friend Joel was ready, too, though it had taken him far longer to make up his mind. Indeed, given Cuba's racial history, it is hardly surprising that black

Cubans have generally been far less eager than whites to flee to America. After all, in pre-revolutionary Cuba, blacks and whites had lived largely segregated, separated by huge disparities in economic and social standing. But two months after he seized power in 1959, Fidel Castro ordered whites to look upon blacks as equals and began leveling the economic and educational playing fields.

When Joel was very small, his family lived crammed into one room of an old carved-up mansion. Soon, the government gave them a three-bedroom apartment in a development that Joel's father had helped build. Before the

Librado Romero/The New York Times

Joel Ruiz cannot forget about race. But instead of limits, he focuses on the opportunities.

revolution, Joel's mother had made a living cleaning white people's homes. It was Fidel, she told him over and over, who had given her the chance to become a nurse. And so Joel came to believe that it was no big deal, being black in Cuba.

As for America, he had seen the images on government television: guards beating black prisoners, the police loosing dogs or training hoses on civil-rights marchers.

But as Cuba's economy fell apart in the 1990's, he began to see things differently. He left military school for a cooking program, hoping for a well-paying job at a tourist hotel. Once he graduated, the only job available was washing windows. Look around, co-workers told him, look who's getting the good jobs. The answer was whites.

He noticed, too, when he watched the American channels at Achmed's house, that some blacks seemed to live well in America. He saw black lawyers, politicians, wealthy athletes. It made him think: "It's not so bad over there. Blacks are all right."

On Aug. 21, 1994, he climbed onto a raft and made for Florida. Like his friend before him, he was intercepted by the United States Coast Guard and sent to the American base at Guantánamo. The next year, they were freed—first Mr. Valdés, then Mr. Ruiz—and headed straight to Miami.

A Shock of Identity

In Miami, Joel Ruiz discovered a world that neither American television nor Communist propaganda had prepared him for. Dogs did not growl at him and police officers did not hose him. But he felt the stares of security guards when he entered a store in a white neighborhood and the subtle recoiling of white women when he walked by.

Miami is deeply segregated, and when Mr. Ruiz arrived, he settled into one of the black urban sections, Liberty City. He had family there. His uncle Jorge Aranguren had arrived in 1980 and married an African-American. Mr. Ruiz took a job at his uncle's liquor store and started learning English.

The first thing Mr. Ruiz noticed about his new world was the absence of whites. He had seen barrios in Havana with more blacks than others, but he had never lived in a place where everybody was black. Far from feeling comfortable, he yearned for the mixing he had known in Cuba.

In Cuba, he says, he had been taught to see skin color—in his case, the color of chocolate milk—as not much more important than, say, the color of his eyes. But this was not Cuba. This was Miami, and in Miami, as the roughly 7 percent of the area's Cubans who are black quickly learn, skin color easily trumps nationality.

Mr. Ruiz began to understand that in earnest on Valentine's Day 1996, three

> "In Cuba, I walked as I owned the streets. Here I have to figure out where, what, when, everything."
>
> —Joel Ruiz

months after his arrival in Miami. He had gone to dinner with his uncle Ramón Suárez at Versailles, a popular restaurant in Little Havana, a bastion of white Cuban-Americans. They took three light-skinned girlfriends along. Mr. Ruiz wore one of his nicest outfits—black jeans and a red-and-green checked shirt. He was new to the country and unsure how to behave, but he felt comfortable at Versailles. After all, he remembers thinking, he was among Cubans. He knew the food, he could read the menu, and he could talk to the waiters.

The five sat in the back. Mr. Ruiz concentrated on the conversation and on his meal. More than four years later, he remembers what he ate: a breaded steak with rice and beans and fried plantains.

Shortly before midnight, the five left in a new red Nissan. One of the women drove. Mr. Suárez sat next to her, taking pictures of his nephew and the other women laughing in back. Twenty blocks from the restaurant, four police cars, lights flashing and sirens wailing, stopped them. The woman who was driving saw them first and yelled for Mr. Suárez to drop the camera.

The officers, with weapons drawn, ordered them out of the car. Terrified, Mr. Ruiz did as he was told, spreading his legs and leaning face down on the car as the officers frisked him. It seemed like a very long time before they were allowed to go.

That was when one officer, a white Cuban-American, said something in Spanish that forever changed Mr. Ruiz's perspective on race. "I've been keeping an eye on you for a while," Mr. Ruiz recalls the officer saying. "Since you were in the restaurant. I saw you leave and I saw so many blacks in the car, I figured I would check you out."

Mr. Ruiz and his uncle stood speechless until an African-American officer approached them, apologized and sent them on their way. Afterward, his uncle said he was sure the police had been called by restaurant patrons uncomfortable with Mr. Ruiz's racially mixed group. His English teacher, an African-American, told him that white police officers liked to single out blacks driving red cars. Mr. Ruiz is not sure what to believe, but the truth is not in the details.

> "I've been keeping an eye on you for a while," Mr. Ruiz recalls the officer saying. "Since you were in the restaurant. I saw you leave and I saw so many blacks in the car, I figured I would check you out."

"Up until that day, I thought all Cubans were the same," he says. "It took a while to sink in, but that incident made me start thinking in a different way."

All at once, he had to learn how a person with dark skin should behave in this country: if an officer is following your car, do not turn your head; the police don't like it. Do not stare at other drivers, especially if they are young and white and loud. He has even learned how to walk: fast in stores, to avoid security guards; slower in the streets, so as not to attract the attention of the police. On the street, he avoids any confrontation.

He pays bills in cash because of an incident at a bank two years ago. When he asked to buy a certificate of deposit with $6,000 in lottery winnings, the bank officer, a white Cuban woman, looked puzzled, he recalls, and told him: "This is different. Your kind likes to spend the money, not save it." Since then he has not had a checking account.

And, of course, he avoids Cuban restaurants in white neighborhoods.

"In Cuba, I walked as if I owned the streets," he says. "Here I have to figure out where, what, when, everything."

He often finds himself caught between two worlds. Whites see him simply as black. African-Americans dismiss him as Cuban. "They tell me I'm Hispanic. I tell them to look at my face, my hair, my skin," he says. "I am black, too. I may speak different, but we all come from the same place."

Librado Romero/The New York Times
For Joel Ruiz, there is little time for relaxation. On this night, he collects cover charges at his uncle's bar in a black Miami neighborhood.

He has started to refer to himself as Afro-Cuban, integrating, indeed embracing, the ways of his black neighbors. He enjoys what he calls black food—fried chicken, collard greens, grits—though he still lusts for a Cuban steak and plantains. He listens to rhythm and blues at home and at work; in the car, though, he listens to a Cuban crooner whose romantic ballads he has memorized. He dresses "black," he says, showing off his white velvet Hush Puppies and silk shirts. When he speaks English, he mimics black Miamians, but his words carry an unmistakably Spanish inflection.

Some months after the Versailles incident, when Achmed Valdés first saw his old friend, he was puzzled. "Joel has changed," he said. "He is in another world now."

A Seamless Transition

Pretty much anywhere else in America, Mr. Valdés would fit nicely into the niche reserved for Hispanic immigrants. If the question of race came up, he would be called a light-skinned Hispanic. Here in Miami, such distinctions do not apply. Here he is not a member of any minority group. He is Cuban and he is white.

This, after all, is a city run by Cubans, white Cubans. Not only are the mayors of Miami and Dade County Cuban, so are 7 of 13 county commissioners and 3 of 5 city commissioners. Spanish is the dominant language heard in the streets.

Mr. Valdés's transition to this world has been seamless, so much so that he does not really think of himself as an immigrant at all. His self-image is of someone well along on a sure, quick path to the middle class, someone who would be right at home in a quiet neighborhood of well-kept houses and neatly mowed lawns. And that is where he lives, with his wife, Ivette Garcia, and his mother in a one-bedroom apartment off 17th Avenue in southwest Miami.

He drives the car he likes, a 1998 Nissan that he plans to trade in soon for a newer model, says whatever is on his mind and dreams of opening his own business selling mattresses in a strip mall.

He has had to learn about punctuality and paying bills on time, but being white and Cuban, he has not had to learn how to behave. His English is tentative, but that does not matter too much here. His childhood friend may wrestle with a new identity, but when Mr. Valdés is asked how he has adapted in a strange land, he looks dumbfounded and jokes: "What are you talking about? I was born in Hialeah Hospital." Hialeah is south Florida's most Cuban city, often the first stop for Cuban exiles.

Still, he struggles the immigrant struggle. He has held a dozen jobs, from delivering Chinese food for tips to cleaning monkey cages for $6.50 an hour. Each time, he has traded up a bit, to the point where today he makes $9.60 an hour, with paid vacations and frequent overtime, to drive an 18-wheel Restonic mattress truck all over the state.

Librado Romero/The New York Times

Achmed Valdés, in hat, plays a game of soccer in his off hours.

On weekends, however, he looks refreshed and energized, positively glow-ing with the middle-class knowledge of having earned his weekly respite.

It is 2 p.m. one recent Saturday, and Mr. Valdés is home from his soccer game. Before he is out of the shower, the apartment fills up with his crowd—athletic white couples, all friends from Cuba. The men drive delivery trucks. The women, like his wife, work as medical or dental assistants.

The men plop themselves on the couch and watch soccer on television. The women cluster around the kitchen table, talking about the pill. They are all in their late 20's, all still childless, focused on the English classes or profes-sional courses that will advance their careers. The pill is pharmaceutical insur-ance for their dreams: eventually having children, owning businesses, buying suburban homes. It is all planned.

With some pride, Mr. Valdés shows recent pictures of his house in Cuba. When he comes to one of his father with his new wife, his mother recoils at the sight of her ex-husband with his arm around a black woman. Mr. Valdés con-centrates on the coconut trees he planted in the backyard years ago. "Look how tall they are," he says, as if surprised that his house, his father, his trees have gone on without him.

The talk drifts back to Cuba, as it so often does in Miami. Like much of Miami's Cuban community, Mr. Valdés is quite conservative politically. A favorite topic is how much he says he has learned about the Cuban government since arriving here—the political prisoners, the human-rights abuses.

He listens to Miami's Cuban exile radio every day, particularly enjoying a program in which the host regularly reads the names of the men and women who have died in prison or were killed trying to overthrow the Castro government. Like most Cubans in Miami—but unlike Mr. Ruiz and most Americans—he believes that Elián González, the 6-year-old shipwreck survivor, should stay in this country rather than return to Cuba with his father.

Ninety miles and four and a half years later, Mr. Valdés has ended up back in Cuba—albeit a new and improved Cuba.

"The only thing I miss from Cuba is being able to see the ocean from my windows," he says. "Everything else I need and want is right here. This is exactly the country that I always imagined."

Confined in a Comfort Zone

"Qué bolá, acere?" ("What's up, brother?") Joel Ruiz asks a friend who has stopped to share neighborhood gossip. It is noon on a Tuesday, Mr. Ruiz's only day off.

The friend leans in the window of Mr. Ruiz's 1989 Buick, and they talk about a shootout in front of the friend's house the day before. Drugs, for sure. Both men know the shooters from the neighborhood, and his friend is worried that they may come back. His little daughter was in the front yard when the gunfire started.

Mr. Ruiz cuts him off politely and heads to the house of another friend, a middle-aged Cuban woman who, he says, loves him like a son. What she would really love today,

> For the most part, blacks are outsiders in this racially charged city, the scene of some of America's worst race riots. Blacks, especially black Cubans, lack economic and political power and resent the white Cubans who have so much of both.

though, is $30 for rice and meat. "I don't have any money in the house," she says, lighting a cigarette. "It's terrible."

Having just cashed his paycheck—$175 for six days of work at the bar—Mr. Ruiz has money in his pocket. He peels off two 20's, and as he drives away, the woman yells after him, "Come by tonight and I'll make you dinner." He waves her off. He is in a rush. As always on these days of rest, relaxation is in short supply.

Like Achmed Valdés, Mr. Ruiz is a man of middle-class ambitions. He is studying English and wants to be a physical therapist. With the help of his uncles, he bought a house in Allapatah—a neighborhood of dark-skinned Latinos and African-Americans—and rents out half of it for extra income. Sure, he would like to be spending his day off hanging out, having a beer, watching sports on TV. But this day, like all his days, is circumscribed by race and the responsibilities that come with being a black man in a poor place.

For the most part, blacks are outsiders in this racially charged city, the scene of some of America's worst race riots. Blacks, especially black Cubans, lack economic and political power and resent the white Cubans who have so much of both. Steadily, relentlessly, the problems of Miami's poor have become Mr. Ruiz's, too.

When his uncle was imprisoned for drug-dealing, Mr. Ruiz was shamed and told almost no one. But the uncle had helped him get started in Miami, and so he stepped in to keep his bar going and help support his little girl. When another uncle was killed by a drunken driver and left his family with no insurance, Mr. Ruiz stepped in to help the widow and her 3-year-old daughter. He also sends money to his 11-year-old son in Cuba.

His entire routine, almost his entire life, is focused on a 20-block area around his home. Occasionally he ventures to South Beach, the fashionable zone where race is not much of an issue. Once, he went to a park in Little Havana, where Cubans, mostly retirees, gather to play dominoes and reminisce.

"But I left right away," says Mr. Ruiz, whose politics, despite a dislike of the Castro government, are more moderate than Mr. Valdés's. "I couldn't be sitting around talking about Cuba and Fidel all day."

Indeed, if his life is confined, he also feels comfortable in this place where he can be black and Cuban, where he can belong. As he drives with the windows down, he waves at people he knows, black men and women, Cubans and non-Cubans alike.

He has ambitions for the evening—some basketball, a date with his girlfriend, a black Cuban, to see "Best Man," a film about successful black professionals.

But 4 o'clock finds him at the bar, Annie Mae's, getting things ready for the night. He puts beer in the cooler, sweeps the floors, cleans the bathrooms, polishes the tables and waits for the women who are supposed to run the bar when he is off. He waits, goes out for a while, then waits some more. Still no relief. He turns on the TV and begins watching the news.

"Have you noticed there are no blacks on television?" he says suddenly.

He should have been playing basketball by now, but instead he begins to play video tennis, his eyes fixed on the ball's glowing path through the darkness of the bar.

Encountering the Unknown

When Mr. Valdés arrived in Miami, friends and relatives did not just give him the obligatory immigrant lessons on how to fill out forms and apply for jobs. They also sent him a clear message about race, one shared by many, though not all, white Cubans: Blacks in America are different from Cuban blacks. Do not trust them and do not go to their neighborhoods.

Mr. Valdés has visited his old friend's home just once. In late 1995, when he heard that Mr. Ruiz had arrived in Miami, he went to see him in Liberty City. Following his friend's directions, Mr. Valdés found the place—a small wood house set back in a huge grassy lot. A chain-link fence surrounds it, and there is an air of abandonment about it, but it does not inspire fear.

Still, he felt uneasy, the only white man in a black neighborhood. The houses were ugly, he says; the few people on the streets stared at him.

Librado Romero/The New York Times

Achmed Valdés lives in an all-white neighborhood and only goes to black neighborhoods when his job, as a deliveryman for a mattress company, requires it.

"It's not that I'm racist," Mr. Valdés says. "But even in Cuba, I had a vague sense blacks were different. That becomes more real here. In Cuba, everybody's the same, because everybody's poor. Not so here."

"Maybe it's just because, for us, that world is the unknown, but we felt uncomfortable," says his wife, who is as talkative as her husband is reserved. "It's like this: In Cuba I ventured out into the ocean, swimming by myself, because I knew the water, the currents. Here, when I swim, I never stray far from shore because I don't know what's out there."

One of Mr. Valdés's early jobs was delivering Ritz soda. Twice, he says, his truck was broken into in black neighborhoods. He lost 16 cases of soda and $2,000 in checks. "Everywhere else you leave the truck open and nothing happens," he says.

Those experiences have left him with no interest in the black world and not a kind word for African-Americans. "They basically have kids and go on welfare," he says. "What else is there to know?"

In Cuba, he says, he grew up with blacks. It was almost impossible not to, and so he never gave it much thought. His immediate neighbors were mostly white, and he never dated a black woman—"I just don't find them attractive," he explains—but he attended racially mixed schools, and several of his soccer buddies were black.

Here, his contacts with African-Americans are limited to chance encounters at work, his relationships with blacks to those he knows from Cuba. "As far as blacks," he says, "I only trust those I know, because I know they are not delinquents."

Mr. Valdés does not flinch when expressing his feelings about blacks. He is passionate and definitive, but he can also be generous and kindhearted, a man who shared his food with children in Guantánamo and regularly sends care packages to his friends, black and white, in Cuba.

> "To eat a good steak in Cuba, I had to steal it from the restaurant where I worked. Here, I may not want to go to Versailles because I feel uncomfortable, but I can go anywhere else I choose, and no one can stop me at the door because it is illegal and I know my rights."
>
> —Joel Ruiz

Mr. Ruiz, he explains, is not his only black friend here. He is also friendly with Fernando Larduet, a man he knew marginally in Cuba but grew to like at Guantánamo. In a video of their time there that Mr. Valdés likes to watch to relive his daring escape from Cuba, there is an image of Mr. Valdés, who, for lack of a mirror, is gently shaving Mr. Larduet.

"It's not that I'm racist," Mr. Valdés says. "But even in Cuba, I had a vague sense blacks were different. That becomes more real here. In Cuba, everybody's the same, because everybody's poor. Not so here."

Soon after arriving in Miami, Mr. Valdés and his wife went to visit a friend at a hotel downtown. On their way, they made a wrong turn and ended up deep in black Miami.

"It was a cold night and it was really dark, even though it was early," his wife says, over dinner at a restaurant in Coral Gables, a fashionable and very white area of Miami. "People were walking around with sheets over their heads, and there was a fire in a trash can in every corner."

"And the houses were boarded up with pieces of wood to keep the cold away," her husband chimes in, barely lifting his eyes from his lasagna. "And people were smoking crack in the middle of the street."

She shudders. "We got out of there fast," she says.

In Cuba, the Limits of Equality

The soccer field where Joel and Achmed played back in Guanabo is still a busy place, a scrum of young men vying to put the ball into a goal strung together with scraps of fish netting. On this January day, the game is still an easy mix of blacks and whites.

A few miles away, in the main plaza of the University of Havana, about 200 students of all colors form a circle around a troupe of dancers. They are not clustered by race. At one point they form a human chain and then they, too, begin to dance, a rainbow of Cuba's best and brightest bathed in sunlight.

At first blush, Cuba might seem to be some kind of racial utopia. Unlike the United States, where there is limited cultural fusion between blacks and whites, Cuban culture—from its music to its religion—is as African as it is Spanish. But despite the genuinely easy mixing, despite the government's rhetoric, there is still a profound and open cultural racism at play.

The same black students who were part of that dancing rainbow say it is common to call someone "un negro," or "black," for doing something inappropriate. "When a man insults a woman in the street, I will shout at him, 'You are not a man, you are black!'" said Meri Casadevalle Pérez, a law student who is herself black.

And a white mechanic named Armando Cortina explained that he would never want his daughters to marry a black. "Blacks are not attractive," he said.

Blacks, he added with conviction, commit the overwhelming majority of crimes in Cuba—a statement impossible to assess in a country that seldom publishes crime statistics. Even Cuba's racial breakdown is uncertain, with a black population thought to be as large as 60 percent.

What is clear is that while the revolution tore down most economic barriers between blacks and whites, there is inequality at the top. Blacks hold few important positions in government or tourism. They are underrepresented at the university and in the nicest neighborhoods. And the few blacks who have tried to organize around the issue of civil rights have been jailed or ostracized.

Bill Brent, a former Black Panther leader who lives in Cuba, said he had arrived full of hope that the government had found the "antidote to racism." Not only does racism persist, he lamented, but black Cubans lack the racial identity to do anything about it.

"The revolution convinced everyone that they are all Cuban and that their struggles were all the same, not separate or different because of their race," he said. "If a Cuban raises his voice to say, 'I am being discriminated against because I am black,' then he would be labeled a dissident."

Still, a voice of black identity can occasionally be heard.

In a sun-scorched neighborhood outside Havana, that voice resonates in the angry rap of Tupac Shakur. It blasts from a boombox at the feet of a group of young black men propped casually against a wall, dressed in a fair imitation of American hip-hop fashion: baggy jeans, oversize T-shirts, Nike sneakers and khaki caps with the brims turned down.

Relatives in Miami sent them the clothes and the rap tapes, they say. As they listen to the music now, it is clear they have not mastered the English lyrics and have only a sketchy sense of the song's meaning. But it does not seem to matter.

"It's about the lives of black people," says 18-year-old Ulysses Oliva. "It is for us. That is why we love it."

Two Men in Two Miamis

When Joel Ruiz told his mother that he, too, would be joining the migration to America, she fell to her knees and begged him to stay. Only when she realized she could not change his mind did she get up, dry her tears and cook him his favorite meal—sugar-coated ham with rice and black beans. Then she accompanied him to Guanabo and cried and cried and waved his wisp of a raft out toward the horizon.

Mr. Ruiz rarely talks about his mother; at the thought of her, his eyes seem to melt under a curtain of tears. But he says he does not for a minute regret leaving Cuba. It's not that he isn't acutely aware of the way his blackness has guided his story so far in America. He understands the bargain he has made. In Cuba, he says, he did not think about race, but he had no freedom and few options.

Here he cannot forget about race, or his many responsibilities, and he has grown apart from his best friend. But instead of the limits, he focuses on the opportunities.

"To eat a good steak in Cuba, I had to steal it from the restaurant where I worked," he says. "Here, I may not want to go to Versailles because I feel uncomfortable, but I can go anywhere else I choose, and no one can stop me at the door because it is illegal and I know my rights."

Librado Romero/The New York Times
Achmed Valdés, with his wife, watches a video of his time at Guantánamo.

Along with his identity as a black man, he has found refuge in a community that welcomes him. And he has acquired an American vocabulary to frame his Cuban past. Thinking back, he points to instances of racism that he once shrugged off.

Once, on a bus in Havana, he got into a scuffle with a man he felt had stolen his seat. Afterward, a white friend's mother told him he had behaved like a black man.

"*'Te portaste como un negro,'* that's what she told me," he says. "Now, what could she possibly have meant by that, and how come I didn't see it then?"

Another time, at one of those special birthday dinners with Mr. Valdés, the maître d'hôtel stopped him at the door and asked, "And who is this?"

"What he really meant was, 'Who's the nigger?'" Mr. Ruiz says. "If that happened to me now, I would know."

Mr. Ruiz insists he does not dislike whites. He cites his friendship with Mr. Valdés as an example of his open-mindedness, just as Mr. Valdés uses their relationship to establish that he is not racist. And talking to the two men, watching them in one of their rare times together, it is impossible not to feel their fierce loyalty and genuine affection.

Yet both also know that theirs is now mostly a friendship of nostalgia. They are adults with ambitions and jobs and bills to pay, they point out, with

Librado Romero/The New York Times

Joel Ruiz has found refuge in a community that welcomes him.

little time to talk on the phone. When they do they seldom discuss anything be-yond their families in Cuba or how busy they are with work.

When it comes to race, Mr. Ruiz will give his friend the benefit of the doubt. Mr. Ruiz is proud that when he turned 30 in February, Mr. Valdés ventured to black Miami for the party at Annie Mae's. "I understand that it is more difficult for him to cross the line than it is for me," Mr. Ruiz says. "It's not his thing and I respect that."

Mr. Valdés seems uncharacteristically thoughtful when discussing his friend's life. His friend, he says, has chosen to live as a black man rather than as a Miami Cuban.

"If I were him, I would get out of there and forget about everybody else's problems and begin my own life," he says. "If he stays it is because he wants to."

Mr. Ruiz thinks his friend cannot possibly understand. Even after he moved in April to an apartment south of Miami to escape the pressures of his needy relatives, Mr. Ruiz could not cast his family or his blackness aside. He spends most of his time back in Allapatah, near the bar and the neighbors who have embraced him.

"I know he would do anything for me if I ask him to, but the one thing he can never do is to walk in my shoes," Mr. Ruiz says of his old friend. "Achmed does not know what it means to be black."

Mr. Valdés and Mr. Ruiz have never talked about race. When told of his friend's opinion of blacks, Mr. Ruiz shifts uncomfortably in his seat.

"He said that?" Mr. Ruiz asks, lifting his eyebrows. "I don't know why he would think that blacks are delinquents. I know he doesn't think that of me, and I'm black. I've always been black." A pause. He thinks some more. "He grew up with blacks," he says. "I don't understand it. Maybe something bad happened to him. I am sure he is talking about American blacks."

Mr. Valdés has never told him about his experiences in Miami's black neighborhoods, just as Mr. Ruiz has never told him about the police outside the Versailles.

Yet Mr. Ruiz says he understands his friend's fear of crime in black neighborhoods. There are parts of Liberty City even he avoids. What he is wariest of, though, are white neighborhoods. Thinking back on that encounter outside the Versailles, he says: "Now I know enough to be grateful we weren't killed that night. The police could have thought Ramón's camera was a gun."

In Mr. Ruiz's new world, whites, even white Cubans, have become a race apart, and while they are not necessarily to be avoided, they must be watched and hardly ever trusted. He can no longer see himself in a serious relationship with a white woman. "Not for marriage," he says. "Not for life."

When he is working in the bar, the only man running a place where money, alcohol and loud music flow into the early hours of morning, the customers who catch his attention are the white men who sometimes wander in.

As he sat at a corner table right before Christmas, a black plastic Santa smiling down at him, Mr. Ruiz was relaxed, debating whether to leave for a quick basketball game or stay to help out.

Just then, two white men walked in. It was easy to tell they were Cuban. They walked as Mr. Ruiz does, that chest-first Cuban walk. Mr. Ruiz perked up. He trailed the men with his eyes. They ordered beers, and as they walked over to the pool table they were momentarily blinded by the light reflecting from a hanging ball of mirrored glass. Averting their eyes, they looked toward the darkness. There they found Mr. Ruiz's cold stare. He stared them down until they left.

"You see," he said, relaxing again, "this is why I can't leave this place. You never know who is going to walk in."

THE MAKING OF

BEST OF FRIENDS, WORLDS APART

By Mirta Ojito
New York Times Staff Writer

The *Best of Friends, Worlds Apart* story was among the first to run in *The New York Times's* Pulitzer–winning series *How Race Is Lived In America*. Like much of the series, the idea emerged at an emotional planning meeting at the home of *Times* assistant managing editor Soma Golden Behr. Here, reporter Mirta Ojito, who emigrated to the United States in 1980 during the Mariel boat lift, talks about the evolution of the story and the time she spent with Joel Ruiz, who is black, and his white friend, Achmed Valdés, to produce a story with insights that only a native Cuban could provide. The techniques she employed in reporting this story hold valuable lessons for every journalist, no matter his or her ethnic background. Shortly after this story appeared, Ojito took a leave from *The Times* to write *Finding Mañana, A Memoir of a Cuban Exodus.*

Keith Woods: How did this story bubble up from that meeting?

Mirta Ojito: I'm used to either generating an idea or being given an assignment. I'm not used to analyzing my work before, during, or after. I didn't quite understand why this particular assignment necessitated a meeting in which people would talk about their feelings. That, to me, was very strange. Some people knew they were expected to come to the meeting with an idea, but I didn't have one. I truly went to the meeting blind. I knew it was a project that had to do with race, but I hadn't thought about it. So when [project editor] Mike Winerip asked, "What happens to a black Cuban when he arrives from Cuba? What happens to him in Miami?" I just blurted out, "He becomes black." Mike asked, "And to a white Cuban?" And I said, "Well, they're still Cubans." And he said, "Well, that's really interesting."

Everyone seemed to think that was a really interesting response. I said that I really hadn't done any research, but I could base it on my experiences in Miami. Sitting there at that moment, I could only remember meeting two black Cubans in Miami in the sixteen years that I lived here. And I knew that had to be wrong.

Woods: So how did you come across these two men?

Ojito: I didn't come across them. I had no idea how to find them. The first thing I did was to call everybody I knew in Miami and ask if they knew of any such relationship [friendships between black and white Cubans]. Coincidentally, there were two very important meetings going on at that time. One, in Washington,

Arlene Morgan

Keith Woods interviews Mirta Ojito about her story.

D.C., was a meeting of U.S. and Cuban academics on the issue of race. Several Cuban academics attended. They lived in Cuba, so their point of view was very important.

The second was a meeting in Miami of an important exile organization composed mainly of academics, and I was hoping to see a lot of blacks at that meeting. There were at least three or four there, and we got together after the conference was over. All of them left with the marching orders to help me find people. I remembered that when the rafters (the more than thirty-five thousand Cubans who fled to Miami in the rafts in the summer of 1994) came, there was a local organization that helped them. I tracked them down. . . . They received federal money to help these people establish a life here, go to college, find jobs. It's sort of a resettlement process. I reached the woman who ran the center, and she remembered me from my years at *The Miami Herald*. She helped me tremendously.

Basically, her staff looked through at least thirteen hundred files of Cuban refugees in the rafters' crisis of 1994 that got help from that organization. After they located the files and looked through the pictures, made the lists, and contacted the people, they contacted me and said, "We have six people willing to meet with you." Through them, I ended up talking to about twenty-four people.

Woods: Did you take notes of things that you learned?

Ojito: Oh, absolutely. I interviewed them thoroughly and learned a lot from them about what life in Cuba was like; about being black in Miami, how they viewed the United States, how they viewed Cuba. One of the black professionals I talked to told me that the reason I wasn't finding more people was because a lot of black Cubans feel more comfortable in so-called black neighborhoods in Miami and that I should go there to find them. But I couldn't just walk the streets and stop every person I saw and ask, "Are you Cuban?" So he suggested I go there with his wife's cousin Joel, who lived in the neighborhood and was very knowledgeable. I met with Joel in the bar where he worked. He was going to take me to find these black Cubans. Many of them married or were living with Americans. Joel asked me what I was looking for. I told him, and he said, "Well, my best friend is white." And then he led me to his friend. I always knew that I needed to begin with the black person to then find the white, instead of the other way around.

Woods: Why is that?

Ojito: Because most of the Cubans who live in Miami are white. It would be like finding a needle in a haystack. But if I began with a black person, it was quicker. There were fewer of them.

Woods: How did you explain the story to Joel?

Ojito: I just said, "I'm writing about the relationship between a black and a white person in Miami. I want to know how your relationship to your best friend is different or equal to what it was in your life in Cuba, and I want to be able to witness this relationship. I want to be with you as much as I can while you're with him and also when you're alone. I'm going to be spending some time with you and some time with him and I'll just watch you. If you can, pretend I'm not here."

Woods: Joel got it right away?

Ojito: Yes. The one who didn't get it was Achmed. I told him exactly the same thing, but he always said, "Yes, OK, fine." But every time I showed up he would look at me as if to say, "Why are you here again?" He thought he would talk to me one time, and I would disappear from his life. I don't think he ever understood how often I was going to be there. In fact, he never returned my phone calls. He wasn't a hostile subject, because I would have dropped him. But he wasn't cooperative either. When I wanted to talk to him or ask him a question, I had to physically fly from New York to Miami and show up at his house or in the one place I knew he would be, which was playing soccer at a field near his house on Saturday morning. So that pretty much ruined my weekends for about a year.

Woods: As you went through the interviews with these two young men, they were slowly revealing their own biases. Were you playing back their words for them so they could hear this for themselves?

Ojito: Interesting. I did not repeat their words back to them. I tended to let them talk. I would realize the significance of what they had said, and then in my next trip I would say, "You know, last time I was here, you told me such and such. What did you mean by that?" Or, "What else can you tell me about it?" Or, "Were you really that afraid?" I wanted to make sure I had it right and that I had understood. I didn't do it immediately, but eventually I got around to it. We always explored the same subject at least twice.

Woods: What would you have done if one of them had said, "Don't write that because that will make me sound like a bigot."

Ojito: I think I would have stepped back and tried to clarify the rules of the game in a more precise way. Once a person says that, then it's obvious that the rules have not been clear from the beginning. So you need to go back to whatever ground rules you have established. I could not have worked with a person who was constantly self-editing. I didn't mind a person who thought about the answer before they said it. In fact, that's good. But there's got to be a level of trust. And if you don't have that after a few weeks or a few months, I think clearly you're in the wrong relationship, and you're following the wrong people.

Arlene Morgan

Author Mirta Ojito during her interview with Keith Woods.

"I think that if you manage to tell a story that others have told, but in a compelling way, people who read it will think about it, and that may impact behavior. In the end, that's why we all write."

—Mirta Ojito

Woods: When doing stories on race, journalists will often say, "This is going to be very difficult because people don't like to talk about it." Yet you got some very candid remarks from both of these men. How did you accomplish that?

Ojito: I couldn't have done that story in a week or even in a month. I think it was just being with them for so long and really trying to understand who they were.

Woods: How were you correcting for whatever biases you might have brought to the story?

Ojito: I guess I knew, before Joel and Achmed acknowledged they knew it, that life in Cuba has not been as ideal as Joel had portrayed it. I have lived here for a long time, longer than they have. I studied Cuba as a reporter and returned to Cuba as a sort of socialized American, understanding the language of race better than they do. I knew that it wasn't the way Joel was telling it. Every time he said, "I never saw racism in Cuba," I knew that wasn't true. Evidently, he didn't recognize the racism, because I knew that it wasn't as perfect as he thought it was.

Woods: Did you think he was going to reach the conclusion that you wound up reaching?

Ojito: No, that was a total surprise. I remember it clearly, that moment. We were in his car, and he mentioned that thing about going to the restaurant and how he got into a fight on a bus [in Cuba] and it was because he was black. He had gotten too close to a white woman or something when the bus was full. There was just so much pain when he told me those things. It was very difficult for him to admit to himself that, yes, it was racism and at the time he hadn't seen it, but now he knew it. That was a surprise to me.

Woods: I often hear from reporters that it's difficult if you are white to get people who are black to talk candidly about race.

Ojito: I would agree with that, but in my conversations with Joel and Achmed, nationality trumped race. We were Cuban first, and that played a very important role. I understood their language—not only the Spanish, but the language of Cuba at a certain time in history. I knew the nuances and I knew where they were coming from. I went to school with boys like them. Remember that I lived in Cuba until I was sixteen. I think it would have been a lot more difficult for a white American reporter, especially if she or he did not speak Spanish. [It's] sometimes a very dangerous role because [Cubans] assume you know why they left Cuba, their reasons for leaving, their relationship—or lack thereof—with the government. In all of those things, they assumed I knew. So I think sometimes when you're too similar to the people you're interviewing, there are a lot of assumptions that you have to overcome by telling them, "No. Even though I understand, I don't know."

Woods: One of the traps awaiting writers when they're telling a story like this is that they paint a picture in which there is clearly a villain and a victim. These men come out somewhere in the middle.

Ojito: I worked very hard on that. With Achmed, frankly, we had some difficult moments because I had never dealt with anyone who was so unresponsive. He did not return my calls, yet he never said, "Disappear from my life." That ambivalence was very unsettling and uncomfortable for me. I purposely looked for ways to understand him and to humanize him in the story. I did not want the resentment that I sometimes felt to taint what the story was about. The story wasn't about whether or not he was polite or had come to the telephone or whether or not he offered me a chair when I showed up at his house. It wasn't about manners. I had to put that aside. In time, other aspects of his personality were revealed. I learned that he cried sometimes, that he expressed tenderness and vulnerability. I realized he was not introspective. He much preferred to talk about the accomplishments he didn't think he was capable of, like escaping from Cuba. He was very proud of that. Allowing him to talk at length about his decision to leave made him trust me more. After that, I would always begin our conversations by talking about his journey here.

Woods: When you step back and think about this experience, would you say it taught you anything about race relations?

Ojito: You know, I have been asked that so many times, and I'm afraid to sound stupid when I say no, but unfortunately what I see in Miami is really the way it is.

Woods: In a nutshell, what is that?

Ojito: Oh, I think segregation is alive and well. Not, perhaps, the way we read in history. I still go to a Cuban restaurant in Miami, and I look around and only see white faces. And by white faces, I don't mean American white faces, I mean Cuban white faces. I went the other day to the same restaurant where Joel had the problem with the car, and I thought about him. Not one black person, Cuban or non-Cuban, was there, not even the employees. But I already knew that going in. I can't say it's something I learned.

Woods: If the story is as we already think it is, then what's new to tell about it?

Ojito: It's not new. I think it's the way you tell it. The beauty of that series is that we told it in a way that was easily relatable to people, as opposed to an occasional op-ed piece. I think that if you manage to tell a story that others have told, but in a compelling way, people who read it will think about it, and that may impact behavior. In the end, that's why we all write.

Woods: So if you were going to push forward from here and visit the issue of race again as a newspaper, what would you do?

Ojito: Personally, because I am raising three kids, I think I would look at schools. I wonder if anybody can capture the moment in which these racial identities begin to take shape. I'm always on the lookout for that in my own kids. I gently quiz my oldest as to how he sees himself. I'm waiting for the moment when he says, "I'm an American" or "I'm Cuban" or something. I am very curious about that because I think that's what it's all about.

To screen the Mirta Ojito interview, select IDENTITY on the DVD Main Menu then "Best of Friends, Worlds Apart."

DISCUSSION POINTS

- The story offers insights on the impact of ethnic culture and race. What did you learn from Mirta Ojito's reporting that can help define the similarities and differences that affected the lives of these men?
- Discuss the implications of how skin color impacts economic and lifestyle opportunities in Miami.
- Examine the similarities and differences among immigrants in your community and compare them with the experiences that Achmed and Joel reveal in their story.
- *The New York Times* series *How Race Is Lived in America* focused mainly on the influence of black and white skin color in its portrayal of the racial climate in America. Discuss how effectively Ojito's story plays out that theme.
- Ojito talks about how hard she worked against her own biases to do this piece. Discuss if she succeeds.

SUGGESTED READINGS AND WEBSITES

Books

Ojito, Mirta. *Finding Mañana: A Memoir of a Cuban Exodus*. New York: Penguin, 2005.

> *Mirta Ojito marks the twenty-fifth anniversary of the Mariel boat lift, which brought her to America, with her memoir of this historic event, which to this day impacts the Cuban community in Miami.*

Rodriquez, America. *Making Latino News: Race, Language, Class*. Thousand Oaks, Calif.: Sage, 1999.

> *This book examines Latino news as part of a larger narrative: the cultural productions and conceptions of Latinos. The author traces historical and commercial contexts of Latino-oriented news production, beginning with late-nineteenth- and early-twentieth-century U.S. Spanish-language newspapers.*

Pulera, Dominic. *Visible Differences: Why Race Will Matter to Americans in the Twenty-first Century*. New York: Continuum International Publishing Group, 2003.

> *Dominic Pulera presents coverage of America's five "racial" groups—whites, blacks, Hispanics, Asian Americans, and Native Americans—and contends that race will continue to matter to Americans during the twenty-first century because of visible differences, including differences in physical appearance. The book takes into account the social, cultural, economic, and political ramifications that accompany these differences.*

Websites

www.nytimes.com/library/national/race

> *The Website address of the total How Race Is Lived in America series, which won the 2001 Pulitzer Prize for National Reporting.*

www-new.latinosandmedia.org/media/index.html

> *A directory of the major Latino-oriented media in the United States and links to their respective Websites.*

journals.dartmouth.edu/latinox/resource_center/media.shtml

> *A list of journals, newspapers, and books dealing with Latino issues.*

www.nahj.org/home/home.shtml

> *The Website of the National Association of Hispanic Journalists.*

www.hispaniconline.com

> *This Website features links to stories—from various news organizations, including the Associated Press—that relate to Latino/Hispanic issues.*

CHAPTER 4

STORY

THE FAMILY SECRET
ALICE IRENE PIFER AND LYNN SHERR
ABC NEWS, 20/20

ALICE IRENE PIFER

Alice Irene Pifer is director of professional education at Columbia University's Graduate School of Journalism as well as an adjunct professor. Before joining the school in 2003, Pifer was a producer at ABC News for twenty years with the newsmagazine *20/20*. Her 2000 story *The Family Secret* was honored by the National Association of Black Journalists.

LYNN SHERR

Lynn Sherr is an award-winning correspondent with ABC News. Since 1977, Sherr has covered a wide range of stories, specializing in women's issues and social change, as well as the space program. She is a graduate of Wellesley College, where she serves as a trustee and was honored with the Alumnae Achievement Award for her distinguished career.

The Family Secret

This ABC News *20/20* report utilizes the journey framework to unfold Jill Atkin Sim's search for her racial identity. As we follow this journey, we learn several important lessons.

First, there's the use of historical context, which is integral to revealing the pain and discomfort of talking about how the United States' unquestioned racism forced on Jill's great-grandparents the practice of passing as white.

Every reporter says it's critical to build trust with sources, but this was especially important for producer Alice Irene Pifer and correspondent Lynn Sherr as they faced reporting the sensitive issues related to Jill's decision to go public with her family's secret on national television. In many ways, Jill's appearance on *20/20* represented a stepping away from her lifelong identity as a white person, much as her ancestors stepped away from their black identity.

The essay in this chapter outlines the decisions Pifer and Sherr made about what to include in the story and how those decisions affect how the viewer understands Jill's journey and, ultimately, a major segment of the nation's racial history.

Gaining a source's confidence when the story involves race poses special challenges. As Pifer says in her essay, "We live in a society where, so often, black and white people see the same events through very different eyes. . . . This divide can lead to misunderstandings and blind spots, as well as clear-cut bias in reporting." She made a point of seeking out different voices as a check against the distortions those perspectives may impose on the story. The broadcast shows why it is critical to put together a team that will foster conversation across racial, ethnic, sexual, gender, and class lines.

The late Robert Maynard, the first African American to own a mainstream newspaper, called the philosophy Pifer utilizes the "fault lines" theory. Though it's sometimes impossible to assemble a "fault lines" team, the chapter provides a platform for thinking about the concept.

"THE FAMILY SECRET" (TRANSCRIPT)

ABC News 20/20
Airdate: April 14, 2000
Correspondent: Lynn Sherr / Producer: Alice Irene Pifer /
Editor: Joe Schanzer

Lynn Sherr: [voice-over]	All her life she felt alone, disconnected from a family that was split by divorce and enveloped in silence. Jill Atkin Sim says no one spoke about it but she always had a sense there was a family secret.
Jill Atkin Sim:	I thought it could be anywhere from illegitimacy to incest to prostitution to all sorts of things.
Lynn Sherr: [interview]	You imagined the worst, as it were.
Jill Atkin Sim:	Of course, yes.
Lynn Sherr: [voice-over]	Not even the relative she felt closest to, her father's mother, Ellen, would tell.
Jill Atkin Sim:	I'd say, "Well, was your mother born in Boston?" She'd say, "'Yes.' And I'd say," Well, where was her mother born?" And she'd just sort of pause and say, "Virginia," and just look at me in a way that I knew the discussion was closed.
Lynn Sherr:	The abrupt silences left Jill with a feeling of undefined shame.
Jill Atkin Sim:	There was always just a sense that you just kept your head down and low and you didn't talk about yourself. You didn't advertise yourself in any way. And you basically hid yourself.
Lynn Sherr:	After Jill got married and later had a son, her grandmother started to open up, finally showing her a photograph of Jill's great-grandmother.
Jill Atkin Sim:	She just quickly showed it to me and said, "This was my mother." And I couldn't see it all that well because it was a very dark photograph. And my grandmother just sort of took it back and said, "Well, that was my mother." And that was it.
Lynn Sherr:	That was it until a year later, when her grandmother died and the secret started seeping out. Jill learned that her great-great-grandfather had been black. It was a stunning revelation. But, surprisingly, Jill shrugged it off.

Courtesy of ABC News, 20/20
Anita Hemmings in her Vassar graduation photo.

Jill Atkin Sim: I immediately thought that he had to be the only one.

Lynn Sherr: Why did you think that?

Jill Atkin Sim: Because my family looked so white.

Lynn Sherr:
[voice-over]   Family therapist Dr. Elaine Pinderhughes is familiar with the problem some whites have absorbing the discovery of black ancestors.

[interview]   Is that typical to think, "Oh, he must have been the only one?"

**Dr. Elaine
    Pinderhughes:**   Oh, sure. The standard reaction is, "It ain't so," or "I don't want it to be so," or "I'm not even thinking about it."

Lynn Sherr: It was a mark of shame for a long time.

Dr. Pinderhughes: Absolutely.

Lynn Sherr:
[voice-over]   But Jill was intrigued. And following her only lead, eventually e-mailed Vassar College where her great-grandmother, Anita Hemmings, the woman she'd seen only once in that fuzzy photo, had gone. The news exploded on her computer screen the next day. Anita Hemmings, according to Vassar, was the first African American graduate of this college, although apparently for most of her college career, she passed as white.

Jill Atkin Sim: I burst into tears when I read the e-mail. I just was overwhelmed. I—I had no idea that my family had such a history.

Lynn Sherr: Desperate to fill in the gaps, Jill headed for Vassar, where, with the help of Professor Joyce Bickerstaff, she finally saw her great-grandmother clearly for the first time.

Professor Joyce Bickerstaff:	She just sat, I think, for about five minutes and just looked at the picture, and she kept saying, "She's beautiful. She's beautiful." And then she got very, very leary.
Jill Atkin Sim:	I saw so many of my own family in her, my immediate family, my brother, my father. And I was so proud of her. And I just was overcome, overcome.
Jill Atkin Sim: [dialogue]	*Could you tell me some more about the sophomore class tree?*
Professor Bickerstaff:	*Oh, yes.*
Lynn Sherr:	When Jill heard the full story of Anita Hemmings' time at Vassar she was even more overwhelmed. In 1893, the year Anita arrived at Vassar, the school didn't admit blacks so Anita, whose mixed heritage gave her very pale skin, presented herself as white. It's called passing, and it wasn't uncommon.
Professor Bickerstaff:	Passing was a survival technique because of the terrible social restrictions, the Jim Crow laws, every kind of restriction on a black person.
Lynn Sherr: [voice-over]	Anita was living a double life, until the end of her senior year, when her roommate, who discovered the truth, viciously outed her. The story became a major scandal. Aristocratic Vassar, of all places, harboring a black student. In a secret session, Vassar's authorities considered withholding Anita's degree.

Courtesy of ABC News, 20/20

Jill Atkin Sim during the ABC *20/20* interview.

"I did not realize how many forms racism took in this country until I started looking into my own family. And I really started looking at the world in a new way."

—Jill Atkin Sim

[interview]	When you heard that story, tell me how you reacted.
Jill Atkin Sim:	I hated her roommate. I hated white people. I hated the ugliness that people are capable of when it comes to race.
Lynn Sherr: [voice-over]	In the end, Anita did graduate, but Jill was in for more. Next, she discovered that Anita's brother had been one of the first black graduates of MIT.
Jill Atkin Sim:	A photograph of Frederick arrived in the mail, and he was definitely a black-looking young man.
Lynn Sherr: [voice-over]	With Frederick, Jill realized that an entire branch of her family had been black. Now she wondered, what was she?
[interview]	Did you look at your hands?
Jill Atkin Sim:	Oh, yeah.
Lynn Sherr:	Did you say, "Who am I? What am I?"
Jill Atkin Sim:	Yes, I used to look in the mirror and I looked at my blue eyes and my red hair and white skin and I just thought, "Gosh," you know, I won—I started wondering what is blackness and what is whiteness?
Lynn Sherr: [on camera]	What, indeed? Today on official records like birth certificates and census forms, race is up to the individual. You are who you say you are. But before the civil rights era, racial identity was often imposed by laws that were used to discriminate. In a number of states, for example, the one-drop rule applied.
[voice-over]	Even a trace of African ancestry meant you were considered black and thus deprived of many rights. Jill was startled to learn that she, too, would have been restricted by those laws.
Jill Atkin Sim:	I did not realize how many forms racism took in this country until I started looking into my own family. And I really started looking at the world in a new way.
Lynn Sherr:	In particular, Jill wanted to know how her family had faded to white. She found out that Anita Hemmings returned to this black community in Boston after Vassar and later married another light-skinned African American, Andrew Love, a physician. But in 1907, they moved to New York and made the dramatic decision to live as whites for the rest of their lives. Their decision to pass gave Anita, Andrew and their three children opportunities in the white world. But it also brought anguish.

Dr. Pinderhughes:	I think that it caused a lot of pain very often to the person who was passing and the persons who were left behind.
Lynn Sherr:	Take Anita's daughter Ellen, Jill's grandmother. She was raised as white and isolated from her cousins, grandparents, aunts and uncles. If word got out about their black heritage, her parents could have lost their jobs, even their home and friends. So they kept their black family a secret. The only way Ellen's grandma Dora could see her grandchildren would be to steal a glance on carefully planned vacations.
Jill Atkin Sim:	They would meet at an appointed place and the grandmother would just look and watch her grandchildren from a distance.
Lynn Sherr:	That's so sad. Doesn't that just break your heart?
Jill Atkin Sim:	The whole thing breaks my heart. Yeah.
Lynn Sherr: [voice-over]	And once, just once, Dora came to Anita's home in New York.
Jill Atkin Sim:	Anita made her use the servants entrance to visit her. This was done so that Andrew and Anita would not be outed because they lived in an all white building.
Lynn Sherr:	Are you angry at her at all?
Jill Atkin Sim:	Yes. I—I have—I go through periods where I'm very angry at her because I feel that she denied her children and her grandchildren a wonderful family. And they—they needed that family.
Lynn Sherr:	But Jill was able to focus on the bigger picture at Boston's public library. Here, genealogist Neil Todd gave her the first real look at her great-great-grandfather Robert Hemmings, Anita's father, the black ancestor who had inspired her journey.
Neil Todd:	Let me see if I can get a larger lens and we'll blow it up.
Jill Atkin Sim:	OK.
Neil Todd:	Yeah.
Jill Atkin Sim:	Oh, wow.
Neil Todd:	Now you can really—you can really see what the gentleman looked like.
Jill Atkin Sim:	Yeah.

Neil Todd:	So, he's your great-great-grandfather.
Jill Atkin Sim:	Yes.
Lynn Sherr:	Through Robert Hemmings, Jill has found a way to link her past to the present.
Jill Atkin Sim:	OK.
Neil Todd:	The census says he's born in Virginia.
Lynn Sherr:	She's been told that her great-great-grandfather is somehow related to Sally Hemings, the slave who is said to have had at least one child with Thomas Jefferson. Robert Hemmings was born near Jefferson's plantation at Monticello in Virginia.

Jill Atkin Sim: [dialogue] *OK, let's go.*

| Lynn Sherr: | So when Jill was invited to the historic meeting of Jefferson and Hemmings' descendants at Monticello last May, she was delighted. It would be her first chance to meet some living black relatives, admittedly very distant, but to Jill, relatives nonetheless. |
| Jill Atkin Sim: | I'm really excited to meet my black cousins and see if there is a connection there, if I—if I feel that there is an ancient bond there that can't be defined but is felt. |

Jill Atkin Sim: [dialogue] *Nice to meet you.*
1st man: *This is my father-in-law.*

| Lynn Sherr: | Once at Monticello, Jill and her family felt instantly connected. |

2nd man: [dialogue] *I was saying the same thing about you.*
3rd man: *Thank you.*
Jill Atkin Sim: *And this is my husband, Al.*
Al Sim: *Nice to meet you.*
Jill Atkin Sim: *And my son, Harrison.*
1st woman: *Harrison, good to meet you.*
Harrison: *Are you part of our family?*
1st woman: *I am.*
Jill Atkin Sim: *Yes.*

Lynn Sherr: [interview]	You said before you got there, you were anxious to see if there will be an ancient bond there.
Jill Atkin Sim:	Yes.
Lynn Sherr:	Was there?

Jill Atkin Sim:	Yes. I really felt very attached to a lot of people there very quickly. I felt like I truly belonged some place for the very first time in my life. I felt like family.
4th man: [dialogue]	*If everyone could come to the steps, please. We're gonna take a family portrait here.*
Lynn Sherr:	Tell me about the group photo.
Jill Atkin Sim:	The group photo was amazing. I was ecstatic to be there.
Lynn Sherr:	Was it a better feeling than being in a family photo at home when you were a little kid growing up?
Jill Atkin Sim:	Yes.
Lynn Sherr:	Why?
Jill Atkin Sim:	They weren't holding anything back.
Group: [dialogue]	*Yeah!!!*
Jill Atkin Sim:	Whereas in a family gathering, there's still the family secrets.

Courtesy of ABC News, 20/20

Jill Atkin Sim greets relatives at Monticello.

"I really felt very attached to a lot of people there very quickly. I felt like I truly belonged some place for the very first time in my life. I felt like family."

—Jill Atkin Sim

Lynn Sherr: [voice-over]	Jill's new understanding of the secrets that had so pained her family has transformed her sense of who she is.
[interview]	So how do you work it out? How do you think of yourself? What box do you now check on the form?
Jill Atkin Sim:	Well, I check "other."
Lynn Sherr:	And, in fact, how do you think of yourself racially?
Jill Atkin Sim:	I think of myself as—as white and black.
Lynn Sherr: [voice-over]	And she is determined that her son will also know exactly who he is.
Harrison: [dialogue]	*Yippy!*
Lynn Sherr:	Jill never wants him to feel that he has something to hide, as she once did.
Jill Atkin Sim:	I tell him, you may look white, but you're black, too. And I show him pictures of black people and I say, these are your cousins. It's just family to him.

THE MAKING OF

THE FAMILY SECRET

By Alice Irene Pifer

The Family Secret is the story of Jill Atkin Sim's personal journey as she unravels a secret kept hidden for ninety years. As Jill's journey evolves, she encounters both painful and proud chapters of her family's story, one that reflects in so many ways the racial history of America.

Jill always thought of herself as white until she discovered that an entire branch of her family was black. That branch had been hidden since 1907, the year her great-grandparents, Andrew Love and Anita Hemmings Love, decided to pass and live as whites. For African Americans who were light-skinned, passing was not uncommon during the first half of the 1900s. In fact, when Jill's great-grandparents made their decision, passing was at a peak. The monumental decision to live as a white person was driven by the severe limits placed on all aspects of black life.

Since childhood, Jill had had a gut feeling that her family's history contained a well-hidden secret. But it was only after her grandmother's death in 1994 that the first inkling of her black ancestors emerged. This revelation led to Jill's quest to understand her family's true history, a quest that ultimately transformed Jill's own racial identity and sensibilities.

The story aired on the ABC newsmagazine *20/20* on April 14, 2000, and ran eleven minutes. Lynn Sherr, a hands-on correspondent, was assigned to the story. Our collaboration was a crucial part of the process. Yet, as is typical in a TV newsmagazine shop, the producer is usually working on two or three stories at once, while the correspondent is working on ten to fifteen stories all at different stages in terms of research, shooting, and editing. So the producer often takes the lead in reporting the story. This was the case in "The Family Secret."

Finding the Story

I found this story the way that so many are found. I set out with one focus and stumbled upon another.

In early 1999, plans were under way for a historic gathering at Monticello, Thomas Jefferson's plantation in Virginia; it would take place in mid-May. Controversy was swirling. For decades, the descendants of Thomas and Martha

"Sherr was one of the main reasons
the interview was a success. Among
her many talents, she excels at
interviews. She always arrives
thoroughly prepared and is the
ultimate pro at establishing a quick
rapport with a subject"

—Alice Irene Pifer

Lynn Sherr discusses the ingredients of "The Family Secret" story.

Jefferson have been holding an annual get-together at Monticello, but at the upcoming meeting, for the first time, descendants of Sally Hemings would also be there. Hemings had been one of Jefferson's slaves and for two centuries the subject of debate about whether Jefferson had been the father of some or all of her children. In November 1998, the British journal *Nature* published the results of DNA tests that provided biological evidence that Thomas Jefferson was the father of at least one of Hemings's six children. That led to the Hemings descendants being invited to the reception, but the invitation caused a bitter split among the descendants of Martha and Thomas Jefferson.

I was busy working up the reunion story when the Associated Press ran an item about the gathering. In one day, dozens of news organizations from around the world contacted the Monticello press department. Realizing that this story would get saturation coverage, I concluded that it would look old by the time it aired on *20/20*. When I phoned my source to let him know *20/20* would not be there, he pitched Jill's story, explaining that her great-grandmother Anita Hemmings and Sally Hemings were apparently related (the two spelled their last names differently). He told me Jill had written an article about her family for *American Heritage* magazine.

Reading the article, I was mesmerized. It had the potential for a very strong TV piece, but there were a lot of questions to answer: Would Jill want to be involved? Was she a strong enough talker to be the main character in a magazine-length story? Would the authenticity of her story hold up when I cast my reporter's eye on it? Would *20/20*'s executive producer be interested? These are the kinds of questions a producer faces with any story. But since this was a story about race, there were particular areas where awareness about race mattered: gaining trust, building a diverse in-house team, providing context, shooting, and writing.

Gaining Jill's Trust

The first time I called Jill, who lived in Virginia, she was quite friendly, but it became clear that she had some serious reservations. For one, Jill didn't really watch television and basically disapproved of it. More important, a few of her relatives were upset with her for revealing the family's black ancestry in *American Heritage*. A story on *20/20* would likely upset her relatives even more. Finally, Jill had to decide whether she wanted to share her own deepest feelings about her discoveries with a national TV audience.

Creating trust is a basic currency of the profession. Many of the steps I took to earn Jill's confidence were race neutral, but gaining someone's confidence when the story involves race poses a special challenge because of the history of racism in the United States. As a reporter, understanding that we live

Jill's great-grandparents, Andrew Love and Anita Hemmings Love, in the 1930's.

"When we spoke, Jill seemed very protective of her great-grandparents and wanted their story told fairly. She was equally concerned that her own journey be respected, especially in a world where there is so much miscommunication about race."

—Alice Irene Pifer

in a society where, so often, black and white people see the same events through very different eyes is critical. This divide can lead to misunderstandings and blind spots, as well as clear-cut bias in reporting.

When reporting on people who are outside of your own ethnic or racial background, it's important to realize that they may be wary because they've seen prejudice distort reporting.

Why would Jill be wary? After all, she had lived almost all of her life with the experience and perspective of a white person. But in the process of unveiling her family's story, her eyes opened about the privilege of being white. In the *20/20* segment, Jill acknowledges that she did not "realize how many forms racism took in this country until I started looking into my own family. And I really started to look at the world in a new way."

When we spoke, Jill seemed very protective of her great-grandparents and wanted their story told fairly. She was equally concerned that her own journey be respected, especially in a world where there is so much miscommunication about race.

Once, during one of our many telephone conversations, my instinct told me Jill wanted to know my race. So I found a natural way to weave the fact that I am white into the conversation. Of course, I also wanted to go beyond that and convey more complex information about myself to let her know that my life experiences had given me a broad enough awareness about race to tell this story. This was obviously not something achieved by declaring "you can trust me when it comes to race." In fact, that would have been the equivalent of saying, "some of my best friends are black," and could have killed my credibility. A more subtle approach was required.

First, I told Jill about some of the reporting I had done concerning race. We spoke most about a profile of Rosa Parks I'd produced for *20/20* on the fortieth anniversary of the Montgomery bus boycott. In hindsight, I should have sent her a videotape of that story rather than describing it. Nonetheless, Jill's trust seemed to deepen after our conversation.

What if I hadn't produced any stories on race? Another approach could have been to send her *20/20* segments on race that I admired to give her a sense of my journalistic values.

I also gained Jill's confidence by keeping her informed about the ways we were planning to tell her great-grandparents' story. For instance, I told her about the archival footage and photos of segregation scenes that I believed would help convey the restrictions Anita and Andrew Love faced. These shots would also provide the viewers with some historical context with which to judge the Loves' decision to pass.

On another front, I respected Jill's strong request not to contact the relatives who were upset with her for talking publicly about their African heritage.

She was convinced that even a telephone call could cause them to cut off contact, and once I understood this, I assured Jill that I had dropped the matter. To me, it would have been unethical to pursue her relatives after she had explained what was at stake.

Getting the Executive Producer's Approval

As I worked on gaining Jill's trust, I simultaneously was persuading then–20/20 executive producer Victor Neufeld to approve the story. When I first pitched the idea, he wasn't excited, so I had to do a better job of captivating his imagination. Here are the steps I took:

- Provided Neufeld with more details about the pivotal moments of this family's saga to illustrate how it was a dramatic and emotional story.
- Emphasized that Jill was a strong enough talker to be able to connect with the viewers and carry the piece. Since the focus of the segment was Jill's experience, she would be doing most of the talking.
- Pointed out that this was a "crossover" story. While it certainly was about race, it had a universal theme: the power of family secrets.
- Remained enthusiastic. My passion helped sway Neufeld to give me the go-ahead.

Team Building

Things were starting to gel. I had an OK from the executive producer, and Jill had said yes. It was time to put an editorial team together.

When you're doing a story concerning race, I believe it's best to have at least one person from the racial or ethnic group that is the focus of your report on the team. Is it absolutely essential? No. Is it always possible? No. Does it increase the odds that the story will avoid the usual biases and blind spots to offer a more authentic and nuanced feel? Yes. A racially mixed team helps ensure that reality will be reflected more accurately, and that is simply good journalism.

Our team began with three white journalists: correspondent Lynn Sherr, then–senior producer Meredith White, and my-

> *The Family Secret* is a story involving racial sensitivities in a society where people often find it difficult to be honest about race.

self. Sherr had a very strong track record on social justice stories. White was a leader when it came to covering race and ethnicity. During her fifteen years at 20/20, she either originated or shepherded many of the program's stories about race. But I did not want to do this piece with an all-white team. Even white reporters experienced in covering race have blind spots. I requested that

Susan Welsh and Donna Hunter, both African American, be assigned to the project. Welsh was an associate producer at the time; Hunter was a production secretary who also did research.

Welsh, Hunter, and I had many discussions that helped shape the story. We talked about the racial divide at the center of the phenomenon of passing and about how, while many black people know or know of someone who has passed, others know very little, if anything, about the subject. Our team discussions, as well as talks with colleagues who are not black, helped me realize that I'd need to assume zero knowledge on the part of most viewers when discussing passing.

The three of us also talked about the emotional pain passing caused. We tried to imagine what it was like for black Americans when Anita and Andrew Love decided to live as white people and leave their relatives and friends behind. These discussions deepened my commitment to finding a powerful way to communicate the pain and complexity of passing. I wanted the viewers to feel the humanity of it all.

Our team had intense debates. Did Andrew and Anita Love betray their families and the black community? In their circumstances, wouldn't many of us have made the same choice to pass? These debates helped me realize how essential it would be to provide strong historical context. Otherwise, viewers across the racial spectrum might judge Anita and Andrew Love by today's standards, even though they made their decision to pass in 1907, a time marked by institutionalized racist restrictions, cruelty, and indeed terrorism.

Providing Context

Context is always important, but it's particularly critical in stories on race because of the racial divide. Without it, a story has a greater chance of failing to communicate. Historical context was especially important here because the story of Jill's family was not just one isolated, fascinating tale. Their lives represent what so many African American families experienced. Here are some of the techniques we used to build context:

- Reporting: We provided solid information in the narration to explain passing and convey the tenor of the time in which Jill's great-grandparents lived.
- Interviews with experts: Dr. Elaine Pinderhughes, a family therapist and noted expert on black families, and Dr. Joyce Bickerstaff, a Vassar professor who was researching Anita Hemmings's life—offered crucial understanding about the motivations for and ramifications of passing.

- Archival footage and photographs: The images of Jim Crow constraints showed just how repressive the system was for black people. Also, photos of Jill's black family were essential in making the story come to life.
- Newspaper headlines: The fact that Anita's secret was considered such a scandal that it was headline news ("Negro Girl at Vassar: She Was Graduated This Year After Confessing Her Father's Race") spoke volumes about American society then.
- Well-planned "b-roll": The b-roll includes all video other than interviews and stand-ups. It should be as engaging and visual as possible yet, of course, adhere to journalistic standards. For instance, *The Family Secret* contained two point-of-view (POV) shots—Dora Hemmings's POVs at the playground and at the servants' entrance—both used to convey painful aspects of passing for the family left behind.

Shooting

The Family Secret is a story involving racial sensitivities in a society where people often find it difficult to be honest about race. Operating in a way that would allow Jill and the people around her to act naturally took on added importance. As I planned each shoot, I asked myself how should we operate—interpersonally, technically, and otherwise—so that people can be themselves?

In covering Jill at Monticello, for instance, *20/20*'s mission was to record the reality of what transpired in a way that was as untainted as possible by the presence of a camera—in a setting with unknown racial dynamics. We had no idea how Jill's distant black cousins would respond to her. In this large, spontaneous setting, I believe there were three factors that enabled us to capture a natural flow of events:

- Trust. The trust had been established with Jill.
- "Fly-on-the-Wall" approach. My instructions to the cameraman and soundman were to operate as invisibly as possible. Using wireless microphones and a long lens helped. They allowed us to shoot from a distance (but not surreptitiously) and avoid being intrusive.
- Setting expectations. I explained to Jill and her husband, Al, that once we arrived at Monticello, they should ignore us. I took a more creative approach with their six-year-old son, Harrison, telling him that once we got to Monticello, we would start playing the "invisibility game." The only rule was to pretend that the camera crew and I were not there. The invisibility game is just one solution for working with children.

One scene in particular at Monticello illustrates that our approach worked. There came a moment when Jill and a Hemings descendant were introducing themselves to each other. Jill then introduced her husband and son. At that point, Harrison said, "Are you part of our family?" The woman responded: "I am." Harrison then hugged her. Most people find this to be one of the most evocative moments of the story. Yet this exchange might never have happened had 20/20 been operating in a way that made people self-conscious.

While the conditions of each shoot will vary, the key at every location is to operate in a way that gives authenticity a chance to flourish. This certainly was of paramount importance when Lynn Sherr interviewed Jill. Whether an interview goes well depends so much on the rapport established long before cameras are rolling.

But TV is a funny animal. As the producer, I'd spent hours on the phone with Jill and had traveled to Virginia to meet her. Her connection to 20/20 was through me. Yet Sherr was conducting the interview. It was essential to help cultivate a connection between Jill and Sherr. This is what worked:

- We provided Sherr with everything necessary to be thoroughly immersed in Jill's story: detailed memos, Jill's *American Heritage* article, articles about the Monticello gathering, and the video of Jill at Monticello. I also planned the schedule so that Sherr and Jill would have some time together before the interview began.
- I explained to Jill well before the day of the interview that while I would be there, Sherr would actually be the one to interview her on camera. I also told her a lot about Sherr: her excellent work, what a warm and friendly person she is, how much she cared about this story, and how well Sherr and I had teamed together on previous stories.
- Sherr was one of the main reasons the interview was a success. Among her many talents, she excels at interviews. She always arrives thoroughly prepared and is the ultimate pro at establishing a quick rapport with a subject. If the interview takes a turn in an unanticipated direction, Sherr can improvise beautifully and come away with gems.

Writing and Editing

Sherr and I collaborated on writing the script for *The Family Secret*. While most of what we did was not specific to race, there were certain aspects of the process where race did matter:

- Context: We kept our commitment to providing context. You can have the best research, interviews, b-roll, and archival footage, but if you don't make good use of them while scripting and editing, context will be lost. Skillful use of strong sound bites, powerful images, and meaningful narration achieves a lot in a small amount of time.

- Complexity: Too often with racial stories, journalists see things in polarized terms and overlook shades of gray. For instance, Jill was proud of her great-grandmother yet also angry with her for passing. Oversimplifying her emotions would have been inaccurate and could have hurt Jill's credibility as well as that of the story.

- Working with a manager who cares: Senior producer Meredith White noticed a major flaw in an early draft of the script because we never addressed what defines blackness and whiteness. So after additional reporting, Sherr did a stand-up laying out the legal definitions of race in both the past and the present. The lesson here is, if possible, work with a strong manager who has an awareness about race. If not, show the piece to someone in your office who does.

- Multiracial collaboration: Susan Welsh and Donna Hunter continued to contribute their ideas. I also asked my colleague Lynn Redmond to critique the script. Redmond is an African American producer who has done an excellent job tackling some of the most complex and sensitive stories on race.

The day of reckoning arrived after about three weeks of writing, rewriting, and editing. It was time to show the story to Neufeld, White, and the other senior producers. With Neufeld's reluctance about the story, we felt nervous going into the screening. But Neufeld not only liked the piece, he asked us to add more detail, an unusual request in a business where the usual mantra is "make it shorter."

> We kept our commitment to providing context. You can have the best research, interviews, b-roll, and archival footage, but if you don't make good use of them while scripting and editing, context will be lost.

On the night *The Family Secret* aired, the ratings told an interesting story. While *20/20* didn't win the time slot (NBC came in first, ABC second, CBS third), the ratings went up one share during the second half hour. That's when *The Family Secret* aired.

Viewer reaction fell into three main categories: black and white viewers who felt moved by the story and either affirmed or enlightened in terms of their knowledge about passing; white viewers who had also discovered hidden black ancestry; and, finally, white skeptics who simply could not accept that

Anita Hemmings was black. One went so far as to say that Hemmings must have been switched at birth in the hospital and accidentally sent home with an interracial couple. "Only whites have the rosebud mouth of this . . . woman's great-grandmother," the viewer wrote. Denial about race can still hold a powerful grip.

As for Jill, she has continued the quest to connect with her black relatives and has widened her circle beyond the Hemmings side of her family. In recent years, she's met some members of Andrew Love's family, her great-grandfather. But the key breakthrough—discovering the secret that her grandmother Ellen would not speak of—took Jill on an unexpected odyssey that changed her sense of self forever.

To screen the Alice Irene Pifer and Lynn Sherr interview, select IDENTITY on the DVD Main Menu then "The Family Secret."

DISCUSSION POINTS

- Producer Alice Irene Pifer discusses how to build trust with Jill, conscious of Jill's fears. How did that impact the story?
- Pifer decided not to pursue Jill's relatives for interviews. What do you think of those decisions? Is it ever ethical to "out" someone regarding their racial heritage?
- What did you discover about your own racial or ethnic awareness from this chapter? How did that affect your view of Jill's story?
- In the story, correspondent Lynn Sherr talks about passing and the one-drop rule. How does the inclusion of such historical context help your understanding of American race relations?
- The story refers to Jill's racial identity in different ways. How would you describe Jill racially and why?

SUGGESTED READINGS AND WEBSITES

Books

Davis, F. James. *Who Is Black? One Nation's Definition.* University Park: Pennsylvania State University Press, 1991.

> *James documents the changing definition of race throughout American history.*

Kelly, Robin D. G. *Race Rebels: Culture, Politics, and the Black Working Class.* New York: Free, 1994.

> *A forthright analysis of how the struggles of African Americans in the twentieth century affected U.S. history.*

Kroeger, Brooke. *Passing: When People Can't Be Who They Are.* New York: PublicAffair Books, 2003.

> *This book explores the phenomenon of passing, revealing the poignant and complicated stories behind people of all races, genders, classes, ethnicities, and cultures who have chosen to pass.*

Malcomson, Scott L. *One Drop Rule: The American Misadventure of Race.* New York: Farrar, Straus and Giroux, 2000

> *This comprehensive and introspective study of the United States' obsession with color scrutinizes everyone from white supremacists to Indians, Hispanics, and African Americans.*

O'Toole, James. *Passing for White: Race, Religion, and the Healy Family, 1820–1920.* Amherst: University of Massachusetts Press, 2002.

An exploration of racial identity, religious tolerance, and black-white passing through the 100-year history of the Michael Morris Healy family.

Robinson, Eugene. *Coal to Cream: A Black Man's Journey Beyond Color to an Affirmation of Race.* New York: The Free Press, 1999.

Robinson uses his assignment in Latin America to explore questions of race and identity, producing a memoir on the meaning of blackness in America.

Sim, Jillian. *"Fading to White." American Heritage* (February–March 1999).

This first-person magazine exploration of the meaning of Jill Sim's family secret— the decision to pass as white—is the basis of The Family Secret *story broadcast on the ABC News program, 20/20.*

Websites

www.jimcrowhistory.org/resources/lessonplans/hs_es_passing_for_white.htm

Teacher resources on the history of Jim Crow.

www.pbs.org/wgbh/pages/frontline/shows/jefferson

The PBS Website "Jefferson's Blood" tells the story of Thomas Jefferson, his slave and mistress Sally Hemings, their descendants, and the power of race.

Courtesy of ABC News, 20/20

Phyllis Everett, Jill Atkin Sim and her son, Harrison, at the Jefferson and Hemings family reunion at Monticello in 1999.

CHAPTER 5

STORY

THE COLOR LINE AND THE BUS LINE

TED KOPPEL, ERIC WRAY AND TOM BETTAG

ABC NEWS, *NIGHTLINE*

TED KOPPEL

Ted Koppel served as *Nightline* anchor and managing editor from its introduction in March 1980. As the principal on-air reporter, Koppel led *Nightline* to numerous awards, including thirty-seven Emmys, six George Foster Peabody Awards, and ten duPont-Columbia Awards, including the first Gold Baton in 1985 for a weeklong series from South Africa. Koppel left *Nightline* in November 2005 and joined the Discovery Channel in a newly created position of managing editor.

ERIC WRAY

Eric Wray is an award-winning editor/producer at *Nightline*, where he has worked almost since its inception in 1980. Wray initiated the story "The Color Line and the Bus Line," which became the linchpin of *Nightline*'s *America, in Black and White* series. Among Wray's honors are two Emmys, three Emmy nominations, and the 1985 NAACP Image Award for his work on a weeklong series in South Africa.

TOM BETTAG

Tom Bettag served as the senior executive producer of *Nightline* from 1991 to 2005, developing the broadcast into television's premier source for in-depth news, investigative reporting, and on-air interviews. He left ABC to join Ted Koppel at the Discovery Channel. Before joining ABC, Bettag spent twenty-two years at CBS News, where he produced *The CBS Evening News* with Dan Rather.

The Color Line
and The Bus Line

America's racial and ethnic minorities have fought a long history of discrimination as they seek jobs, obtain educations, use transportation, or even go shopping. *Nightline*'s *The Color Line and the Bus Line* probes the obstacles that low-income black people in Buffalo faced on all these levels through the investigation of what looked like a routine traffic accident.

When the death of a young teenage mother spurred cries of racism, *Nightline* decided to go beneath the surface. The result, created through *Nightline*'s use of separate black and white reporting teams, was a disturbing revelation of how systemic racism created unequal services for black residents traveling to a suburban mall from one of the poorest sections of Buffalo.

The story teaches how to question assumptions by using a variety of voices and perspectives to examine a racially divisive issue. It also teaches the value of using street reporting to combine a variety of conflicting viewpoints, creating a narrative that allows the audience to reach its own conclusion through the facts that are laid out.

Ted Koppel, the highly respected journalist and anchor of *Nightline* for twenty-five years, had his doubts about the national merits of this story but trusted producer Eric Wray to lead the way in reporting this tension-filled local event. The result displays the value of what a diverse staff can bring to the newsroom.

"THE COLOR LINE AND THE BUS LINE" (TRANSCRIPT)

ABC News Nightline
Airdate: May 22, 1996
Correspondent: Ted Koppel / Producers: Joe O'Connor, Leroy Sievers,
Artis Waters, and Eric Wray / Editor: Eric Wray

Ted Koppel: [program open]	It could have happened anywhere in America, a teenager hit and killed jaywalking across a seven-lane highway. But when that teenager is African American, it becomes, for some, a lot more.
Andre Clark: (Cynthia's friend)	It's racism, and that's what caused her death.
Prof. Henry Taylor: (University of Buffalo)	The kind of racism that people can engage in in the quietness of their suburban homes.
Ted Koppel:	And for others, a lot less.
1st white Buffalo resident:	Race is an excuse for everything these days.
2nd white Buffalo resident:	We do not view this as an issue of race.
Ted Koppel:	Part three in our series, *America in Black and White*—tonight, *The Color Line and the Bus Line.*
Announcer:	This is ABC News *Nightline.* Reporting from Washington, Ted Koppel.
Ted Koppel: [studio intro]	It is, we pointed out at the beginning of the week, largely a matter of perspective. This business of how we perceive the reality of racism in America depends, in large measure, on who we are, where we live, how much money we earn, and of course, whether we are white or black. About five months ago, something happened in Buffalo, New York. It was a traffic accident which made some news for reasons you'll understand in a few minutes. I may have been aware of the incident at the time, but if I was, it didn't really register. I may have read about it in the paper and then, almost immediately, forgot about it.

"It could have happened anywhere in America, a teenager hit and killed jaywalking across a seven-lane highway. But when that teenager is African American, it becomes, for some, a lot more."

—Ted Koppel

Courtesy of ABC News, Nightline

Cynthia Wiggins, the victim of the Buffalo traffic accident.

Several of my black colleagues here at ABC heard about the incident and were outraged. This, they argued, was a clear example of the sort of insidious racism that white people rarely notice and almost never acknowledge.

Early this spring, with the last vestiges of a hard Buffalo winter still visible in occasional piles of gray ice, I flew up to Buffalo to look into a traffic accident.

Leonard Wiggins:
(Cynthia's father)

I know how much you loved roses. I brought you a rose here.

Ted Koppel:
[voice-over]

Which brings us to Cynthia Wiggins. Cynthia was only 17 when she was hit and killed by a truck last December.

Leonard Wiggins:

How you doing, huh?

Ted Koppel:

Now, that just makes her one statistic among tens of thousands of other traffic fatalities last year. What else can we tell you about Cynthia? She was an unwed mother, attended school sporadically, and she died after a truck ran over her, but people do not agree on why she was killed. Cynthia, you see, was African American.

Andre Clark:

It's racism, and that's what caused her death, racism. Nineteen-ninety-six, racism is still alive.

Ellen Lucas: (teacher)	I don't know if you can call that anything except racism.
Ted Koppel:	Within Buffalo's white community, you will find just as many people just as sure that race had absolutely nothing to do with Cynthia's death.
3rd white Buffalo resident:	I think it's, to be honest with you, utterly ridiculous that racism was even brought into a situation such as this.
1st white Buffalo resident:	Race is the excuse for everything these days. I mean, anything that happens that's bad, it seems like that's the excuse.
Gary MacNamara: (radio talk show host)	There have been many cases, many things that happen in our society, where automatically racism is thrown out, that it's got to be racism, it's got to be racism, without any proof. Well, that's crying wolf.
Ted Koppel: [on camera]	Remember now, we're talking about a traffic accident. No one has charged that Cynthia Wiggins was run down deliberately. No one has even suggested that she was killed intentionally because of her race. So why do feelings run so high? Why is there such a difference of opinion, clearly split along racial lines? Part of the answer may flow directly out of the fact that Cynthia Wiggins was not really all that extraordinary. She was,

Courtesy of ABC News, Nightline
The bus heads from Buffalo's poor neighborhoods toward suburbia.

"No jobs in the neighborhood; that was one part of the problem. Cynthia didn't have access to a car. That was another part. The only way that she could get to where there were jobs to be found was by city bus."

—Ted Koppel

	in so many ways, a typical teenager, with perhaps a few more problems than her family and friends like to remember.
Andre Clark:	A true friend, and it's so hard to find a true friend, right, at this time, a true friend.
Leonard Wiggins:	She loved kids, and her goal in life was to be a pediatrician.
Ellen Lucas:	She was bright and determined. Why couldn't she be a doctor? Sure, she could have been a doctor.
Ted Koppel: [voice-over]	Perhaps. But Cynthia was part of another huge statistical profile. Buffalo, it turns out, has one of the highest teen pregnancy rates in the country. According to Cynthia's father, the birth of her son, Takilyu, was the proudest moment in her life.
Leonard Wiggins:	She said, "I'm having one child, and one child only, you know, and I'm going to love him to death."
Ted Koppel: [on camera]	The baby had become Cynthia's primary concern. She dropped out of high school and enrolled in a part-time satellite program. She was eligible for some public assistance, but she needed to get at least part-time work.
[voice-over]	But finding a job close to home, here on Sycamore, one of the main streets in east Buffalo, was almost impossible.
Prof. Henry Taylor:	Buffalo is a poor community by national standards, something like 37 to 38 percent of the people live below the poverty line. Unemployment across the city is about 18 percent, and in the—many of the black neighborhoods, as high as 25 to 30 percent.
Ted Koppel:	In fact, more than twice as many blacks are unemployed as whites, and twice as many blacks live below the poverty line. On Cynthia's street, half of the families earn no wages or salary.
Donn Esmonde: (Buffalo News)	There are stretches of the east side of Buffalo that look like downtown Beirut, just bleak. Plywood is almost the—the signature emblem of the east side—boarded-over windows, boarded-over doors, graffiti-strewn storefronts. This is really, you know, urban America in 1996, in some ways at its worst.
Ellen Lucas:	It's a rough neighborhood. She grew up in a rough neighborhood.
Ted Koppel: [on camera]	Finding a job could be even rougher. Cynthia was 17, hadn't finished high school, and had no real job skills. But she was

determined. If there were no jobs to be found in her neighborhood, she would go somewhere else.

Donn Esmonde: There is no big supermarket on the east side of Buffalo. Try and find a hardware store. Try and find a family restaurant.

Prof. Henry Taylor: The irony is that many of the entry-level jobs, the jobs that people use as stepping stones to—to higher forms of occupation, are located in the suburban region.

Ken Cowdery:
(Job Placement Center) Last year, we were unable to place well over a hundred people in a lot of jobs that were being offered, simply because we couldn't get them out to where the jobs are.

Ted Koppel:
[voice-over] No jobs in the neighborhood; that was one part of the problem. Cynthia didn't have access to a car. That was another part. The only way that she could get to where there were jobs to be found was by city bus.

Prof. Henry Taylor: If you're poor, or if you're black, or you're without an automobile in the central city, you've got to depend on that bus as a form of transportation.

Ted Koppel: In fact, roughly a third of the people in Cynthia's neighborhood rely on public transportation to get to work. The bus that Cynthia Wiggins would come to depend on was city bus number six. It started down Sycamore Street to Walden Avenue, and about a half-hour later it would drop her off across the city line in the suburb of Cheektowaga. She would step off the bus into a different world.

[Commercial break]

Ted Koppel:
[voice-over] The suburb of Cheektowaga is everything that east Buffalo is not. It is more attractive. It has more jobs. It is predominantly white. Its residents are also looking nervously over their shoulders at what they see happening just a few miles down the road.

Young black man:
[excerpt from *He was just walking around with guns and taking*
WKBW-TV] *lives for no reason.*

WKBW-TV *Glenwood Avenue is one of many Buffalo streets on the*
correspondent: *edge.*

Dennis Gabryszak:
(Cheektowaga town
supervisor) We're very concerned about some of the problems on the east side as they come closer and closer to our town, so what we wanted to do was make sure that we're taking the steps to

maintain our property values. I don't want to lose a neighborhood.

Capt. John Howlett:
(Cheektowaga Police
Department)

I don't see any racial tension. I don't see it as being a problem, and I wouldn't, in any way, shape or form, consider this a segregated community, although our population, in terms of blacks that would actually be residents in our community, is probably around 3 to 4 percent.

Ted Koppel:

The percentage of African Americans in the police department is even lower than that. In fact, it's zero.

**Cheektowaga police
officer:**

It's pretty much the kind of an opinion that within the not-too-distant future we'll have a black officer on this department.

Ted Koppel:

When officers on the Cheektowaga police force tell you that their department does not discriminate in its hiring practices, you get a strong sense that they really mean it. But before you can even apply to take the exam here to become a police officer, before you can apply for any city job in Cheektowaga, you have to have been a resident in this community for at least six months. And for people living in east Buffalo, that is

Courtesy of ABC News, Nightline

A chained fence marks a boarded-up factory in Buffalo.

"There are stretches of the east side of Buffalo that look like downtown Beirut, just bleak. Plywood is almost the—the signature emblem of the east side—boarded-over windows, boarded-over doors, graffiti-strewn storefronts."

—Donn Esmonde

the functional equivalent of saying "Blacks need not apply." Nobody puts it that way, of course, anymore than people talk about the Thruway Mall, one of the older shopping centers in Cheektowaga, as having a predominantly black clientele. People do talk, though, about the high crime rate at the Thruway Mall.

Ken Cannon:
(former Pyramid
Companies executive)

There had been some knifings, and there had been some other instances related to drugs, and alcohol, which we were not interested in moving down the highway. And nor was the town, for that matter.

Ted Koppel:

And when the Pyramid Corporation came to Cheektowaga to build the Walden Galleria, a huge regional shopping mall, there was clearly some nervousness about the crime rate at the Thruway Mall, just down the road. Cheektowaga police now say that the level of crime at the Thruway Mall was no different than at any other shopping center in the region. But when the transit authority tried to make arrangements for the number six bus to stop at the new Galleria, it ran into resistance.

Gordon Foster:
(former transit official)

I was surprised, but they had mentioned one route that they did not want to have serve the mall, which was route six, which is the Sycamore line, from downtown Buffalo, that currently, at that time, went right by the area where they were building the mall, and had been there for many years.

Ken Cannon:

They did ask us about access for the bus traveling down Walden Avenue, and I said to them that we had these concerns about security, and we really weren't interested in moving that problem down the highway.

Gordon Foster:

My sense was they weren't too friendly, but they, you know, they were careful, fairly careful, in what they said.

Ted Koppel:

About a year after the Galleria opened, the bus stop was set up on the road that ringed the shopping mall, and two buses did stop there, one from north Buffalo, the other a shuttle from the nearby Thruway Mall. That shuttle was an option for people like Cynthia coming from east Buffalo, but it would entail a transfer and a 30- to 90-minute wait which, in Buffalo, in the winter, is a very long time. The number six bus could have dropped passengers at the same stop, but that would have entailed a one-mile detour, which the transit authority didn't want to do. So the number six continued to let its riders off on Walden Avenue, at a place where there was neither a sidewalk nor a crosswalk.

Donn Esmonde: You've got seven lanes of traffic going across—across Walden Avenue, and it's also—also a thruway entrance and an exit there, as well.

Andre Clark: You're dodging cars, trucks, vans, and it's—it's difficult. You fear for your life every time you get off that bus.

Prof. Henry Taylor: Danger? Yeah. A tragedy waiting to happen? Lots of tragedies in black Buffalo waiting to happen. That's just one of them.

Ted Koppel:
[voice-over]   With a baby to support, Cynthia Wiggins got a job at this fast-food restaurant inside the Galleria. She got to work aboard the number six bus, which dropped her off on Walden Avenue.

[on camera]   One morning last December, the number six made its usual stop here. It was Christmas rush. Traffic was heavier than usual. Several feet of piled-up snow made it almost impossible to get out of the road. Cynthia got off the bus and started to cross the street, weaving between the cars stopped at the light.

Tom McKenna
(witness):   And she walked alongside of my van, crossed my van, went in front of me. The light was still red at that time. To my right was a 18-wheeler dump truck. She walked up to about the center of the dump truck, turned, and began to walk along the side of the dump truck. And just about the time she gets to the front of the dump truck, by the bumper area, fender and bumper area, the light's starting to change, and by that time I can see what's happening. It's almost like slow motion. She was struck and basically collapsed, fell, collapsed, however you want to word it, and the truck had no idea she was there. It happened so slow but so quickly, the truck just went over. There was nothing you could do. Both set of tandems went over the girl, it was like she couldn't—there's no way she could get out of the way of the wheels.

Ted Koppel: Cynthia's injuries were massive, and three weeks later she died.

Prof. Henry Taylor: It sounds so innocent. Don't let the buses roll into the suburban regions. Don't let the buses roll into the malls. Don't let the buses roll into the industrial parks. But there are major consequences to this. That's why I refer to those transportation issues as racist. Sanitized, guiltless racism, the kind of—of racism that people can engage in in the quietness of their suburban homes.

[Results of ABC News poll onscreen. "Blacks complain too much about racism": Whites: Yes, 64%, No, 31%; Blacks: Yes, 56%, No, 37%]

[Commercial break]

Ted Koppel:
[voice-over]

To some people, maybe even most people in Buffalo, the charge of racism still seems like a stretch. A tragedy? Certainly. But racism?

James Pitts:
(president, Buffalo City Common Council)

The racist act was the mall management not allowing that bus from the inner city that carried African Americans, primarily, on the site.

Tim Ahern: (Pyramid Companies director)

This is a tragic accident, the accident that occurred on Walden Avenue, that was then pieced together to be a race issue. Quite frankly, you know, we do not view this as an issue of race.

Bud White: (former owner, White's Shoes)

They told me in 1988 they definitely did not want the black inner-city community. They just didn't want them.

Ted Koppel:

Back when the Galleria first opened, Bud White wanted his shoe store to be one of the original tenants.

Courtesy of ABC News, Nightline

"Cheektowaga police now say that the level of crime at the Thruway Mall was no different than at any other shopping center in the region. But when the transit authority tried to make arrangements for the number six bus to stop at the new Galleria, it ran into resistance."

—Ted Koppel

Bud White:	I was negotiating a lease. Tim Ahern, sitting at a desk, and Mark Congell were talking about demographics, and what they were going to bring to us if we became a tenant. And I asked about the black community, and he said, "You know, don't worry about the black communities." He said, "We're not going to—we don't want 'em, and we're not going to let 'em"— you know, "In fact," he said, "Bud, we're not going to let the buses come in."
Tim Ahern:	We had Mark Congell, you and I had him on a conference call yesterday. He emphatically denied that conversation took place. Now it's a new twist. Now I was in attendance at the meeting. Those statements are emphatically false.
Ted Koppel:	There are always reasons why buses and trains are routed through certain neighborhoods and not others. Race is certainly among those reasons, but it is rarely acknowledged.
Prof. Henry Taylor:	The lack of transportation imposes a second-class citizenship standard on those people who cannot get to those locations and places.
Ted Koppel:	But what seems so clear to one person is just a new version of an old story to others.
3rd white Buffalo resident:	People should stop coming up with the excuses and try to find solutions to the problems, rather than wasting their time trying to point the finger and put the blame onto—onto other reasons.
4th white Buffalo resident:	I don't think race is really a big problem anymore. I just think it's a—it's—it's a good way to get a scam out of something, to say, "Hey, you know, I was turned down because of this reason" or whatever. And I don't think it really goes on as much as everyone thinks it does.
Ellen Lucas:	I hear that frequently. "Well, black people call this racist, black people call that racist." It's not racist. It's easy to say when you're not the one feeling it. I face racism every day. It makes me tired.
Ted Koppel: [on camera]	How can people live side by side and yet have such different experiences? Part of the answer may come from the fact that, for the most part, blacks and whites really don't live side by side.
Richard Swist: (executive director, Transit Authority)	It is a segregated town. I don't know if it's uncomfortably or comfortably segregated, but you know, there are clearly demarcations between the—the white neighborhoods and the black neighborhoods, and you know where they are.

Father Walter Matuszak:
(Resurrections Catholic Church)

Whether they're black or white, we should get along with each other and live together as good neighbors should, but sometimes people don't consider all these things, and they just want to be by themselves, you know. The blacks want to be with the blacks and the whites want to be with the whites.

Leonard Wiggins:
[dialogue]

Daddy loves you.

Wiggins relative:

We love you, Baby.

Ted Koppel:
[voice-over]

After Cynthia Wiggins' death, the bus company and the mall agreed on the need for a new bus stop, on the grounds of the mall. Passengers on the number six bus will no longer have to dodge traffic on Walden Avenue. It is, in a manner of speaking, Cynthia's legacy.

Andre Clark:

It took her to die for people to finally look and open their eyes, to say that this policy isn't right.

Dennis Gabryszak:

When it first happened, from my standpoint, it was a safety issue, and it still is a safety issue, and it's very important. I guess, since this has happened, I guess I'm a little more sensitized to—to the racial issue.

Donn Esmonde:

The problem has been alleviated at the Galleria mall. No one else is going to die or be hurt crossing that street. Whether it changes things in the larger picture, I just—I don't see it happening.

Prof. Henry Taylor:

We cannot change history, but we can write new histories, and those new histories are only limited by the boldness of our imagination and by our commitment to creating real change. So that's what she means to me, and I hope that's what she means to this region and this nation, hope.

THE MAKING OF

THE COLOR LINE AND THE BUS LINE

By Eric Wray, producer and editor, *Nightline*

The racism controversy that was triggered by the death of a black teenager, Cynthia Wiggins, was already a pretty big story in Buffalo when the *Nightline* crew arrived in town. It wasn't hard to find people who had an opinion about the case. Donn Esmonde, the editorial writer for the *Buffalo News*, had written a strong editorial on the subject. The story also had been picked up by several wire services. I read about it in *The Washington Post*.

I was in the midst of an ongoing discussion with *Nightline* anchor Ted Koppel, executive producer Tom Bettag, and other members of our staff on issues relating to the coverage of race and segregation. My gut told me that this incident was a perfect example of the consequences that racial discrimination and segregation inflict on a minority community. But to confirm my hunch, I had to investigate.

Our research showed that the city had a history of race-related problems. That is almost a given in any city where black and white segregated living is stark and long-standing. Segregation leads to oppositional and confrontational relations. The majority and minority communities fight for their own interests, with the majority community too often using its superior numbers to get its way. We were aware of the powerful press generated by this story and decided that some of our sources should be from the news media. We looked for people to represent the various viewpoints in the tragedy. Gary MacNamara, a popular local radio talk show host, was referred to us as an articulate voice for the "no, it wasn't a race issue" perspective. In contrast, Donn Esmonde and Professor Henry Davis were powerful voices claiming race had everything to do with Ms. Wiggins's death.

Preparing for the Story

The issues we were investigating were not new for *Nightline*. We already had done several compelling stories on the impact of race in America and had been having all sorts of discussions, including working with an advisory group, on how to report the story using a different tactic from the conflict-ridden approach that usually characterizes accounts of this type. Meetings with two black academics who had written extensively about race—Dr. Cornell West and Professor Henry Louis Gates—turned out to be very fruitful. Andrew Hacker's book *Two Nations* also provided great insight, as did *American Apartheid*, by Douglas Massey and Nancy Denton.

But, as in any newsroom, this story needed buy-in from the top, particularly since it would help launch *Nightline*'s *America in Black and White* series, which has been an ongoing part of our program since 1996. The Buffalo project would involve two teams of four producers, two camera crews, and myself as the editor/producer. I first pitched the story to Richard Harris, a senior producer, and to Leroy Sievers, a former *Nightline* executive producer but at the time producer of all special projects. We also secured Tom Bettag's backing before we went to Koppel for the final OK. We estimated that we would be gone for at least a week, maybe two—a considerable expenditure of Nightline resources. It was imperative that Ted Koppel believe this story was worth it.

In television news, producers and correspondents always work collaboratively on projects. But, with someone of Koppel's stature, it is vital that his exceptional judgment, writing skills, and experience drive the process. Koppel devised the *Rashomon* strategy of attacking the story piece by piece, constructing it brick by brick, showing all perspectives until the whole case was made.

Selecting the Team

There was a consensus among Sievers, Koppel, and myself on who would cover the story. Since I had found it and pitched it, naturally it was my story. I suggested Leroy, Artis Waters, and Joe O'Connor as the team. Two black producers, two white producers: a conscious decision based on the necessity to inject a sense of ease into the interview process, which was certain to include people who had never encountered a network news reporter.

Leroy Sievers, who was picked to lead the white team, has a reputation as one of the best road producers. From Somalia to Buffalo, Sievers hits a town, figures it out, and gets the material he needs to make a story work. Joe O'Connor, a big thinker, would join Sievers. A senior producer at ABC's *World News Tonight* before he joined *Nightline,* O'Connor sees the big picture clearly. His job was to keep the team focused on our mission and to ensure that we fairly represented all sides of the story.

Artis Waters joined me as the other African American producer. His record of covering issues of race and politics is second to none at *Nightline*. He has pushed hard to make certain that people of color are fairly represented and their issues covered. When the Columbia Graduate School of Journalism's *Let's Do It Better!* project recognized the *America in Black and White* series with its top award in 2001, Bettag cited Waters for his integrity, influence, and insights.

As far as the racial aspect of the team, there wasn't much controversy within the staff. Most decisions about whom we were going to interview were made once we were in Buffalo. The four of us had no doubt that the white interviewees—the shoe store owner, Bud White, and the Pyramid Corporation executives—would feel more comfortable with Sievers and O'Connor. Obviously, we thought that the Wiggins family would open up more readily to Waters and me because we were black. We also thought that *Nightline*'s reputation for fairness in covering racial issues would induce them to cooperate. Our show was one the family said they trusted.

But we did not stick with straight white-on-white, black-on-black assignments. I interviewed McNamara, the radio talk show host, and Donn Esmonde, both of whom are white men. We made calls on a case-by-case basis, though most involved matching the producer and interview subject based on race. This extended even to the camera crews.

This racial breakdown isn't always essential. But we had learned a lot about explorations of race in our storytelling and had the experiences of other examples of what happens to a community when racial differences abound. Throughout the country, we found evidence of segregation: schools with separate proms for black and white students, incidents of environmental racism,

"Our research showed that the city had a history of race-related problems. That is almost a given in any city where black and white segregated living is stark and long-standing."

—Eric Wray

Courtesy of ABC News, Nightline
Nightline producer/editor Eric Wray during the interview.

housing discrimination, racial redlining by banks—the list is endless. In staff meetings and in smaller groups, many of us had discussed how best to cover these issues for a skeptical white audience. For me, this approach rang true, and I imparted that belief to my fellow producers. At first, they just trusted in my vision. Further research confirmed we were on to something real.

Giving the Audience Context

The employment stats in Buffalo spoke for themselves. The bleak employment prospects in the poor and deteriorated neighborhoods of Buffalo were evident to Cynthia Wiggins when she went looking for a job. She had to go outside the city, and the Galleria Mall, despite its distance from her home, was a logical place to look.

Creating the context for what Cynthia Wiggins faced is where the genius of Koppel's *Rashomon* approach worked. Plank by plank, he wanted us to nail every part of the story: the bleak job opportunities, the city bus serving as a crucial lifeline for poor inner-city residents without cars, the fact that employment agencies in the suburbs had difficulty getting urban job seekers out to jobs because of limited public transportation, and the dangerous crossing from the roadside bus stop that Cynthia had to navigate to reach the mall.

Most important were the interviews with Bud White, the shoe store owner, who recalled his conversation with Pyramid Corporation officials about not allowing the number six bus into the Galleria Mall to drop off passengers. The White interview was Leroy's shining moment. Without White bearing witness to what he had heard, this story would have been another "he said, she said" conflict over whether Cynthia Wiggins's death was the result of a racist decision or just a tragic accident. That smoking gun was crucial to getting the doubtful white public to see the truth. If African Americans are sometimes too quick to charge racism, we have often found that many white people, even in the face of overwhelming evidence, are all too eager to deny it.

Working with the Local Press

Most national news crews depend on the local press when they parachute into a situation. The circumstances here weren't any different. Donn Esmonde of the *Buffalo News* was a relentless voice speaking for Cynthia Wiggins. His editorials were instrumental in keeping the story alive. The local press explored the issue as well as it could. It is possible that battle lines had already been drawn between the black and white communities on this issue and that it took an outsider like *Nightline* to come in and offer an opportunity for all sides to look at the evidence anew.

Admittedly, this is touchy territory. Often, the big bad national media is resented as an intruder in local communities. A thoughtful, reasoned step-by-step approach was critical if we wanted respect from all sides. After our story aired, we contacted Gary MacNamara, the talk show host, and several other white residents who had been interviewed to gauge their reactions. They thought we had been fair and that our story did open some eyes to new realities.

Understanding Why People Went on Camera

Leroy Sievers remembers being surprised by how willing white residents were to speak to us, whether in the malls, on the street, or in bars or restaurants. That is not always the case. Having white producers and white camera crews approach white subjects helped a great deal. White people did not feel so threatened. On the other side, black residents opened up quickly to Artis Waters and me. Often, black people tell me they feel ignored or misrepresented by majority media. I believe they felt we understood their plight, and they seemed grateful to have a prominent show like *Nightline* pay attention to their concerns.

One interesting glitch in the interview process arose with Bud White. When Leroy located White by phone in North Carolina, where he had relocated, he was very forthcoming about the Pyramid Corporation meeting. But when we got down there to interview him in person, he was less talkative. He was still an important source, but he was noticeably restrained compared to his manner during his phone interview. As I said before, this is touchy territory, and you have to keep your source's fears and sensitivities in mind when embarking on interviews dealing with race.

An Assessment

I thought the comments on this examination of a slice of life about the racial health in the Buffalo area were, for the most part, positive, though I do remember that some black residents thought we didn't go far enough in condemning racism in Buffalo as a whole. But that was not the purpose of this story. By focusing on a personal tragedy, the story had larger implications and lessons for the entire country. It was also perfect as a culmination of all the brainstorming on these kinds of questions that we had been pursuing literally for years.

Nightline has been a very open shop, where internal criticism of the program's performance has been aired constantly. Ted's door was always open to me, and all the staff, from the beginning. From the moment I started out as an editor assigned to *Nightline*, I have been interested in issues of social justice. When the show missed a story opportunity or did a story about African Americans in a way I felt was incomplete or biased, I would tell Lionel Chapman, a

Nightline producer. Lionel, who is black, had a long relationship with Koppel that dated back to Ted's days covering the State Department, when Lionel was his producer. Finally, after hearing several of my critiques, Ted asked Lionel to tell me that if I had something to say about the program, I should say it to him directly. This started a dialogue between Ted and me that has lasted for years. Ted is unique in his ability to encourage criticism and advice from all staff members and use them to produce a better program. Based on my experience with other anchors and shows, Ted is the exception. Minorities have a very difficult challenge in most major media getting their voices heard. Office politics, racial resentment, and the media's inherent bias in favor of white viewers often interfere with people of color getting a fair shake when their issues are being covered.

Risks We Took, Lessons for the Rest of the Series

Anytime you address the issue of race in the United States, you run a risk. It is a polarizing topic, and attempts to discuss it often satisfy no one. It is also too important to ignore. *Nightline* has over the years tried to address this subject. With the *America in Black and White* series, we tried to develop a vehicle to alert the *Nightline* audience to the fact that (1) we placed a high value on

Courtesy of ABC News, Nightline

Ted Koppel on the *America in Black and White* set

"Often, the big bad national media is resented as an intruder in local communities. A thoughtful, reasoned step-by-step approach was critical if we wanted respect from all sides."
—Eric Wray

covering this area of American life and (2) we were going to cover this issue regularly.

The Buffalo story was important to the *Black and White* series for a couple of reasons. First, it was a story so powerful that it served as the anchor for the entire week of shows. Second, it reinforced the belief that, if done well, programs covering race could be done thoroughly and reach a large audience.

To screen the Ted Koppel and Eric Wray interview, select EQUALITY on the DVD Main Menu then "The Color Line and the Bus Line."

Reporting the Rashomon Way

By Eric Wray

The Rashomon approach to reporting, named after the famous film of the same name by Japanese filmmaker Akira Kurosawa, involves looking at a story through multiple perspectives. This is especially important when a story is steeped in racial or ethnic conflict.

Rashomon holds many lessons for journalism students. The story is simple: a woman is raped and her husband murdered. The complexity of the event unfolds when viewed through the eyes of four different people: the woman, the murderer, a witness, and, through a medium, the murdered man. Each has a different perspective that leads to differing conclusions and reveals different "truths" about what actually happened.

In many ways, the Cynthia Wiggins tragedy is its own Rashomon. Clearly, white and black Buffalo area residents had different opinions about the circumstances that led to her death. Differing notions about the placement of the bus stop—sinister to some; incidental to others—point up different perceptions of racism. Buffalo's, and to some extent, America's stance on racial justice issues appears quite adequate to some but unfair to others. For journalists, this is a major point of conflict in the story. The same event was viewed by many people differently and was clearly based on their vantage points.

Internalizing the Rashomon method is perhaps the greatest lesson from "The Bus Line and the Color Line." Each perspective has its own biases and prejudices. The "truth," if there is such a thing in journalism, can only be determined by looking at an event from multiple points of view. This is especially important if you are trying to reach a large and diverse audience and maintain your journalistic ethics and objectivity.

THE MAKING OF

AMERICA IN BLACK & WHITE

By Tom Bettag, former *Nightline* executive producer

The decision to do the *America in Black and White* series really had to do with diversity in an increasingly diverse America. While the series was to be about the white majority and racial/ethnic minorities, we decided to make the initial focus on black and white people, believing that this was where the issues were most glaring.

To get started, we had a series of meetings, asking, "What is it that white people don't get?" Then we brought in two groups of community leaders and interviewed them for several hours. We kept the minority residents in one group and the white residents in another, because we found that people pulled their punches when the races were mixed. Those sessions were invaluable. We learned to listen to one another. A black Ph.D. told of checking out of a hotel and having a white man approach him with his car keys assuming that he was the person who parked cars. Everyone roared when a prominent African American Washington columnist recounted the day he was mowing his grass in the Maryland suburbs when a white woman driving past stopped and said, "Boy, how much does the lady here pay you to cut her grass?" Without missing a beat, he shot back, "Oh, she doesn't pay me; she let's me sleep with her."

What white people don't get about race can fill volumes. Cultural differences are subtle yet incredibly significant. A theme designed to help white viewers understand what they don't get also should make for great television. But we needed to find the right story to get white viewers into the tent. The Buffalo story was it.

One morning, one of our editors, Eric Wray, a brilliant, outspoken African American man, called in from the road. He told a senior producer he had seen a story in the morning papers that was perfect. When we looked at it, many of the white staff members couldn't figure out why Eric thought it was a story. At the same time, we trusted Eric. If he was outraged, we knew we must be missing something. It was another O. J. Simpson moment. White people were confused. Black people couldn't figure out why we couldn't see something that was so obvious to them.

When Ted Koppel, the producers, and a camera crew went to Buffalo, they were still a bit skeptical about whether the story was really there. As they continued to report, they called back to the office more and more outraged. By the time they had finished, the white producers working on the story were livid and felt they had unearthed an astounding scandal. Another O. J. moment. The black producers couldn't figure out why their white colleagues were so surprised; in their eyes, this was a fairly routine incident.

America in Black and White tries to show how much the European American or Caucasian cultural prism distorts what is called "reality." The notion of the melting pot masks significant differences among Americans. Our series offers an ongoing look into everyone's reality.

DISCUSSION POINTS

- Producer Eric Wray cites the so-called *Rashomon* approach as being critical to reporting this story. Explain how that technique worked for the *Nightline* team.
- For the most part, this broadcast used a black team with black sources and a white team with white sources to get the story. Was that necessary? Had *Nightline*'s newsroom not been diverse, how could they have produced the same result?
- Some of the interviews with white people in this story take place in a nightclub and at the mall, while all black sources are shown in more formal interview settings. Discuss how that contributes to or detracts from your response to this piece.
- What elements in this investigation set it apart from the traditional "he said, she said" accusations that so often characterize reporting on racial issues?
- How does reporting on this Buffalo accident speak to the larger issue of the state of race relations in the country?
- Discuss how the news media contribute to Americans' perceptions of race.

RESEARCH

SUGGESTED READINGS AND WEBSITES

Books

Barker, Lucius J., and Mack H. Jones. *African Americans and the American Political System.* 3rd ed. Englewood Cliffs: Prentice-Hall, 1994.

The authors present a systematic appraisal of how African Americans work with the prevailing theoretical, structural, and functioning patterns of the U.S. political and governing systems.

Entman, Robert M., and Rojecki, Andre. T*he Black Image in the White Mind: Media and Race in America.* Chicago: University of Chicago Press, 2001.

This book offers a comprehensive look at the patterns of racial depiction in the mass media and how those images influence the way white people view black Americans.

Hacker, Andrew. *Two Nations.* New York: Ballantine, 1995.

Hacker uses statistical evidence to argue that black and white residents live in two different worlds: a world that is hostile, separate, and unequal based on skin color.

Massey, Douglas S., and Nancy A. Denton. *American Apartheid: Segregation and the Making of the Underclass.* Cambridge: Harvard University Press, 1993.

The 1995 cowinner of the American Sociological Association Distinguished Publication Award, this book links persistent poverty within the African American community to the deliberate segregation of American cities.

Sears, David O., James Sidanius, and Lawrence Bobo. *Racialized Politics: The Debate About Racism in America.* Chicago: University of Chicago Press, 2000.

> *A range of perspectives and essays is offered to illustrate the continuing debate surrounding the sources of racism in America.*

Sigelman, Lee, and Susan Welch. *Black Americans' Views of Racial Inequality: The Dream Deferred.* Cambridge: Cambridge University Press, 1991.

> *A study of black Americans' perceptions of race and inequality, including the sources of inequality and the means for redressing the imbalance.*

Websites

www.unc.edu/~bsemonch/afrlinks.html

> *A resource that provides collections of numerous Website links on various topics related to African Americans, including issues of media and communications.*

mumford1.dyndns.org/cen2000/report.html

> *The Lewis Mumford Center for Comparative Urban and Regional Research Website carries studies about demographic, social, and economic conditions of minorities and about policies that impact them in the United States, based on the 2000 census.*

Courtesy of ABC News, Nightline

Ted Koppel outside the Walden Galleria, near the traffic accident site.

"How can people live side by side and yet have such different experiences? Part of the answer may come from the fact that, for the most part, blacks and whites really don't live side by side."

—Ted Koppel

CHAPTER 6

STORIES

BROKEN TRUST SERIES

JODI RAVE

LEE ENTERPRISES NEWSPAPERS

JODI RAVE

Jodi Rave is a national reporter and columnist who covers
Native issues for fifty-eight newspapers in twenty-two states
for Lee Enterprises newspapers. Rave started working out
of the *Missoulian* newspaper in Missoula, Montana, after
completing a 2004 Nieman Fellowship at Harvard
University.

She won the 2002 Thomas C. Sorensen Award for distinguished
Nebraska journalism for the *Broken Trust* series, written when she
was assigned to Lee's *Lincoln Journal Star* in Nebraska.

Jodi Rave's series *Broken Trust* is a complicated story about Indian land rights and federal bureaucracy. But more than that, it's a tale of how discrimination older than the United States conspired with neglect and malfeasance to bleed millions of dollars from a struggling people.

Rave hung the series on the peg of a remarkable event—a contempt charge brought against a presidential cabinet member—and then mined many of her stories from a single court document that proved to be a mother lode.

Throughout this chapter, journalists will see how sourcing, most of it methodical, some of it serendipitous, led to a greater understanding of an issue's breadth and to the human interest profiles that gave the series its depth.

Rave provides insights into the universal challenges of swimming through a bureaucratic morass and the reporting problems specific to Indian Country. Hers is a lesson in how a reporter can work at recognizing and mitigating biases about the government—federal and tribal—to produce a story that sticks to the facts. It's one of the hardest tasks any journalist can undertake.

The chapter shows the benefits, costs, and limitations that come with sharing an ethnic or racial identity with sources. Rave discusses how she used deep cultural knowledge to advance her reporting but also challenges the notion that there is an automatic advantage to being Indian when covering Indians. This chapter invites discussion about the degree to which journalists can—or should—bring their racial or ethnic identity to bear on their journalism. And it begs the question: why did it take so long for the media to tell this story?

The series is, unto itself, a lesson in history. It also provides a wealth of context for journalists trying to comprehend the ongoing issue of tribal sovereignty or gain perspective on the racial schism that provides the title of the series, *Broken Trust,* with its double meaning.

LAND OF CONFUSION

Part I of a series.

Native landowners say billions of dollars have been lost through misman-agement by the Bureau of Indian Affairs. Complicating matters for BIA record-keepers is this fact: A single tract of land may have hundreds of owners.

"The earth was created by the assistance of the sun, and it should be left as it was. . . . The country was made without lines of demarcation, and it is no man's business to divide it. . ."

—Chief Joseph, Nez Perce

By Jodi Rave
Lee Enterprises Newspapers
Published September 20, 2002

Picture this piece of land four, three, even two centuries ago.

Eighty acres of hardwood forest in Wisconsin's upper reaches. Ojibwe country. Maybe they hunted there. Maybe they fished. But they didn't own the land; most tribes didn't think anyone could own the land.

Today, that land—on the Lac Courte Oreilles Reservation—likely hasn't changed. It's still 80 acres of hardwood forest, still Ojibwe country.

But you could fill a small city with the number of tribal citizens sharing ownership in the 80 acres: at one point, the local Bureau of Indian Affairs of-fice struggled to simply keep track of the parcel's 2,400 owners.

And they can all be traced to Git-chi-i-kwe Sr., and the U.S. government's controversial introduction of land ownership to tribal citizens.

He was 82 in 1881, when Washington assigned him the 80 acres. The land that stood without owners for so long now had a title. And boundaries. And heirs. When the old man died 17 years later, the government transferred his land to the next generation. As the years passed, the number of owners grew.

Across Indian Country, where hundreds—even thousands—of owners share single tracts of land, this has become the joke: sure, you might own land, but just enough to stand on.

Git-chi-i-kwe's 80 acres and thousands of other parcels are known as fractionated land—pieces of property shared by multiple owners and held in trust by the U.S. government.

And Washington's failure to manage the land and the income it generates is at the core of a class-action lawsuit against the U.S. Department of Interior on behalf of an estimated 800,000 past and present Native landowners.

The landowners contend up to $100 billion has been lost, misappropriated or never deposited into their accounts.

Courtesy of North County Times

Thomas Slonaker, former head of the Office of Special Trustee for American Indians, participates in a discussion in San Diego between tribal leaders and Interior Department officials about Native trust fund reform. Slonaker later resigned after criticism from Interior Secretary Gale Norton.

The case, which has triggered a sweeping reform movement involving all three branches of the federal government, could change the way Washington does business with Native America.

Picture a family farm that's been divided and subdivided again and again and again, as each generation passes its holdings to the next. The land doesn't grow, but the number of owners does.

Dozens at first, then hundreds, then thousands.

All heirs, all owning interest in the same piece of land.

But none of them allowed to manage their own assets on their own terms because of the government's role as trustee.

Now picture you're that trustee—responsible for managing 11 million acres nationwide for these owners, and the money generated by leases for farming, minerals and timber.

How do you keep track of 230,000 current owners?

How do you manage the records?

How do you handle probate cases?

How do you divide the income?

"It's meticulous, tedious, pain-in-the-ass work," said Michael Hackett, superintendent of the Winnebago BIA Agency in Nebraska.

Finally, imagine you're sued by an angry and determined landowner.

Six years ago, Elouise Cobell of Montana's Blackfeet Nation asked a judge to force the Interior Department to provide an accurate accounting of its Individual Indian Money trust fund account, which collects and distributes lease payments and royalties for tribal members who own trust land.

The class-action suit has generated thousands of pages of testimony and documents that depict a broken system: inadequate account statements, destroyed and missing records, lack of security for landowner information stored on computers.

Since the lawsuit was filed, two Interior Department secretaries—members of the Clinton and Bush cabinets—have been held in contempt of court for failing to comply with the judge's requests for trust fund records.

Cobell's suit, however, has done more than expose problems with how the government manages tribal citizen trust funds.

It's sparked a reform movement now spreading across Indian Country with the speed of a prairie fire. And it could restructure how the Interior Department and the BIA manage trust assets and resources for tribes and tribal citizens—undoing federal policy that started 212 years ago.

The roots of government-managed trust lands can be traced to the Trade and Intercourse Act of 1790, which required federal approval of any sale of Native lands.

Roy Dabner, Journal Star

Sara Bernal and her uncle, Kenneth Hayes, both own land on Arizona's Gila River Reservation. Both are dissatisfied with the government's management of their land and the income it earns. "We get lease checks, but it doesn't say where it's from—[the] person leasing it or who the pay's coming from," Bernal said.

"The trust responsibility was initially created as a way to justify how the United States had power over people who had never consented to the Constitution," said Kenneth Bobroff, a University of New Mexico assistant law professor.

A century later, the Dawes Act, or General Allotment Act of 1887, decimated reservation land bases by assigning parcels to individual tribal citizens.

The law didn't allow landowners to make wills until 23 years later, setting the groundwork for fractionated land inheritance.

The problem was instantly clear to some.

"After a few subsequent deaths of the heirs the title becomes so interminably mixed that it is next to impossible to clear it up," an Indian agent on Washington's Puyallup Reservation said in an 1892 complaint to superiors.

> The class-action suit has generated thousands of pages of testimony and documents that depict a broken system: inadequate account statements, destroyed and missing records, lack of security for landowner information stored on computers.

Fast forward 110 years.

Ernie Pourier, BIA realty director at Nebraska's Winnebago Agency, helps manage thousands of acres shared by thousands of owners on the Omaha, Santee and Winnebago reservations. One 80-acre tract on the Winnebago Reservation has 600 owners.

Among his duties: Negotiating leases on behalf of owners and notifying them about lease changes.

On those days, he said, the office printer runs all day.

Nationwide, it's an extensive—and expensive—duty. In 1999 the BIA spent 50 percent to 75 percent of its $33 million realty budget managing fractionated land interests alone, according to congressional testimony by Kevin Grover, former head of the BIA.

But critics say the Interior Department and its bureaus are failing in their trust fund management duties:

Some probate cases—which determine heirs for ownership—haven't been resolved for decades, creating a backlog that prevents efficient records management.

Most BIA workers manage assets with two obsolete computer systems that can't interact with each other. A new, $40 million computer system that began to be developed in 1998 was deemed a failure by Interior Department and BIA officials. Work was halted on the system in January.

Landowners say they are denied basic information about their land and assets.

Diane Rasmussen, who inherited land from her grandmother on South Dakota's Rosebud Reservation, remembers a relative giving her a check for about $800.

"I thought at the time, 'Gee, I didn't know when you own the land you get that much.'"

Now her lease earnings have dwindled to as low as 36 cents, she said. But the 58-year-old Sicangu Lakota said she can't find out why.

"I don't know who to call, who to discuss it with or where to start," she said.

In Idaho, Shoshone-Bannock landowners are suing the BIA. They claim the BIA provided land ownership information to non-Native lessees and a power company but that they were denied the same information.

While fractionated land problems have long been acknowledged as an obstacle to trust land management, interest in the issue has been renewed because of the Cobell litigation.

A trust reform task force of Interior Department officials and tribal leaders recently created a committee to find ways to solve the problems of fractionated land. The group had its first meeting in August.

And now an effort is under way to amend legislation that would alleviate related problems. Sen. Ben Nighthorse Campbell, R-Colo., plans to introduce amendments to speed up land consolidation efforts.

Congress tried nearly 20 years ago to fix those problems when it passed the Indian Land Consolidation Act of 1983. The law allowed tribes—with approval from the interior secretary—to buy, sell or exchange lands to consolidate tribal holdings.

The idea was good, said Teresa Carmody of the Indian Land Working Group in Wagon Mound, N.M.

But the language was flawed and the results ineffective, she said.

The act stripped landowners of their property and gave it to the tribes if people owned less than 2 percent of the total land interest. The Supreme Court ruled the provision unconstitutional in 1997.

Congress decided to amend the act in 2000. Carmody's group—with input from tribes, landowners, probate and realty officers—had developed a comprehensive legislative proposal for solving fractionated land problems, she said.

Congress ignored the proposal. And the group does not support the amendments lawmakers ultimately passed.

"Once again, the administration's attempt to come up with a cheap, quick fix for managing trust allotments and fractionated ownership has produced a complex and ill-fated law," Carmody said.

The act gave tribes—but not individuals—more control over land acquisition and consolidation efforts. The act did, however, create a pilot program allowing individuals to sell fractionated interests to tribes.

The BIA has administered the pilot program on five Wisconsin reservations.

Meanwhile, tribes and Native organizations are undertaking their own reform efforts.

Oregon's Confederated Umatilla Tribes is consolidating land for the tribe and individuals.

"This tribe has been sort of fortunate that they have bought back tens of thousands of acres of land over the last, probably, six years," said Scott O'Daniel, Umatilla's general information systems manager.

In 1946, legislation allowed the Rosebud Sioux Tribe to create the Tribal Land Enterprise program. In 59 years, the tribe has bought 500,000 acres and is slated to begin a BIA program similar to the one in Wisconsin.

But many say sweeping changes must come from Congress—which introduced allotment and fractionated land.

"The allotment property system is broken," said New Mexico's Bobroff. "It doesn't allow for rational inheritance. It doesn't allow for rational transfers among tribal members."

All mixed up

Land ownership on most reservations is often a complicated mix of trust lands and taxable private (fee) property, as shown on the Winnebago and Omaha reservations in northeast Nebraska. The United States holds land in trust for tribes and individuals while fee lands are privately owned and typically taxed by the local non-Native governments.

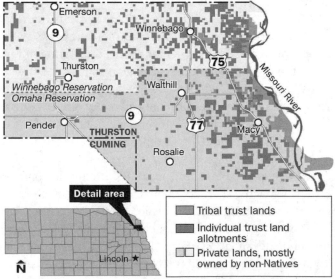

D. Matt Van Driest, Journal Star

Land Allotments Proved Devastating to Native Land Holdings

By Jodi Rave
Lee Enterprises Newspapers

Their land atop one of the largest oil fields in North America once made Osage tribal citizens among the richest people in the world.

And among the most murdered.

In a deadly Oklahoma land grab, as many as 6 percent of Osage citizens died in the early 20th century—many victims of shootings and poisonings by those who coveted their land and the oil it cradled.

It started in 1906, when the tribe was forced to carve up its reservation and distribute 640-acre allotments to Osage tribal citizens.

By the 1920s, the land's underground riches were too tempting.

Washington's rules governing Osage land ownership were too easy to exploit.

The killing spree was under way.

"The Osage story makes it clear that allotment was not done for our benefit," said Dennis McAuliffe, a University of Montana associate professor whose grandmother was killed for her land.

Across Indian Country, tribes watched as their land bases were decimated by the 1887 Dawes Act, or General Allotment Act, which divided reservations into individual parcels of lands. Nationwide, tribes lost two-thirds of their land base because of the act.

The U.S. government became trustee of the allotted property. Its management of the land and the income it generated is at the heart of a class-action lawsuit filed by Native landowners against the Interior Department.

In Cobell vs. Norton, individual landowners contend $10 billion to $100 billion has been lost, misappropriated or never deposited into their trust accounts.

Tribal governments and members earn income from their land by leasing it for farming, pasture, timber, and coal or oil extraction.

And it was the oil that killed the Osage.

The tribe originally lived in southeastern Kansas. But when settlers—including the family of Laura Ingalls Wilder—sought their territory, the tribe sold its land. In 1872, it moved south to Oklahoma's Indian Territory.

There, it bought a new reservation. And it struck gold.

Frank Phillips, founder of Phillips Petroleum Co., moved to Indian Territory in 1905 after learning of the area's oil fields. Today, the company's headquarters are based in Bartlesville, adjacent to the Osage Reservation.

Although the Osage held title to its 1.4 million-acre reservation, the federal government still forced the tribe to allot its land. In 1906, the Osage assigned land tracts to its 2,229 tribal citizens.

All tribal citizens on the original allotment rolls, including children, received headrights, or quarterly royalty payments from oil.

By the 1920s, the annual spending power of each tribal citizen was the equivalent of $1 million today, McAuliffe said.

But there was a catch: Congress allowed non-Osages to inherit the headrights. And it required Osages—half-bloods to full-bloods—to have appointed guardians. These guardians received the royalty checks, not the landowners.

Greed took over. Non-Osage men married tribal women, killed them and inherited their royalties.

"Well, why stop with one headright?" McAuliffe said. "You start by murdering the grandparents, and you murder the aunts and uncles and you murder the sisters, and the cousins to where your wife ends up with 12 headrights, and then you murder your wife."

McAuliffe's grandmother, Sybil Bolton, received an oil headright when she was 3.

In 1925, Bolton was killed by her guardian. The 21-year-old mother left behind a 16-month-old baby, McAuliffe's mother. The baby was later stolen by her estranged non-Osage father.

"The moral of the story is this was overly complicated on purpose," said McAuliffe, who has written a book on the Osage murders. "And you can translate that to the current mess. It's overly complicated, and it didn't just happen this way, it started out this way."

Only a handful of reservations withstood allotment.

"The act came about when Eastern liberal elites—who loosely styled themselves as friends of the Indians and thought they knew what was best for the Indians—tried to impose their vision of what should become of the Indian," said Robert N. Clinton, chairman of American Institutions at Arizona State University in Tempe.

Across Indian Country, tribes lost 90 million acres—lands that were not assigned as allotments to tribal individuals—from 1887 to 1934.

Former Commissioner for Indian Affairs John Collier ended allotment with the 1934 Indian Reorganization Act.

His reasoning: "The allotment system has not changed the Indian into a responsible, self-supporting citizen. It has merely deprived vast numbers of them of their land, turned them into paupers and imposed an ever growing relief problem on the federal government."

Allotments brought additional mayhem.

The Dawes Act complicated land ownership because the government had extended its trust responsibility from tribes to individuals, "which is of course the current basis of the Cobell litigation," Clinton said.

Today, most reservation lands look like checkerboards. Property inside reservation borders is owned by tribes and Natives and non-Natives. Also, 56 million acres are held in trust by the government for tribes and tribal members.

At the time of its introduction,

Dawes Act proponents argued allotments would force Natives to assimilate by becoming property owners and farmers.

But others had a hidden agenda, said Sam Deloria, director of the American Indian Law Center at the University of New Mexico in Albuquerque.

"It was essentially to make this land available to non-Indians to use with the Indians being the nominal owners," he said.

Among the greatest opponents were Native people themselves, but their dissent barely rose above the din of "friends of the Indian," said Kenneth Bobroff in "Retelling Allotment: Indian Property Rights and the Myth of Common Ownership."

Tribes feared allotted lands would be sold, that people were not prepared to support themselves through agriculture, that there wasn't enough tillable land or water for farming, that parcels were too small and that non-Natives would move onto their lands.

"All their fears," Bobroff said, "came true."

WHO'S GOING TO PAY?

Part II of a series.

By Jodi Rave
Lee Enterprises Newspapers
Published September 30, 2002

After a century of mismanagement, a Blackfeet woman's lawsuit over Native trust money could be a turning point

Missing money. Shredded documents. Arthur Andersen accountants. Congressional hearings.

Enron? WorldCom? Global Crossing?

How about Uncle Sam?

"I say this, and I really mean it," said 56-year-old Elouise Cobell, a citizen of Montana's Blackfeet Reservation. "The United States government just robbed people out of a whole entire quality of life."

And Cobell expects someone to pay for it.

The banker from Browning, Mont., and four others sued the U.S. Department of Interior six years ago, claiming the department has historically mismanaged the Individual Indian Money, or IIM, trust fund.

About 230,000 Natives own trust land. For more than a century, the government has been responsible for collecting and distributing income the land earns through leases and mineral royalties.

Specifically, Cobell is asking the federal government to correct its "grossly mismanaged" trust duties and provide an accounting for an estimated 500,000 to 800,000 past and present Native landowners. A federal judge since has ordered the government to document accounts dating to 1887.

The suit has been described as "one of the most complicated pieces of litigation in federal court history," by Stephanie Mencimer, a Washington Monthly editor.

This much is clear:

- The stakes are high. Cobell's lawyers have estimated $100 billion is owed to landowners, and they've urged the Interior Department to settle for more than $10 billion. A department spokesman calls their claims overstated.
- The outcome likely will change the way the government manages Native trust funds. The Cobell suit is prompting Congress, the court, In-

terior Department officials and tribal leaders to try to overhaul the system.

■ It has exposed the government's failure to uphold its responsibility to manage Native trust land and assets.

"It would be difficult to find a more historically mismanaged federal program than the Individual Indian Money trust," U.S. District Judge Royce C. Lamberth wrote in a December 1999 opinion.

"The United States, the trustee of the IIM trust, cannot say how much money is or should be in the trust. . . . Notwithstanding all of this (government officials) continue to write checks on an account that they cannot balance or reconcile."

Interior Secretary Gale Norton and Bureau of Indian Affairs director Neal McCaleb were held in contempt of court Sept. 17 for failing to comply with Lamberth's orders.

Nearly four years ago, Lamberth held two Clinton cabinet members in contempt in the same lawsuit.

Courtesy of North County Times

Thomas Slonaker, left, participates in a discussion in San Diego between tribal leaders and Interior Department officials about Native trust fund reform.

As the suit was moving toward its seventh year of litigation, comparisons to 2002's business scandals were easy to make.

"They are our first Americans. They have died in our wars. They have invested and contributed to our society," said Rep. Nick Rahall, D–W. Va. "And today they are being treated with most callous disregard, no better than the heads of Enron and WorldCom treated their investors."

Louis LaRose of the Winnebago Tribe of Nebraska, one of five lead plaintiffs, sees only one difference:

"They got 401(k) accounts. We got IIM accounts."

> "People cannot get the government to issue title status reports because the records are in such a mess. So when you do a home mortgage loan, it takes a year. Now, that should not be happening to Indian people."
>
> —Elouise Cobell

Dennis Gingold, a 20-year banking attorney, was introduced to Native trust funds about a decade ago, after being invited to meet with "Indians."

He expected to see people wearing turbans, he said.

He found Plains-style headdresses instead.

Then he heard a "three-hour horror story" about trust accounts.

Today, as lead attorney in the Cobell vs. Norton lawsuit, Gingold has made a dramatic shift for a lawyer accustomed to representing people with power, money and respect.

Now, his clients are among the nation's poorest people.

When he met Cobell, he said, she was "extremely frustrated, and had a right to be, and didn't know what to do about it."

"At the same time, she was unwilling to give up. It was a remarkable impression, because I'd never met anyone in that position before."

Cobell also remembers those days. Too many meetings. Too few results. And all she wanted was answers for other Native landowners: Who leases their land? How much income can they expect to earn from it? Is that fair market value?

"The total arrogance of people in power just made you so upset," she said. "You could go to meeting after meeting and nothing happened."

At one of the last meetings, a Justice Department lawyer provided a turning point.

She remembers his words: "'Don't come here with any false expectations.' They really didn't care. That's when I decided to sue."

The money in question is not an entitlement.

It's not a federal program.

It's not welfare.

It's generated from leases and royalties from land owned by tribal members and managed by the government. More than a century ago, when Washington started dividing and distributing reservation land to tribal members, it gave itself the duties of managing the land and its assets.

"This is the Indians' money, not the government's," Rep. Dale Kildee, D-Mich., said during a July House debate. "The United States has admitted that it mismanaged and lost the money."

How much money?

"If it goes to judgment, we believe the judgment will be $100 billion, over $100 billion, and this is why the government has tremendous incentive to come to the bargaining table," said Keith Harper, a Native American Rights Fund attorney in the case.

"We can establish what went into the system," he said. "They cannot establish what went out of the system. And they owe us everything. That's what trust law says."

But Interior Department officials say Cobell and the other plaintiffs are painting an inaccurate picture.

Eric Ruff, a department spokesman, said a recent review of 8,000 accounts showed an error rate of less than 1 percent.

"So I think the plaintiffs are exaggerating and overstating the case, which is predictable. They've been doing that all along," Ruff said. "They've shown no reluctance at any time to exaggerate and hyperextend their rhetoric."

There's more than money at stake.

Cobell said it's important for Native people to have more information, to have more opportunities. A tribal member with five oil wells producing income on her land ought to be able to walk into a bank with details about how much oil is being produced and how much revenue is expected.

That's not possible now, she said.

Some even struggle to prove they own land.

"People cannot get the government to issue title status reports because the records are in such a mess," she said. "So when you do a home mortgage loan, it takes a year. Now, that should not be happening to Indian people."

Although the case is far from over, it has already generated its share of rulings and revelations.

- February 1999: Judge Lamberth cited then-Interior Secretary Bruce Babbitt, Treasury Secretary Robert Rubin and BIA head Kevin Gover for contempt of court for failing to provide an accounting of the trust land and assets owned by the five lead plaintiffs.

"The way in which the defendants have handled this litigation up to the commencement of the contempt trial is nothing short of a travesty," he wrote.

- December 1999: Citing 11 breaches by the Interior Department of its trust responsibilities to Native landowners, Lamberth ordered a historical accounting of trust accounts dating to 1887. That ruling also called for a court investigator to oversee government compliance with court orders.
- April 2001: Lamberth appointed a court monitor to review the department's reform activities and file written progress reports.
- September 2002: Lamberth holds Norton and McCaleb in contempt.

When the Interior Department estimated this summer that an accounting dating to 1887 could cost $2.4 billion and take a decade to complete, Congress stepped in.

The House Appropriations Committee tried to shorten the accounting by 100 years—proposing to approve only enough money for an accounting back to 1985.

"This is litigation that has absolutely no end in sight. None," said Rep. Jim Kobe, R-Ariz. "There is no prospect of this litigation ever coming to a resolution. We are trying to put some parameters around it so that we can get an historical accounting for the people who really need it."

But to some, the move smacked of an attempt by the Bush administration to shirk a full accounting.

"Does this administration support it?" asked Rep. Jack Kingston, R-Ga. "This administration does know about this language and the administration does support this bill."

Lawmakers killed the proposal.

"We have had problems over the last few weeks and the last few months with the corporate scandals and the accountants that we have had in Enron and WorldCom and everything else," said Rep. Frank Pallone, D-N.J. "We have to take responsibility and do the right thing to make sure that the accounting is proper.

"Why is that any different for the federal government?"

Mike Theiler, Journal Star

As presiding judge in a class-action lawsuit over the government's management of Native trust land and assets, U.S. District Judge Royce Lamberth has held three cabinet members in contempt of court since 1999. The Texan isn't known for pulling punches.

Read the rest of the series at www.theauthenticvoice.org

"I Just Have a Good Time, All the Time"

Federal judge drives government reform of Native trust funds.

By Jodi Rave
Lee Enterprises Newspapers
Published September 30, 2002

WASHINGTON—U.S. District Judge Royce C. Lamberth's persona is as big as the wall of sea green marble behind him in Courtroom 21 of Washington's federal courthouse.

When he's cloaked in his black robe, his reputation bespeaks his home state's saying: "Don't mess with Texas."

But off the bench, he doesn't want to be judged by his hard-hitting courtroom demeanor.

He's smiling underneath.

"You do know I just have a good time all the time," he said, punctuating the sentence with a hearty laugh. "I mean, I'm painted as this raving lunatic, but I'm just having a good time."

That comes from the man who held two Clinton cabinet members in contempt in 1999 for failing to produce documents related to a lawsuit against the Interior Department over its trust fund duties to Native landowners. And in September, Lamberth held another, Interior Secretary Gale Norton, in contempt in the same lawsuit.

Lamberth, 59, has unleashed a flurry of court rulings as he presides over the Elouise Cobell vs. Gale Norton class-action lawsuit, which accuses the Interior Department of mismanaging trust funds for as many 800,000 past and present Native landowners.

He's gained national attention for his actions in the case. In addition to the contempt charges, Lamberth last year ordered the Interior Department to provide security for trust data stored on computers.

Department officials responded by cutting off Internet access to all of its bureaus, including the BIA.

"We have a judge who is out of control who is saying the department cannot use the Internet," Rep. Jack Kingston, R-Ga., said in July during House debate on trust fund amendments to the 2003 Interior Appropriations bill. "To me that is one of the most outrageous things that I have witnessed in my career. We have to stop it."

But the judge also has fans.

"He understands bull—. He sees through the bull—. He's the best thing that's happened to the Native Americans in over 200 years," said Dennis Gingold, lead attorney in the Cobell lawsuit.

Lamberth, an avid reader of John Grisham novels, earned a law degree from the University of Texas in 1967. He decided at age 7 to become a lawyer.

"My twin brother says because we always watched Perry Mason," Lamberth said. His brother, Cloyce, works for the local park service in San Antonio.

One of Royce Lamberth's first jobs led him to Vietnam, where he served in the Army's judge advocate general corps.

Appointed by former President Reagan, the judge has earned a non-partisan reputation in times when politics too often permeate judicial appointments, Gingold said.

"Most judges are appointed because they are political ideologues who support the particular views of the president who appoints them," Gingold said. "They are not appointed because they earn distinction in the practice. Judge Lamberth is one of the few judges in the country today who has that integrity."

Ross Swimmer, head of the Interior Department's Office of Indian Trust Transition, gave a more tempered view of the judge who hasn't been afraid of punishing the department.

"He's very likeable," Swimmer said. "I guess that's dependent on whether you're the plaintiff or defendant, but if you're not in court with him, he's a very likeable fellow and well-respected by a lot of people here."

"They Act like It's Their Money"

By Jodi Rave
Lee Enterprises Newspapers
Published September 30, 2002

Native trust fund system far from user-friendly, account holders say.

When his niece found him, Kenneth Hayes was living in a home without doors, windows or water in the same hardscrabble Arizona town where his older brother had died decades ago.

His brother had been a hero. A national symbol of valor. The Pima tribal citizen and Marine Corps private had helped hoist the flag in the famous image of Iwo Jima.

Johnny Cash had even paid tribute to Ira Hayes.

Ira Hayes died destitute in 1955.

And Kenneth Hayes was close to joining him when his niece, Sara Bernal, returned to the Gila River Reservation from California.

Take care of your uncle, she was told. He's living in the shack his parents used to own.

"I didn't think anybody lived there," Bernal said. "And they said, 'Yeah, he's there.'

"It didn't have no doors, no windows, and he was just in a room by himself and he looked so skinny. It looked like he had the same clothes on for years. He had no water, no electricity."

But he had money in the bank.

Her uncle owned reservation land that was leased to others. The Bureau of Indian Affairs managed the lease proceeds collected from his land.

Bernal approached the Bureau of Indian Affairs but was told her uncle's account was restricted because he had been deemed incapable of managing his money.

Today, nearly 10 years later, Bernal has guardianship over her uncle. She provides the 70-year-old with food, shelter and clothing. But getting money from his account is still difficult.

"I have the paper that says I'm his legal guardian," Bernal said. "But it's still hard for me to try and get anything. They don't send him money; it's just there."

Periodic statements indicate her uncle's account contains about $2,000, she said. But like with her own trust account—she also receives lease payments for land she owns—the statements don't provide such basic details as which tracts are leased or how much each contract earns, she said.

"He knows that it's all his," Bernal said of her uncle's account. "But they act like it's their own money but they don't want to part with it."

The money is available, said Evelyn Roanhorse, a social worker for the BIA's Western Region in Phoenix.

"They [guardians] can come in and ask for funds to provide for food or clothing, but they have to provide receipts for everything," Roanhorse said.

One of the last times Bernal withdrew her uncle's money, she used it to help Hayes buy new clothes. He needed them for a trip to Washington to see the men who served with his brother.

The reunions have become an important part of their lives.

"In 1995, we went to the island of Iwo Jima for the 50th anniversary," said Bernal, who recalled meeting veterans who had survived the historic World War II battle. "They were all in Ira's regiment. They remembered him. It was really a place to be."

THE MAKING OF

BROKEN TRUST SERIES

By Jodi Rave
Lee Enterprises Newspapers

As far back as I can remember, I'd heard about Individual Indian Money accounts.

Because I am a citizen of the Cheyenne River Sioux Tribe in South Dakota, the government created an IIM account in my name. When I turned eighteen, I'd be eligible to receive the balance, which was about $6,500.

The money represented the earnings from two historic land settlements that involved the Mississippi Sioux Claim, owed to direct descendants of Chief War Eagle. A second deposit came from a land settlement that broke the Great Sioux Reservation into five smaller ones in 1889.

I didn't have any access to or control of my IIM account until my eighteenth birthday. As was true for thousands of Native Americans with claims to land rights, the money was in the hands of the U.S. Department of the Interior. It was a situation I took for granted until I had a chance to report on it.

Native-owned lands, I soon discovered, had a long, sordid history, steeped in government bureaucracy and mismanagement that took away Native control of one of society's most valued assets. In today's world, owning property is like money in the bank. But for hundreds of thousands of Native landowners, whose property is held in trust by the government, it is almost impossible to enjoy the full benefits of ownership.

As one of the few beat reporters on Native issues for the daily press, I knew that tribal sovereignty—a tribe's right to govern itself—was one of the top concerns in Indian Country. Sovereignty includes the right to self-determine education, health care, law enforcement, economic development, tribal government, and land management.

The government dismantled all these rights to some degree over the last century. And while tribes have made substantial progress in regaining autonomy, they have never recovered the large land bases Congress stripped from them. Although tribes and individuals did retain millions of acres, much of that land—and the money earned from natural resources found on it—has largely been managed by the Interior Department and its Bureau of Indian Affairs.

I once thought the Bureau of Indian Affairs had the sole responsibility for managing trust lands. But in my reporting I found the bureau merely carries out Interior Department policies. Another surprise surfaced when it became evident that the Interior Department's Office of Special Trustee wielded substantial power, more so than the Bureau of Indian Affairs, when it came to reforming the trust fund system.

I knew the story of Native trust lands needed to be told because it exemplified the jurisdictional battle taking place between tribes and the federal government. No issue better illustrated the tribes' loss of sovereignty than the U.S. Interior Department's century-long mismanagement of individual land and natural resource assets.

Yann Nicolas

"As a Native woman, I grew up witnessing and experiencing the political, social, and economic injustice in the lives of Native peoples. It's the reason I decided early to become a journalist." —Jodi Rave

The money earned is not an entitlement. It's not a federal program. It's not welfare. It's generated from leases and royalties from land owned by tribal citizens and managed by the government.

While the daily press covered certain aspects of the trust fund plight of Native peoples, Lee Enterprises newspapers offered the first in-depth series—and arguably the only one. The Broken Trust series appeared in Lee papers, a chain of small to medium-sized newspapers with a 1.1 million circulation base, including the Rocky Mountain, Great Plains, and Midwest tribes. Those regions are home to the majority of the trust fund account holders.

For the most part, the press had covered these stories in the traditional conflict mode—focusing on the government's victimization of Native Americans—or offered boring "for the record" summaries of legal court cases. I decided I had an obligation to tell this story, to help Native people understand and to make others care. At the same time, I knew I had to keep my own anger about the mismanagement out of my reporting.

It was a test because I could feel the frustration of people like Elouise Cobell of the Blackfeet Nation of Montana, who brought the landmark suit against the government. And I was distraught because this was a century-old problem that had been shuffled from one presidential administration to the next. Finally, I felt outrage each time I heard someone say the trust fund scandal would not be such a mess if the money and land belonged to any other racial or ethnic group.

But it's a different story for Native people. This country can't seem to stop taking from us. That's why tribes cling so hard to the concept of sovereignty. It's one of the most important possessions we have left.

As a Native woman, I grew up witnessing and experiencing the political, social, and economic injustice in the lives of Native peoples. It's the reason I decided early to become a journalist. I wanted to make a difference in my community. I wanted people to know the indigenous side of the story. Since I published my first column in high school—I wrote about the vibrancy of Native traditions—my journalistic ideals haven't changed. I still want to shed light on injustices. I still want to educate. And I'm still working to do it in a way respected and read by everyone.

Going into this project, I was conscious of how much I'd learned about covering Native issues. I'll never forget one editor's warning that a story I was covering couldn't be written by "Indian Jodi." What did that mean? I am Indian. I was dismayed by the comment.

And then there was the editor who reproved me for allowing my anger to seep into stories where it seemed obvious Native people had experienced severe prejudice. His advice was to "let the facts speak for themselves" because readers were smart enough to form their own opinions about injustice.

Following this advice has probably been one of my most difficult challenges, but it has served me well, especially with the Broken Trust series. Emotional reporting wouldn't help anything; the facts would.

I've learned how to become a better journalist while working at daily newspapers. If I'd stayed at a Native-owned newspaper, I might have been labeled an "activist journalist" or reported like one. Although much good work comes from Native-owned newspapers, I feel coming through the ranks of mainstream newspapers taught me early that I couldn't get away with injecting personal bias into a story. For that, I am grateful.

I was able to bring that wisdom to my reporting, setting anger aside, even when dealing with a largely white-controlled accounting system that had left the management of Native land assets in shambles. My initial research uncovered East Coast newspaper reports from the late 1880s revealing a system in trouble. Since then, several government reports have chronicled the mismanagement of these funds.

Despite the billions of dollars that could not be accounted for, the news media has underreported the trust fund story. It might have continued to go unnoticed if not for Cobell, who became so frustrated with the system that she took a courageous step and filed suit against the Interior Department in 1996. She was my inspiration.

A banker by trade and a tribal leader on the Blackfeet Reservation, Cobell had been among the scores of people advocating major changes in the trust fund system. I earned her trust by having a reputation as a good reporter. She knew who I was before I ever called. I'd spent time interviewing dozens of people about how their trust funds were handled, so Cobell never had to review Trust Fund Management 101 for me. These interviews brought out how poorly the trust accounts were being managed.

One of the greatest challenges in my reporting was to get into the belly of the beast: the federal bureaucracy. Among my accomplishments were interviews with people in the Office of Special Trustee and regional Bureau of Indian Affairs offices. My first visit to the Office of Special Trustee in Albuquerque, New Mexico, was off the record. It took place with senior managers who agreed to talk, to offer an insider perspective. They said they could not be interviewed for the record. I agreed just to listen. They helped me understand some of their problems with reforming the system. My meeting with them was invaluable. I ended up not talking to any senior managers again until nearly the end of my reporting. My second visit was with a different manager, and for the record.

Given the complexity of the trust fund system, I needed to report this story from as many perspectives as I could find. One of the voices I needed but which proved more difficult to locate was that of someone who worked at a regional Bureau of Indian Affairs office. But it was tough getting an interview with anyone because the word from Washington, D.C., was that no one working within the bureau was allowed to talk to the press, especially while Interior Secretary Gale Norton was on trial for contempt.

I hit walls time and again. I kept getting referred back to Washington, but I needed a local connection. I managed to convince bureau officials that giving me access would be to their benefit. I needed to hear their side. Finally, I got an interview with the bureau superintendent and his staff on the Winnebago Reservation in Nebraska. I had already cultivated a relationship with some of the workers there, so when I was granted an interview, those workers already trusted me.

It turned out to be one of the best interviews of the series because it illuminated the obstacles bureau workers faced when managing trust funds. They were understaffed and working with an impractical accounting system. I became more sympathetic to their ordeal. I drove away from the reservation with a solid framework in mind for the story. My persistence in getting the interviews ultimately helped the series appeal to all sides represented in the lawsuit.

For reporters handling a complicated legal issue, nothing is more important than finding sources like Keith Harper, a Native American Rights Fund attorney who helped translate the legal jargon into something the average reader could understand. When I became Lee Enterprises' first Native beat reporter, I interviewed Harper, a Cherokee, for a number of stories for which he was a quick and reliable source. That type of relationship, developed over time, is essential when you're embarking on a complicated story.

One of the first things Harper did was help me identify the foundation on which to build the series: a 1999 court opinion handed down by U.S. District Judge Royce C. Lamberth. This 136-page opinion laid the groundwork for how the government breached its trust responsibilities for trust fund beneficiaries. The court described the Interior Department's noncompliance with previous court orders as "the most egregious governmental misconduct that it has ever seen." That opinion became my bible.

Finding sources inside the government was also an essential part of my work. Take Thomas Wabnum, who had twenty-five years of experience in both the Bureau of Indian Affairs and the Office of Special Trustee. When I met him, he was a management analyst for the Office of Special Trustee in Albuquerque, New Mexico. Wabnum helped decipher the roles and duties of employees, including the office structure, allowing me to get a broad understanding of how the bureau worked.

His connections led me to about two dozen Bureau of Indian Affairs and Office of Special Trustee workers who called themselves "the moles." This was a group of frustrated employees who met regularly outside the workplace to discuss the effects of the Cobell lawsuit on them. Many felt overlooked by the Interior Department as it sought to improve the trust fund system as ordered by the court. The moles knew the system better than anyone, yet they were troubled by changes within the department, including a situation where, some complained, they had to train outside contractors to do their work. Distrust was everywhere.

Finding Wabnum was the breakthrough I needed. He and the moles became my sounding boards. Only a few agreed to be quoted because they feared retribution. But they referred me to friends or relatives who were affected by the scandal—the voices I needed to make this story real.

Once I started reporting the series, I realized the problems surrounding Indian land ownership were as relevant now as when Congress first passed the Trade and Intercourse Act of 1790, an act requiring federal approval of the sale of Native lands. My challenge was to humanize this story and find a news peg beyond the Cobell suit.

I had tried two years earlier to convince my editors that the story should be my top reporting project for the year. They said no. The story took on a new urgency in November 2001 when Norton shocked Indian Country by announcing plans to reorganize the Bureau of Indian Affairs, a department that shares trust management duties with the Interior Department and the Office of Special Trustee. Norton unveiled her reorganization plan in Spokane, Washington, during an annual meeting of the National Congress of American Indians.

Tribal leaders were alarmed because the proposed reorganization would remove the core of government trust responsibilities from the Bureau of Indian Affairs. They were also outraged because Norton didn't consult with them before creating the new department, the Bureau of Indian Trust Assets Management. Many tribal leaders wondered what the reorganization would mean to their sovereign status and their relationship with the federal government.

> . . . it was tough getting an interview with anyone because the word from Washington, D.C. was that no one working within the bureau was allowed to talk to the press. . . .

Probably one of the most outspoken tribal leaders on this issue was Tex Hall, president of the National Congress of American Indians. Hall, who was also chairman of my tribe, the Mandan, Hidatsa, and Arikara Nation in North Dakota, spoke across the country on this issue. He proved to be a reliable source and was one of the few tribal leaders to take the stand during Norton's contempt trial.

The timing was right for an in-depth series. The issue now was to convince my editors at the *Journal Star* in Lincoln, Nebraska, that this story was worth the time it would take to investigate. The last time I tried, my then-editor rejected the story as too bureaucratic. But this time I had great characters and a human narrative that would counter the stilted bureaucratic and legal jargon that accompanies land dispute stories.

Journal Star city editor Peter Salter pushed me further to find voices in the communities. I eventually found people like Gary Loudner, a Crow Creek Sioux from South Dakota. He typified the frustration of so many trust fund account holders. He had simple questions about his land lease payments but could find no simple answers. He was furious it took so long and that he had to do it on his own.

But a good story needs more than good interviews. I armed myself with facts, something I was able to do thanks to the Website *http://indiantrust.com,* operated by Cobell, which made all the land trust court documents readily available. Another site, *http://www.Indianz.com*—a Native news Website— became an invaluable source because it provided timely updates on the case and direct links to several types of documents. Without the Web it would have been difficult to report on a court case unfolding in Washington from my desk in Lincoln.

After several months of interviews and trips to Washington and Albuquerque, I had collected a tremendous amount of paperwork. The issue, as it is for any reporter doing an investigative story, was how to make sense of it all.

The answer turned out to be simple, and I found it at my local stationary store. Highlight markers! I used them on every other page of the court opinion and referenced those pages often. I also used fluorescent sticky notes extensively on the huge volume of documents I'd collected. And I recorded most of my phone and in-person interviews so I could refer to them during subsequent reporting and writing.

Following the paper trail proved a truly educational experience. Everything I didn't understand was documented somewhere. I just had to find it.

Ultimately, the series taught me a lot about investigative reporting and how important it is to create the documentation necessary to support one's claims—in this case, the Native complaints. I was forced to dig through piles and piles of records and to understand complicated legal maneuvers. It was certainly the most complex case I've ever written about.

The reporting also reminded me how important it is to work through my biases in order to present all perspectives fairly. Still, I didn't check my heritage at the door. The sources I brought to the story and my awareness of how Native people feel about the land and justice gave me a definite advantage. They allowed me, the sole reporter on this series, to maneuver through a complicated landscape and bring nuance to a story most reporters would miss.

It's very common for Native people to tell me: "You understand. You get it." This is a point of pride, not as a Native American but as a journalist determined to report accurately this largely untold chapter of America's history. As a reporter, my agenda must be grounded in telling my people's stories through a cultural awareness and professional integrity that lead me to do the right story and to get it right as well.

To screen the Jodi Rave interview, select EQUALITY on the DVD Main Menu then "Broken Trust."

DISCUSSION POINTS

DISCUSS

- Discuss the importance of this series in light of what you understand about the history of injustices against Native Americans.
- Does Jodi Rave succeed at integrating knowledge of her family's history into the series without taking on an activist role?
- How would a non-Native journalist build Jodi Rave's source list and knowledge?
- Discuss what you have learned about investigating government control over Indian land rights that would be useful in following up on this story.
- In her essay on the Broken Trust series, Rave says that Indians tell her that she "gets it." What do you think it takes for a reporter to "get it" the way Rave does?

SUGGESTED READINGS AND WEBSITES

RESEARCH

Books

Winbush, Raymond. *Should America Pay? Slavery and the Raging Debate on Reparations.* New York: HarperCollins, 2003.

A collection of essays and articles on the reparations movement.

Hightower-Langston, Donna. *The Native American World.* New York: Wiley Desk Reference, 2003.

This authoritative and comprehensive resource provides detailed information on a vast array of topics related to the Native American World, including more than three hundred entries covering major tribes, languages, prominent individuals, and important historical events.

Websites

news.lp.findlaw.com/hdocs/docs/doi/cobellnorton917020pn.pdf

The complete U.S. District Court memorandum of opinion from the groundbreaking Cobell vs. Norton class-action lawsuit. The court ruled in favor of Elouise Cobell, a member of the Blackfeet tribe, finding that U.S. Interior Secretary Gale Norton had been lying about her agency's efforts to handle land trusts from over three hundred thousand Native Americans.

indiantrust.com and www.indianz.com

Cited in Jodi Rave's essay "The Making of Broken Trust."

www.doi.gov/bureau-indian-affairs.html

The Website of the Bureau of Indian Affairs (BIA), which is responsible for the administration and management of over fifty million acres of Indian land.

news.minnesota.publicradio.org/projects/2001/04/brokentrust

The Website for "Broken Trust: Civil Rights in Indian Country," a series on the plight of Native Americans residing in reservations that was aired by Minnesota Public Radio in April 2001. The eight-part series cast a national spotlight on the glaring problem of protecting individual freedoms and justices on these lands.

www.nmai.si.edu

The National Museum of the American Indian site.

wkconlin.nexcess.net/index.php/blogs/nativeamerican/P0

The Covering Indian Country blog is dedicated to fostering excellence in media coverage of Native American issues, communities, and cultures through the sharing of resources, stories, viewpoints, and journalism tips.

CHAPTER 7

STORY

ASIAN-AMERICAN

JOHN DONVAN, ABC NEWS, *NIGHTLINE*

JOHN DONVAN

ABC News correspondent John Donvan has worked for more than two decades as a *Nightline* correspondent, chief White House reporter, chief Moscow correspondent, Amman bureau chief, and reporter in Jerusalem. Donvan, who has been acclaimed by the *Chicago Sun Times* as one of "ten war stars" for his reporting from Iraq, began his career with ABC Radio in 1980. He has been honored by the National Association of Black Journalists, the Committee of 100, and the Media Action Network for Asian Americans.

Asian-American

The story that veteran *Nightline* correspondent John Donvan tells is about fear, perception, and bigotry. But above all it's about what it means to be an American. Donvan pulls the curtain back on the "us-versus-them" atmosphere Asian Americans brought to light in the aftermath of the Chinese fund-raising scandal and the Wen Ho Lee spy investigation that unfolded during the presidency of Bill Clinton.

Donvan shows how a reporter can build a strong, credible story about prejudice without benefit of court documents, hidden cameras, or other fact-based evidence. First, though, Donvan had to challenge what he said were his own blind spots about what constitutes bigotry, blind spots that made him reluctant at first even to pursue the story.

One of network television's most seasoned correspondents, Donvan brings a level of humility and transparency to this story that is rare for journalism. To tell your audience that you did not initially believe the story you are reporting was legitimate is a unique admission likely to provoke debate among journalists of any vintage.

This chapter opens a window on historical events—The Chinese Exclusion Act and the internment of Japanese Americans during World War II, for example—that often form the context for reporting on American race relations. It also will help journalists recognize that they can become increasingly aware of the ways education and life experiences affect editorial judgment. As Donvan and producer Mary Claude Foster debated the information they had uncovered, they wound up questioning their own journalistic notions, instincts they never would have challenged had they stopped listening to their sources.

Reporters writing about race relations need to know a lot about history, stereotypes, and the many forms of prejudice and racism. What Donvan shows in this chapter is that it's equally important for reporters to understand what they do not know if they are to tell complex stories of race in this nation that so proudly thinks of itself as a "melting pot."

"ASIAN-AMERICAN" (TRANSCRIPT)

ABC News, *Nightline*
Airdate: June 28, 1999
Correspondent: John Donvan / Producer: Mary Claude Foster / Editor: Russ Freeman

John Donvan: [voice-over]	Sometimes the way things look depends on how you connect the dots. Right now, with the U.S. in the midst of a spy scare, one group of Americans is very frightened of the picture they see emerging because the face at the center of the scandal, though it belongs to an American, has Asian eyes and an Asian name and Asian Americans, Chinese, Japanese, Korean and others, all say what happens to him is going to haunt us. Talk to an engineer at the Los Alamos weapons lab.
1st Asian American:	The whole group feels that cloud of suspicion over our heads.
John Donvan:	Talk to a doctor in Dallas.
Suzanne Ahn:	I'm personally very tired of being singled out and my patriotism and my Americanness being questioned.
John Donvan:	Listen to an activist for Japanese Americans.
2nd Asian American:	Japanese Americans during World War II were incarcerated for being mistakenly as disloyal [*sic*] and this whole scene today smacks similarly to that.
John Donvan:	This is the fear that eats at Asian Americans, that when the rest of us connect the dots of some recent events, from Wen Ho Lee, to the Cox Report on Chinese spying to anti-U.S. demonstrations outside the American embassy in Beijing, that this will feed a feeling against them that Asian Americans say is always there, just beneath the surface. Consider the May 26th edition of the *New York Post*. The White House selling out to China, is the message. The President caricatured as a Chinese man is the image. Or this recent cover of National Review Chinese Bill Clinton, Chinese Al Gore, Chinese Hillary Clinton. They've even got the buck teeth. Ever see Mickey Rooney in *Breakfast At Tiffany's*?

[Clip from *Breakfast At Tiffany's*]

John Donvan: [on camera]	The truth is that nowadays no legitimate cartoonist or moviemaker would dare to caricature the facial features of,

Courtesy of ABC News, Nightline

Alice Young recalls racial stereotyping during her school days.

" . . . when they showed a film, a social studies film, on communism, there I sat in the third-grade class and when the lights came on all of the, my classmates had moved their chairs further back. At the end of the film they said if you notice anyone suspicious, please call your local CIA or FBI."

—Alice Young

say, a black person or a Jew. Flat noses and hooked noses are taboo. The truth also is that Chinese Americans and other Asian Americans do not enjoy that kind of protection from ridicule.

[voice-over]	Only in rare cases like the people in the film based on Pearl Buck's novel, *The Good Earth* . . .
[Clip from *The Good Earth*]	
1st actor:	My father plowed it and it's mine.
John Donvan:	. . . Lieutenant Sulu in *Star Trek,* do we see Asians playing the parts of people we might like or might want to be like. More often, when an Asian has a part in a U.S. movie or TV show, it's to play the servant—Hop Sing on *Bonanza*.
[Clip from *Bonanza*]	
2nd actor:	Hop Sing think maybe Mr. Ben sailor man, too.
John Donvan:	Or to be the butt of jokes in the movie *Sixteen Candles*.
[Clip from *Sixteen Candles*]	
3rd actor:	Would you like to go to the dance . . . with Sam?

"Anybody that grows up Asian American experiences, 'Gee, you speak English so well,' or hears, 'So, where are you from?' 'I'm from L.A.' 'No, where are you really from?' 'I'm really from L.A.'"

—Angela Oh

Courtesy of ABC News, Nightline

Angela Oh discusses how Asian Americans are made to feel like foreigners.

John Donvan:	Or, most of all, it's to play the villain. Fu Manchu in the '50s, James Bond's nemesis Odd Job in the '60s. And in the '90s Angela Oh served on President Clinton's race advisory panel.
Angela Oh:	I'm told that one out of every six physicians is of Asian descent. Now, we've got a program called *L.A. Doctors*. There's not a single Asian American on that program. You've got a program called *E.R.* There's not a single Asian American doctor on that program. You've got a program called *Chicago Hope*. You don't see any Asian Americans.
John Donvan: [on camera]	Now, what does all this have to do with the spy scare? To a white American, it is not necessarily all that obvious why Asian Americans feel vulnerable in this period of troubled U.S.-Chinese relations. But it was finally hammered home when virtually everyone I spoke to told essentially the same story in different ways, that to be Asian American is to be told at one time or another that you're not quite one of us.
[voice-over]	Attorney Alice Young felt it when she was a child.
Alice Young:	Well, I specifically remember when I was in McLean, Virginia. As the only Asian family in what was then essentially

Pentagon-CIA land that when they showed a film, a social studies film, on communism, the communists happened to be Chinese. There I sat in the third-grade class and when the lights came on all of the, my classmates had moved their chairs further back. At the end of the film they said if you notice anyone suspicious, please call your local CIA or FBI.

John Donvan: Angela Oh feels it because she speaks English like the native born American that she is.

Angela Oh: Anybody that grows up Asian American experiences, "Gee, you speak English so well," or hears, "So, where are you from?" "I'm from L.A." "No, where are you really from?" "I'm really from L.A."

John Donvan:
[voice-over] And Olympic skating champion Kristi Yamaguchi must have felt it when an L.A. disk jockey said on the air about his Wheaties box, "I don't want to see eyes that are all slanted. I want to see American eyes." Yamaguchi was born in the United States. So were her parents. So were her grandparents.

[on camera] The deejay said it was a joke and he apologized. But it hurt a lot of people. And it went to prove a point that a lot of Asian Americans have already made, that in this country, a lot of us see an Asian face, even an Asian American face, and reflexively think foreigner.

[voice-over] Perhaps that is only human nature. But the danger comes when there is also fear. Economic fear. Late last century, Congress passed a law to exclude Chinese workers from coming to America because they were seen as cheap labor threatening American jobs. It was later expanded to cover all Asian workers. The fear that comes with war. In the middle of this century, the U.S. government locked up 120,000 Japanese Americans for the duration of World War II because they might possibly be a threat. And now?

Pres. Bill Clinton: Now we hear that China is a country to be feared.

John Donvan: Now it's the fear of being spied on and Asian Americans, believing they're still not quite seen as American as everyone else, wonder whether human nature will make a threat of them once again.

[commercial break]

John Donvan:
[voice-over] When U.S. scientist Wen Ho Lee was dismissed from the U.S. weapons lab at Los Alamos, reportedly for security violations,

it was U.S. Energy Secretary Bill Richardson who fired him. In the months since, Richardson has spent a lot of time reassuring other Asian Americans that they are not also suspects.

Bill Richardson: Let me be very clear with you. The alleged actions of any one individual are not, are not and never will be a reflection on any other American citizen, whether [sic] his or her race, color, creed, ethnic background or nation of origin.

John Donvan: Richardson was speaking before the prestigious Committee of 100, made up of prominent Chinese Americans and it was what they wanted to hear. But Asian Americans remain dubious. They wonder why no Asian American has ever been appointed to any president's cabinet. And fresh in their minds is another scandal with a China angle. 1996, Bill Clinton was running for his second term. Asian Americans felt he was sincere in inviting them to work for his election.

Sen. Fred Thompson: I speak of allegations concerning a plan hatched during the
(R), Tennessee last election cycle by the Chinese government and designed to pour illegal money into American political campaigns.

John Donvan: And then the campaign finance scandal exploded. The
[voice-over] suspicion that a few Chinese Americans raising funds for the President were actually getting their money from China.

[on camera] The Democratic Party went into a panic and suddenly every Asian American who had ever donated money to the party felt like a criminal suspect, contacted by investigators who appeared to be looking at anyone who had an Asian sounding name. Millionaire businessman Charlie Woo was one of them.

Charlie Woo: The Democratic National Committee had, their investigator contacted me.

John Donvan: So was Suzanne Ahn, a prominent doctor in Texas.

Suzanne Ahn: The questions that this gentleman asked was one, what is your reported income on your tax statement? Two, what are your assets? Three, are you an American citizen?

Charlie Woo: They told me that if I did not cooperate, they would release my name to the news media as one that would not cooperate with the investigation.

Suzanne Ahn: And he said if you do not, you will be listed as being uncooperative. We will return your money and your name will be released to the press.

John Donvan:
[voice-over]

So Woo got called, Ahn got called, but Alice Young did not. Is that because she spells her name Y-O-U-N-G, the English way? And then there is Hoyt Zia, a Clinton political appointee to the Commerce Department whose name showed up in the press in a story linking him to the campaign finance scandal. He was never charged with anything, but he says it cost him his future in Washington. In a blistering New York Times editorial last month he wrote, "Innuendo can ruin a reputation in no time. The link to possible controversy was enough to cause administration officials to withdraw my appointment to a higher position in the Department of the Navy. I will forever have to explain to prospective employers why my loyalty as an American was called into question." We caught up with Zia on moving day. After more than five years in Washington, he's packing it in and heading to Hawaii with his family for a job not in government.

[interview]

Do you think that if you were white you would still have a job in Washington, you'd be staying and none of this would have happened to you?

Hoyt Zia:

Oh, absolutely. If I were white or maybe just non-Asian there wouldn't have been the connections that these conspiracy theorists drew connecting me with China.

Courtesy of ABC News, Nightline
New Mexico governor Bill Richardson, then U.S. secretary of energy

"I understand that Asian-Pacific Americans are concerned that their loyalty and their patriotism are being challenged and that's because of racism."
—Bill Richardson

"If I were white or maybe just non-Asian there wouldn't have been the connections that these conspiracy theorists drew connecting me with China."

—Hoyt Zia

Courtesy of ABC News, Nightline

Hoyt Zia discusses having been fired for "security reasons."

John Donvan: Hoyt, in a lot of ways you, as a child of immigrants who makes it into the Ivy League, who becomes an officer in the marines, you have lived and embodied what we all call the American Dream. And after all that's happened, a presidential appointment and then it ends this way, are you still a believer?

Hoyt Zia: Oh, I'm definitely a true believer. I believe in our system. I believe that what makes this country great is the fact that someone like me and others like me have the opportunity to achieve this success. I think that from the standpoint of the Asian American community, I'm just, as far as I'm concerned, just another booster rocket in what we eventually hope will get us to the level where we are enjoying our full rights as American citizens and being considered full Americans and not foreign nationals or people being suspect of being less than truly American.

[commercial break]

John Donvan:
[voice-over]
There is bitterness now toward Bill Clinton in the Asian American community, a feeling that once they became politically radioactive neither he nor his party wanted anything to do with them, which may explain, in the midst of this new spy scandal, why the President's Energy Secretary is taking their concerns so seriously.

Bill Richardson:	I understand that Asian-Pacific Americans are concerned that their loyalty and their patriotism are being challenged and that's because of racism.
John Donvan: [interview]	Do you think this perception that Asian Americans are being singled out exists more in the minds of Asian Americans than anybody else?
Bill Richardson:	Yes, it exists more in the minds of Asian Americans. There is a perception, more than reality, that there is a discrimination that's resulting from this incident, that it's going to be tougher to get a job, to gain approval for new work.
John Donvan: [on camera]	But are Asian Americans in sensitive positions simply imagining that people are looking at them a little differently these days? Not necessarily, because according to authorities in the FBI, it is a given, first, that China has successfully recruited Chinese Americans as spies in the past and second, that China continues to target Asian Americans much more than white Americans in an effort to compromise them.
[voice-over].	A clip or two from a 1980s Energy Department training film.
Unidentified narrator:	A visitor from overseas, perhaps someone with whom you've worked on joint projects who has become your friend may have ulterior motives in that friendship.
John Donvan: [voice-over]	. . . makes the point not so subtly that the people trying to steal information from our scientists are going to look like that man on the right there.
[interview]	Does that mean in reality that the FBI probably spends more time looking at the Wangs than they look at the Smiths?
Paul Moore: former FBI analyst	Yes, because the Chinese are in contact more with the Wangs than they are with the Smiths. If the Chinese were in contact more with the Smiths than the Wangs, the FBI would forget about the Wangs and go after the Smiths.
John Donvan: [voice-over]	And once they went after a man named Hu. We don't know all that's behind what happened to Chi Ming Hu, only the side of it he tells us, his immigration from Taiwan, earning his Ph.D. in physics from the University of Maryland, the job he went to in 1982 for Computer Sciences Corporation, which subcontracted with NASA. That's when the FBI called.
Chi Ming Hu:	An FBI agent called Henry Belch interviewed me. He said he was investigating a friend of mine who was doing business

with China and he wanted to find out whether my friend did anything illegal.

John Donvan: Two weeks later the agent was back at Dr. Hu's workplace, calling from the personnel office.

Chi Ming Hu: The FBI was quite hostile. He tried to intimidate me. First I said I want to talk to a lawyer first. Then he said if you don't come, I'm going to get you, and second he said he would write a report to NASA and NASA may fire me.

John Donvan: A week later, Dr. Hu was fired for security reasons. The FBI told us it cannot comment on Hu's case because he has never been charged with a crime and, said a spokeswoman, "The FBI does not make recommendations to employers about what they should or should not do about employees." But listen to this man.

Bruce Blalock: The FBI had made the request that Dr. Hu's employment be terminated, that he was suspected of being a spy because of his associations.

John Donvan: Bruce Blalock was Dr. Hu's boss at the time.

Bruce Blalock: I was incredulous. It didn't seem to make any sense to me. I protested to my manager. I protested to human resources. I protested to the NASA managers at the site.

Chi Ming Hu: No one dared to hire a spy after they heard my story. And second is a lot of my friends tried to avoid me.

Bruce Blalock: I think there is a general suspicion of Asians that is not applied to other Caucasians.

Chi Ming Hu: I cannot show you the evidence, but my strong feeling is, you know, if I were a native American, I'm pretty sure I would have been treated differently.

John Donvan:
[on camera] Today, Hu says he is speaking out because he suspects what happened to him may now be happening to Wen Ho Lee, who has not yet been charged with any crime. If China is spying on the United States, and we would be fools to think otherwise, and if China is trying to recruit Asian Americans in the hope of playing on the sort of affection that, say, an Irish American feels for Ireland or a Jewish American for Israel, then the FBI would be under attack for not doing its job if it ignored ethnicity entirely. It is one of those dilemmas for which democracy does not always have an easy answer. As for the

dilemma of Wen Ho Lee, the princip[le] that many Asian Americans say should apply to him, as always, is innocent until proven guilty.

I'm John Donvan for *Nightline* in Washington.

Broadcast scene of *Asian-American,* foreground, with Wen Ho Lee, the scientist charged with espionage, background.

Courtesy of ABC News, Nightline

Courtesy of ABC News, Nightline

Japanese Americans discuss the ramifications of the Wen Ho Lee spy investigation.

"When U.S. scientist Wen Ho Lee was dismissed from the U.S. weapons lab at Los Alamos, reportedly for security violations, it was U.S. Energy Secretary Bill Richardson who fired him. In the months since, Richardson has spent a lot of time reassuring other Asian Americans that they are not also suspects."

—John Donvan

THE MAKING OF

ASIAN-AMERICAN

By John Donvan
ABC News, *Nightline*

The truth about this piece is that I didn't really believe in it at the start. My executive producer, Tom Bettag, had been approached by an old colleague of his, Sam Chu Lin, who suggested that *Nightline* put together a program reporting on the latest "yellow scare" outbreak in the American news media. I was given the assignment and teamed with a first-rate *Nightline* producer, Mary Claude Foster.

It was the spring of 1999, and *The New York Times* had just broken a huge story: the arrest and detention of a nuclear scientist at the U.S. government nuclear labs in Los Alamos. His name was Wen Ho Lee, and according to *The Times* and other news reports, he was accused of passing secrets to the Chinese government. An immigrant from Taiwan, Lee was a naturalized U.S. citizen. He proclaimed his innocence but spent nine months in solitary confinement until the government dropped all but one minor charge against him. But in 1999 he was still being held, and his arrest, detention, and alleged crimes were the story.

But the other story, Sam Chu Lin told Bettag, concerned the tone of anti-Chinese hysteria in all this coverage—classic "yellow scare" stuff—that he felt was blatantly racist and threatening to Americans of Asian heritage.

Born and raised in Mississippi, Chu Lin had earned himself a place in history as one of the first Asian American journalists to break through as a network news correspondent at CBS, back in the early 1970s. By 1999 he was working independently in California, and he pitched the story to ABC's *Nightline* because he considered it important enough for the show to take on.

The trouble, as I saw it, was that *The Times* and the other news organizations reporting on Lee's case had not crossed the line into coverage that could be described as even mildly racist. Chu Lin, Mary Claude, and I met for lunch in Washington, D.C., to talk about this. It was an interesting meeting, during which Sam talked warmly about life in the small Mississippi community. Quite matter-of-factly, without much bitterness, he also talked about the ugly remarks he'd heard throughout life, at various times, about people who looked like him and how they didn't really "belong" in America. Now, he insisted, it was happening again, in the way that the Wen Ho Lee case was being reported.

I knew it broke Chu Lin's heart when we told him we just didn't think there was much of a story there. "We've looked at the coverage," I told him, "and we're just not seeing the kind of stuff you're talking about."

In fact, we had gone through the papers and transcripts of network reporting on the Wen Ho Lee case and had found nothing that was anti-Asian American. No name-calling. No race-baiting. No "yellow scare." In every case, the reports we reviewed simply relayed details of an FBI investigation into a naturalized citizen held on spying charges.

"But you've got to see what that looks like to *us*," Chu Lin said. By *"us,"* he meant Asian Americans. He explained that, to Asian Americans, stories about spy charges—even if they only mentioned one man—put a cloud of suspicion over every other American of Asian heritage.

"No, they don't," I answered. "I mean, they don't to me." I truly did not know what Chu Lin was talking about. Wen Ho Lee was one man. The press was not giving him an unduly hard time, given the fact that the government was investigating him.

"Sorry," I said. "We just can't do a story about a racist backlash that didn't exist."

Next we heard from Henry Tang, like me, a native New Yorker. He'd been talking with Chu Lin about the Wen Ho Lee coverage. A success on Wall Street,

Arlene Morgan

Correspondent John Donvan discusses his story on Asian Americans.

"The trouble, as I saw it, was that *The Times* and the other news organizations reporting on Lee's case had not crossed the line into coverage that could be described as even mildly racist."

—John Donvan

A Wheaties box featuring Olympic ice skating star Kristi Yamaguchi was the topic of radio talk show ridicule.

"You know, the stereotype that has always hurt us, it's the one that we are not real Americans. We're foreigners. We can't be trusted. That's what Wen Ho Lee does. A spy case. A guy from Taiwan. It fits the stereotype."

—Henry Tang

Courtesy of ABC News, Nightline

The National Review magazine cover on the Chinese spy allegations.

Tang had helped organize the Committee of 100, an association of prominent Chinese Americans, of which he is one. Tang phoned me and made the same points we'd heard from Chu Lin, but he had an idea. "I know you missed the ugly stuff in the press," he said. "If I hire a journalism grad student to go through the papers and collect examples, would you be willing to take another look at it?" Mary Claude and I saw no reason to reject this proposal, so Tang put the student to work.

About a week later, Tang called back. He sounded frustrated. His student researcher had, like us, come up dry in looking for anti-Asian expressions in the news media. They just weren't there. Tang also sounded heartbroken. He let out a long sigh.

"You know, the stereotype that has always hurt us, it's the one that we are not real Americans. We're foreigners. We can't be trusted," he explained. "That's what Wen Ho Lee does. A spy case. A guy from Taiwan. It fits the stereotype."

He talked about the times Asian Americans had suffered because of this stereotype. He cited the immigration laws that targeted Chinese in the nineteenth and early twentieth centuries and the internment of Japanese Americans during World War II. "It's the pattern," Tang argued. "I don't know how to get across to you why this is important," he said, sounding practically despondent.

Something clicked inside me in that moment. Henry Tang is a serious man. He knew that the evidence I needed—concrete examples, facts—was lacking. And still he was telling me something concrete was happening in the Asian American community. A sense of foreboding . . . of dread. He insisted it wasn't just him or Sam Chu Lin. Asian Americans everywhere were reading the Wen Ho Lee coverage, and it was scaring them.

I didn't know Tang well, but I sensed that he was giving me something genuine, if elusive: maybe not the story they originally pitched but something about the fear, the discomfort they felt as the Wen Ho Lee story played so prominently.

At this point I should mention, though it has to be obvious, that I am not Asian American. My roots are Irish. I think that says enough to explain why my next move was to phone every Asian American friend and colleague I knew to ask: Is this for real? Have you experienced the feeling that you are perceived in America as . . . exotic, foreign, "other"?

My college friend Mark laughed. "Of course," he answered. "I don't sweat it all the time, but, sure, it kind of is all the time." He told me how a few days earlier, he'd hailed a taxi in Boston, where he lives, and the cab driver had asked, in a friendly way, "So where ya from?" "It was obvious," said Mark, who was born in Los Angeles and whose mother's family spent World War II in an internment camp for Japanese Americans, "that he was asking what country I came from. He didn't mean it as a put-down, and I didn't take it that way. But the assumption is, I'm foreign."

That set the pattern. Every Asian American I contacted had a story to match. A scientist at Los Alamos, where Wen Ho Lee worked, told me how his colleagues began to snicker when he walked into a meeting where classified material was being discussed. "Here comes another spy," was the joke. A lawyer recalled her fellow students in a fourth-grade class shifting their desks away from hers the day they had a lesson on the evils of Communist China. And so on.

And there Mary Claude Foster and I found our story, which our executive producer Tom Bettag embraced enthusiastically: the reason why the Wen Ho Lee case was causing so much upset in the Asian American community.

It was not the media coverage per se, which at the time seemed mostly responsible and accurate. Rather, it was the history of a long-established pattern of Asian Americans being depicted as unreliable. We did not pull together a set of facts in the traditional sense as much as we explored a range of feelings and recognized that these feelings were our "facts."

I suspected, and still suspect, that some of our viewers would consider this a "squishy" kind of journalism about the Asian American community. I can hear the criticism: "This is all in their heads; why don't they get over it; it's yet another group claiming 'victim' status." In fact, this is some of what I kept thinking during those early conversations with Sam and Henry. Over time, however, and through the persistence of both of them, I came to a simple conclusion: if I were in their shoes, I would feel the same way.

Further, I made the assumption that many viewers would be like me: at first unaware of this aspect of the Asian American experience but open to hearing the details and learning something about what our fellow citizens were going through.

During my years as a foreign correspondent, I relied on the basic idea that if I was surprised or amazed or puzzled by some aspect of another culture, chances were my viewers would feel the same way. I called them blind spots, the things I could not know because no one can know everything. I find a lot of stories by looking into my blind spots and trying to shed light on them, trying to understand people whose experience is different from mine, trying to reach the point where I stand in their shoes.

Reporting into your blind spots takes a certain amount of humility, because it means having to admit to yourself, and perhaps your viewers and readers, that there is something you don't get. This becomes particularly sensitive in areas of race relations, where it is easy NOT to know the other person's experience.

We are all vulnerable in that regard. We may have a strong grasp on the concerns, priorities, and grievances of people with whom we share a strong ethnic identity but not necessarily on those of some other grouping. The morning after the *Nightline* program on Asian Americans was broadcast, a black colleague came by my office to discuss the show. She said: "Wow, I just never saw it—what Asian Americans have to go through. The whole thing that they're seen as foreign. Of course, of course. I just never saw it before."

The lesson is that, in reporting on matters of race, there are times when it makes a lot of sense to admit to not understanding. It turns out to be a good starting point. Perhaps not a comfortable one, but a good one.

To screen the John Donvan interview, select EQUALITY on the DVD Main Menu then "Asian-American."

DISCUSSION POINTS

- John Donvan discusses his blind spots about discrimination against Asian Americans. How can journalists test their own blind spots to prevent inaccurate or incomplete reporting?
- Discuss the value and relevance of the television and film clips used to illustrate the complaints aired in this story.
- This is a story about facts versus feelings. How does Donvan come to understand that Asian American citizens' fears are a legitimate story topic?
- Donvan never interviews Wen Ho Lee, but his presence is strongly felt in this story. Should an interview with Lee have been included for this broadcast's context?
- Considering the attacks on 9/11 and the suspicion many Arab Americans and Muslims say they've endured since then, develop parallel stories about those ethnic and religious groups.

SUGGESTED READINGS AND WEBSITES

Books

Lee, Wen Ho, and Helen Zia. *My Country Versus Me: The First-Hand Account by the Los Alamos Scientist Who Was Falsely Accused.* Santa Clara, Calif.: Hyperion, 2002.

> *Dr. Lee speaks of his experience before, during, and after his imprisonment and discusses violations of national security that occur in government agencies. He describes how the FBI infiltrated his private life, lying to him and spying on him for nearly two decades.*

Okihiro, Gary Y. *The Columbia Guide to Asian-American History.* New York: Columbia University Press, 2001.

> *A survey of two hundred years of Asian American experience.*

Websites

www.asian-nation.org/index.shtml

> *Asian-Nation, an information source on the historical, political, social, economic, and cultural elements that make up the Asian American community.*

www.census.gov/pubinfo/www/hotlinks.html

> *Data on racial and ethnic populations in the United States.*

www.sscnet.ucla.edu/aasc

> *The Website of the Asian American Studies Center at UCLA. The center aims to contribute to an understanding of the neglected history, cultural heritage, and present position of Asian Americans in the society.*

www.modelminority.com

A collection of research articles, commentaries, stories, poems, pictures, and other documents on the Asian American experience, including its minority status in U.S. society.

www.aaja.org/resources/apa_handbook/2000aaja_handbook.pdf

The Asian American Journalist's Association official handbook on coverage and terminology.

PART III

Telling the Untold Story

CHAPTER 8

STORY

TORN FROM THE LAND SERIES

DOLORES BARCLAY, TODD LEWAN

AND BRUCE DESILVA, ASSOCIATED PRESS

DOLORES BARCLAY

Dolores Barclay is the Arts Editor of the Associated Press. She joined AP in 1971 as a reporter, covering city hall, federal and criminal courts, and the police beat for the New York bureau. She took a leave from editing to work on *Torn from the Land,* which was awarded the Aronson Prize for Social Justice Journalism, the APME Enterprise Award, and the Griot Award of the New York Association of Black Journalists. She is the author of several books, including *A Girl Needs Cash,* an investment guide for women.

TODD LEWAN

Todd Lewan has been a correspondent with the Associated Press since 1988 and worked as an editor on AP's international desk and as a national features writer. He is the author of *The Last Run: A True Story of Rescue and Redemption* of the Alaska Seas. In 2001, he shared the Aronson Prize for Social Justice Journalism, the APME Enterprise Award, and the Griot Award of the New York Association of Black Journalists for the *Torn from the Land* series.

BRUCE DESILVA

Bruce DeSilva is the writing coach for the Associated Press, responsible for training AP staff worldwide. Previously, he directed the AP's News/Features Department, which specializes in national enterprise reporting including investigations, explanatory journalism, and narrative storytelling. He has worked as a consultant on writing and editing at more than forty newspapers

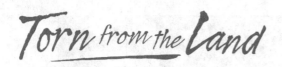

Torn from the Land

The Associated Press project Torn from the Land, which first appeared in 2001, documents a largely untold chapter of America's violent racial history. In this chapter, reporters Dolores Barclay and Todd Lewan and editor Bruce De-Silva teach the importance of investigative reporting in proving the complaints about land thefts that are central to the reparations movement. The series unequivocally proves specific land ownership claims, thus documenting a history of racial injustice that continues to have human consequences. Barclay and Lewan use a compelling set of facts and interviews to spotlight this particular aspect of being black in America.

Obviously, the claims behind this project are not new. But the series is original, and the team relies on its own tenacious approach, illustrated by the amount of shoe leather they wear out to document the paper trail that upholds the claims, which are the basis of an ongoing movement for reparations in the United States. The word "reparations" rarely shows up in the series. According to DeSilva, the decision to let the series speak for itself without connecting it to the drive for compensation was conscious, prompted by fears that the controversy would overwhelm their story.

The story creates a fresh awareness about the history of African Americans and their descendants. The connection of lynchings with land grabs is a feature of American history that has garnered scant attention in the history books but reverberates through the economic fabric of African American society.

Operating in an atmosphere of suspicion and fear, Barclay and Lewan display a set of important skills in this series: tenacity, resourcefulness, and, above all, a desire to put a human face on this sad chapter of the nation's evolution.

TORN FROM THE LAND

Part I of a series.

By Todd Lewan and Dolores Barclay, Associated Press
Published December 2, 2001

For generations, black families passed down the tales in uneasy whispers: "They stole our land."

These were family secrets shared after the children fell asleep, after neighbors turned down the lamps—old stories locked in fear and shame.

Some of those whispered bits of oral history, it turns out, are true.

In an 18-month investigation, the Associated Press documented a pattern in which black Americans were cheated out of their land or driven from it through intimidation, violence and even murder.

In some cases, government officials approved the land takings; in others, they took part in them. The earliest occurred before the Civil War; others are being litigated today.

Some of the land taken from black families has become a country club in Virginia, oil fields in Mississippi, a major-league baseball spring training facility in Florida.

> No one knows how many black families have been unfairly stripped of their land, but there are indications of extensive loss.

The United States has a long history of bitter, often violent land disputes, from claim jumping in the gold fields to range wars in the old West to broken treaties with American Indians. Poor white landowners, too, were sometimes treated unfairly, pressured to sell out at rock-bottom prices by railroads and lumber and mining companies.

The fate of black landowners has been an overlooked part of this story.

The AP—in an investigation that included interviews with more than 1,000 people and the examination of tens of thousands of public records in county courthouses and state and federal archives—documented 107 land takings in 13 Southern and border states.

In those cases alone, 406 black landowners lost more than 24,000 acres of farm and timber land plus 85 smaller properties, including stores and city lots. Today, virtually all of this property, valued at tens of millions of dollars, is owned by whites or by corporations.

Properties taken from blacks were often small—a 40-acre farm, a general store, a modest house. But the losses were devastating to families struggling to overcome the legacy of slavery. In the agrarian South, landownership was the

Rogelio Solis, AP

Griffin McLaurin Jr. points to the Mileston, Miss., farmland and wetlands bordering his 10 acres, May 9, 2001. "Much of that land used to belong to my family," recalled McLaurin. "Now all I have is these 10 acres that I plant my crops on," he said.

ladder to respect and prosperity—the means to building economic security and passing wealth on to the next generation. When black families lost their land, they lost all of this.

"When they steal your land, they steal your future," said Stephanie Hagans, 40, of Atlanta, who has been researching how her great-grandmother, Ablow Weddington Stewart, lost 35 acres in Matthews, N.C. A white lawyer foreclosed on Stewart in 1942 after he refused to allow her to finish paying off a $540 debt, witnesses told the AP.

"How different would our lives be," Hagans asked, "if we'd had the opportunities, the pride that land brings?"

No one knows how many black families have been unfairly stripped of their land, but there are indications of extensive loss.

Besides the 107 cases the AP documented, reporters found evidence of scores of other land takings that could not be fully verified because of gaps or inconsistencies in the public record. Thousands of additional reports of land takings from black families remain uninvestigated.

Two thousand have been collected in recent years by the Penn Center on St. Helena Island, S.C., an educational institution established for freed slaves during the Civil War. The Land Loss Prevention Project, a group of lawyers in

Durham, N.C., who represent blacks in land disputes, said it receives new reports daily. And Heather Gray of the Federation of Southern Cooperatives in Atlanta said her organization has "file cabinets full of complaints."

AP's findings "are just the tip of one of the biggest crimes of this country's history," said Ray Winbush, director of Fisk University's Institute of Race Relations.

Some examples of land takings documented by the AP:

After midnight on Oct. 4, 1908, 50 hooded white men surrounded the home of a black farmer in Hickman, Ky., and ordered him to come out for a whipping. When David Walker refused and shot at them instead, the mob poured coal oil on his house and set it afire, according to contemporary newspaper accounts. Pleading for mercy, Walker ran out the front door, followed by four screaming children and his wife, carrying a baby in her arms. The mob shot them all, wounding three children and killing the others. Walker's oldest son never escaped the burning house. No one was ever charged with the killings, and the surviving children were deprived of the farm their father died defending. Land records show that Walker's 2-acre farm was simply folded into the property of a white neighbor. The neighbor soon sold it to another man, whose daughter owns the undeveloped land today.

—In the 1950s and 1960s, a Chevrolet dealer in Holmes County, Miss., acquired hundreds of acres from black farmers by foreclosing on small loans for farm equipment and pickup trucks. Norman Weathersby, then the only dealer in the area, required the farmers to put up their land as security for the loans, county residents who dealt with him said. And the equipment he sold them, they said, often broke down shortly thereafter. Weathersby's friend, William E. Strider, ran the local Farmers Home Administration—the credit lifeline for many Southern farmers. Area residents, including

Steve Helber, AP

Bryan Logan sits on the granite steps of the Virginia State Capitol in Richmond, Va. The granite used to make the steps was taken from a quarry on land once owned by Logan's ancestors, former slaves who lost the property to whites at the time of the Civil War.

Erma Russell, 81, said Strider, now dead, was often slow in releasing farm operating loans to blacks. When cash-poor farmers missed payments owed to Weathersby, he took their land. The AP documented eight cases in which Weathersby acquired black-owned farms this way. When he died in 1973, he left more than 700 acres of this land to his family, according to estate papers, deeds and court records.

In 1964, the state of Alabama sued Lemon Williams and Lawrence Hudson, claiming the cousins had no right to two 40-acre farms their family had worked in Sweet Water, Ala., for nearly a century. The land, officials contended, belonged to the state. Circuit Judge Emmett F. Hildreth urged the state to drop its suit, declaring it would result in "a severe injustice." But when the state refused, saying it wanted income from timber on the land, the judge ruled against the family. Today, the land lies empty; the state recently opened some of it to logging. The state's internal memos and letters on the case are peppered with references to the family's race.

In the same courthouse where the case was heard, the AP located deeds and tax records documenting that the family had owned the land since an ancestor bought the property on Jan. 3, 1874. Surviving records also show the family paid property taxes on the farms from the mid-1950s until the land was taken.

AP reporters tracked the land cases by reviewing deeds, mortgages, tax records, estate papers, court proceedings, surveyor maps, oil and gas leases, marriage records, census listings, birth records, death certificates and Freedmen's Bureau archives. Additional documents, including FBI files and Farmers Home Administration records, were obtained through the Freedom of Information Act.

The AP interviewed black families that lost land, as well as lawyers, title searchers, historians, appraisers, genealogists, surveyors, land activists, and local, state and federal officials.

The AP also talked to current owners of the land, nearly all of whom acquired the properties years after the land takings occurred. Most said they knew little about the history of their land. When told about it, most expressed regret.

Weathersby's son, John, 62, who now runs the dealership in Indianola, Miss., said he had little direct knowledge about his father's business affairs. However, he said he was sure his father never would have sold defective vehicles and that he always treated people fairly.

Alabama Gov. Don Siegelman examined the state's files on the Sweet Water case after an inquiry from the AP. He said he found them "disturbing" and has asked the state attorney general to review the matter.

"What I have asked the attorney general to do," he said, "is look not only at the letter of the law but at what is fair and right."

The land takings are part of a larger picture—a 91-year decline in black landownership in America.

In 1910, black Americans owned more farmland than at any time before or since—at least 15 million acres. Nearly all of it was in the South, largely in Mississippi, Alabama and the Carolinas, according to the U.S. Agricultural Census. Today, blacks own only 1.1 million of the country's more than 1 billion acres of arable land. They are part owners of another 1.07 million acres.

The number of white farmers has declined over the last century, too, as economic trends have concentrated land in fewer, often corporate, hands. However, black ownership has declined 2-times faster than white ownership, the U.S. Civil Rights Commission noted in a 1982 report, the last comprehensive federal study on the trend.

The decline in black landownership had a number of causes, including the discriminatory lending practices of the Farmers Home Administration and the migration of blacks from the rural South to industrial centers in the North and West.

However, the land takings also contributed. In the decades between Reconstruction and the civil rights struggle, black families were powerless to prevent them, said Stuart E. Tolnay, a University of Washington sociologist and co-author of a book on lynchings. In an era when black Americans could not drink from the same water fountains as whites and black men

> In 1910, black Americans owned more farmland than at any time before or since - at least 15 million acres . . . Today, blacks own only 1.1 million of the country's more than 1 billion acres of arable land.

were lynched for whistling at white women, few blacks dared to challenge whites. Those who did could rarely find lawyers to take their cases or judges who would give them a fair hearing.

The Rev. Isaac Simmons was an exception. When his land was taken, he found a lawyer and tried to fight back.

In 1942, his 141-acre farm in Amite County, Miss., was sold for nonpayment of taxes, property records show. The farm, for which his father had paid $302 in 1887, was bought by a white man for $180.

Only partial, tattered tax records for the period exist today in the county courthouse; but they are enough to show that tax payments on at least part of the property were current when the land was taken.

Simmons hired a lawyer in February 1944 and filed suit to get his land back. On March 26, a group of whites paid Simmons a visit.

The minister's daughter, Laura Lee Houston, now 74, recently recalled her terror as she stood with her month-old baby in her arms and watched the men drag Simmons away. "I screamed and hollered so loud," she said. "They came toward me and I ran down in the woods."

The whites then grabbed Simmons' son, Eldridge, from his house and drove the two men to a lonely road.

"Two of them kept beating me," Eldridge Simmons later told the National Association for the Advancement of Colored People. "They kept telling me that my father and I were 'smart niggers' for going to see a lawyer."

Simmons, who has since died, said his captors gave him 10 days to leave town and told his father to start running. Later that day, the minister's body turned up with three gunshot wounds in the back, the McComb Enterprise newspaper reported at the time.

Today, the Simmons land—thick with timber and used for hunting—is privately owned and is assessed at $33,660. (Officials assess property for tax purposes, and the valuation is usually less than its market value.)

Over the past 20 years, a handful of black families have sued to regain their ancestral lands. State courts, however, have dismissed their cases on grounds that statutes of limitations had expired.

A group of attorneys led by Harvard University law professor Charles J. Ogletree has been making inquiries recently about land takings. The group has announced its intention to file a national class-action lawsuit in pursuit of reparations for slavery and racial discrimination. However, some legal experts say redress for many land takings may not be possible unless laws are changed.

As the acres slipped away, so did treasured pieces of family history—cabins crafted by a grandfather's hand, family graves in shaded groves.

But "the home place" meant more than just that. Many blacks have found it "very difficult to transfer wealth from one generation to the next," because they had trouble holding onto land, said Paula Giddings, a history professor at Duke University.

The Espy family in Vero Beach, Fla., lost its heritage in 1942, when the U.S. government seized its land through eminent domain to build an airfield. Government agencies frequently take land this way for public purposes under rules that require fair compensation for the owners.

In Vero Beach, however, the Navy appraised the Espys' 147 acres, which included a 30-acre fruit grove, two houses and 40 house lots, at $8,000, according to court records. The Espys sued, and an all-white jury awarded them $13,000. That amounted to one-sixth of the

Todd Lewan, AP

Members of the Espy family stand outside the fence around Vero Beach, Fla., airport in summer 2000, as a small plane comes in for a landing. Mary Hoover, 65, right, is the niece of Henry Espy, an NAACP official and lawyer who tried for years to retrieve the family land. Beside Hoover are her nephew, Andrew Logan, 40, and his 10-year-old son, Andrew Logan, both of Ft. Lauderdale, Fla.

price per acre that the Navy paid white neighbors for similar land with fewer improvements, records show.

After World War II, the Navy gave the airfield to the city of Vero Beach. Ignoring the Espys' plea to buy back their land, the city sold part of it, at $1,500 an acre, to the Los Angeles Dodgers in 1965 as a spring training facility.

In 1999, the former Navy land, with parts of Dodgertown and a municipal airport, was assessed at $6.19 million. Sixty percent of that land once belonged to the Espys. The team sold its property to Indian River County for $10 million in August, according to Craig Callan, a Dodgers official.

The true extent of land takings from black families will never be known because of gaps in property and tax records in many rural Southern counties. The AP found crumbling tax records, deed books with pages torn from them, file folders with documents missing, and records that had been crudely altered.

In Jackson Parish, La., 40 years of moldy, gnawed tax and mortgage records were piled in a cellar behind a roll of Christmas lights and a wooden reindeer. In Yazoo County, Miss., volumes of tax and deed records filled a classroom in an abandoned school, the papers coated with white dust from a falling ceiling. The AP retrieved dozens of documents that custodians said were earmarked for shredders or landfills.

The AP also found that about a third of the county courthouses in Southern and border states have burned—some more than once—since the Civil War. Some of the fires were deliberately set.

On the night of Sept. 10, 1932, for example, 15 whites torched the courthouse in Paulding, Miss., where property records for the eastern half of Jasper County, then predominantly black, were stored. Records for the predominantly white western half of the county were safe in another courthouse miles away.

The door to the Paulding courthouse's safe, which protected the records, had been locked the night before, the Jasper County News reported at the time. The next morning, the safe was found open, most of the records reduced to ashes.

Suddenly, it was unclear who owned a big piece of eastern Jasper County.

Even before the courthouse fire, landownership in Jasper County was contentious. According to historical accounts, the Ku Klux Klan, resentful that blacks were buying and profiting from land, had been attacking black-owned farms, burning houses, lynching black farmers and chasing black landowners away.

The Masonite Corp., a wood products company, was one of the largest landowners in the area. Because most of the land records had been destroyed, the company went to court in December 1937 to clear its title. Masonite believed it owned 9,581 acres and said in court papers that it had been unable to locate anyone with a rival claim to the land.

A month later, the court ruled the company had clear title to the land, which has since yielded millions of dollars in natural gas, timber and oil, according to state records.

Ron Frehm, AP
Baseball fans at Holman Stadium in Vero Beach Fla., watch the Los Angeles Dodgers play the Montreal Expos, March 30, 2000, in their last spring training game of the season. The stadium land was owned originally by the Espy family, who settled the area in the 1890s.

From the few property records that remain, the AP was able to document that at least 204.5 of those acres had been acquired by Masonite after black owners were driven off by the Klan. At least 850,000 barrels of oil have been pumped from this property, according to state oil and gas board records and figures from the Petroleum Technology Transfer Council, an industry group.

Today, the land is owned by International Paper Corp., which acquired Masonite in 1988. Jenny Boardman, a company spokeswoman, said International Paper had been unaware of the "tragic" history of the land and was concerned about AP's findings.

"This is probably part of a much larger, public debate about whether there should be restitution for people who have been harmed in the past," she said. "And by virtue of the fact that we now own these lands, we should be part of that discussion."

Even when Southern courthouses remained standing, mistrust and fear of white authority long kept blacks away from record rooms, where documents often were segregated into "white" and "colored." Many elderly blacks say they still remember how they were snubbed by court clerks, spat upon and even struck.

Today, however, fear and shame have given way to pride. Interest in genealogy among black families is surging, and some black Americans are unearthing the documents behind those whispered stories.

Over the past 20 years, a handful of black families have sued to regain their ancestral lands. State courts have dismissed their cases on grounds that statutes of limitations had expired.

"People are out there wondering: What ever happened to Grandma's land?" said Loretta Carter Hanes, 75, a retired genealogist. "They knew that their grandparents shed a lot of blood and tears to get it."

Bryan Logan, a 55-year-old sports writer from Washington, D.C., was researching his heritage when he uncovered a connection to 264 acres of riverfront property in Richmond, Va.

Today, the land is Willow Oaks, an almost exclusively white country club with an assessed value of $2.94 million. But in the 1850s, it was a corn-and-wheat plantation worked by the Howlett slaves—Logan's ancestors.

Their owner, Thomas Howlett, directed in his will that his 15 slaves be freed, that his plantation be sold and that the slaves receive the proceeds. When he died in 1856, his white relatives challenged the will, but two courts upheld it.

Yet the freed slaves never got a penny.

Benjamin Hatcher, the executor of the estate, simply took over the plantation, court records show. He cleared the timber and mined the stone, providing granite for the Navy and War Department buildings in Washington and the capitol in Richmond, according to records in the National Archives.

When the Civil War ended in 1865, the former slaves complained to the occupying Union Army, which ordered Virginia courts to investigate.

> "What I have asked the attorney general to do is look not only at the letter of the law, but at what is fair and right."
>
> —Alabama Gov. Don Siegelman

Hatcher testified that he had sold the plantation in 1862—apparently to his son, Thomas—but had not given the proceeds to the former slaves. Instead, court papers show, the proceeds were invested on their behalf in Confederate War Bonds. There is nothing in the public record to suggest the former slaves wanted their money used to support the Southern war effort.

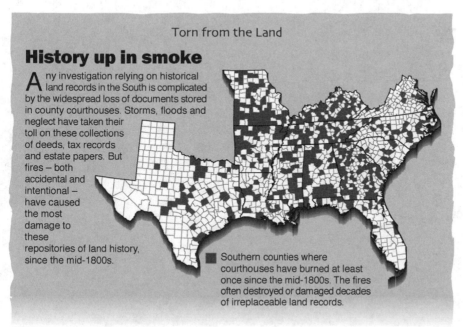

Torn from the Land

History up in smoke

Any investigation relying on historical land records in the South is complicated by the widespread loss of documents stored in county courthouses. Storms, floods and neglect have taken their toll on these collections of deeds, tax records and estate papers. But fires – both accidental and intentional – have caused the most damage to these repositories of land history, since the mid-1800s.

■ Southern counties where courthouses have burned at least once since the mid-1800s. The fires often destroyed or damaged decades of irreplaceable land records.

SOURCE: State libraries and historical archives

John Jurgensen/AP

Moreover, the bonds were purchased in the former slaves' names in 1864—a dubious investment at best in the fourth year of the war. Within months, Union armies were marching on Atlanta and Richmond, and the bonds were worthless pieces of paper.

The blacks insisted they were never given even that, but in 1871, Virginia's highest court ruled that Hatcher was innocent of wrongdoing and that the former slaves were owed nothing.

The following year, the plantation was broken up and sold at a public auction. Hatcher's son received the proceeds, county records show. In the 1930s, a Richmond businessman cobbled the estate back together; he sold it to Willow Oaks Corp. in 1955 for an unspecified amount.

"I don't hold anything against Willow Oaks," Logan said. "But how Virginia's courts acted, how they allowed the land to be stolen—it goes against everything America stands for."

EDITOR'S NOTE—Associated Press Writers Woody Baird, Allen G. Breed, Shelia Hardwell Byrd, Alan Clendenning, Ron Harrist, David Lieb and Bill Poovey, and investigative researcher Randy Herschaft contributed to this report.

DIRECT RESULTS:

Alabama House Votes to Set up Panel Following AP Report on Land Losses

Associated Press
Published January 18, 2002

MONTGOMERY, ALA.—The Alabama House has voted to set up a panel to study whether the state has illegally taken land from some black residents.

The resolution was introduced by Rep. Thomas Jackson, D-Thomasville, who said he became concerned following a series of stories last year by The Associated Press documenting black land losses across the South.

The resolution passed the House on a voice vote Thursday and now goes to the Senate.

One of the AP stories was about Willie Williams of Sweet Water.

The Williams family lost a pair of 40-acre plots to the state in a 1964 court case. The state had claimed the property didn't belong to the family because of a 1906 federal designation as swampland.

Today, the land is vacant, overgrown and posted with signs of state ownership. Some of the area has been opened to timber cutters, state records show.

The AP reported that the family held an 1874 deed and had records dating from the 1950s to show they had been paying taxes on the land for generations. A judge called the state's claim a "severe injustice," but the land went to the state.

Jackson said he has talked to Williams and with two other Marengo County residents, who said their family land was also taken by the state.

"If it was wrongfully taken, we feel the state ought to restore the land to its proper owner," Jackson said.

If approved by the Senate, the 10-member African-American Land Loss Task Force would study the issue and report to the Legislature in 2003.

One member would be appointed by the governor, three by legislative leaders, three by the Legislative Black Caucus and one each by the presidents of Alabama State University, Alabama A&M University and Tuskegee University.

Alabama Family Recovers Land
Taken by State Decades Ago

By Bill Poovey
Associated Press
Published June 6, 2002

MONTGOMERY, ALA. (AP)—A black family whose land was seized by the state under a 1964 court order can return to the farm as its "rightful owners," Gov. Don Siegelman said.

Siegelman transferred ownership of the land to the family Friday, saying it had been taken "by a legal technicality." The family had said for nearly 40 years that the land was rightfully theirs.

"It is a great moment for the family but equally it is a great moment for the state of Alabama," State Sen. Hank Sanders said Friday.

Siegelman reviewed the land-taking claim by Willie Williams of Sweet Water after it was detailed in an Associated Press story. In December, an AP series documented the loss of 24,000 acres by black Americans, through violence, trickery and legal maneuvers. The series, "Torn From the Land," uncovered 107 land takings during an 18-month investigation.

"Thank you for bringing this matter to the public's attention,"

Siegelman said while signing what he described as an unprecedented land grant by an Alabama governor.

The Williams family lost the western Alabama land after the state claimed the property belonged to the government because of a 1906 federal designation as swampland.

Williams was not immediately available for comment Friday.

The property is now vacant and overgrown. Some of it has been opened to timber cutters, state records show.

The AP reported that the family held an 1874 deed and had records to show they had been paying taxes on the land for generations. Records show that a judge in 1965 said allowing the state's claim would create a "severe injustice," but nonetheless signed an order giving the property to the state.

Williams' great-grandfather, named George Washington, bought 240 acres in 1874. The purchase and his conveyance of the land to his children in 1900 are documented in well-preserved, handwritten courthouse records.

State officials secured "quiet title" to the 40 acres Williams' father inherited, based on a 1963 U.S. Bureau of Land Management notice. That notice said a 1906 federal patent classified the Washington property as swampland owned by the state.

Then Circuit Judge Emmett F. Hildreth wrote in a Dec. 13, 1965, letter to state conservation officials that evidence showed the families had "been in possession of these lands about three generations. The effect of a decree favorable to the state of Alabama would be to dispossess these people and deprive them of these lands. Such action would create a severe injustice."

Letters and internal memos on the case in files of the State Lands Division in Montgomery are peppered with references to the family's race. They show officials adamantly opposed allowing "the negro defendants" to keep the land, even while acknowledging that the family could trace its ownership back to 1874.

In 1967, Hildreth, who is now dead, signed a decree awarding ownership to the state, but allowing Williams' father, Lemon Williams, and his wife to remain on the property as long as they lived.

Willie Williams, 51, said that up to his death in 1983, his father was still pleading for the family not to give up trying to reclaim ownership of the land, where they grew beans and cotton.

Siegelman said that "when George Washington bought this property he did everything a reasonable person would have done, got a title and paid his taxes."

Dave Martin, AP

Willie Williams walks near his family's old "home place" which the Williams family bought and occupied from 1874. Williams and his family have been pleading for return of the land in letters to estate officials for three decades.

WEBPAGE Read the rest of the *Torn from the Land* series on *www.theauthenticvoice.org*

THE MAKING OF

TORN FROM THE LAND

By Dolores Barclay and Bruce DeSilva
Associated Press

Black families had a story to tell, but no one was listening.

It was a story of farms, homes, and businesses stripped away, sometimes through chicanery, sometimes through intimidation, sometimes through murder. It was a story of how not only property but also hope was torn away from generations of black Americans. It was a story that had been ignored for so long that many black families had grown mistrustful and reluctant to speak of it.

As the series eventually put it, "These were family secrets shared after the children fell asleep, after neighbors turned down the lamps—old stories locked in fear and shame."

But in the beginning, the writers and editors knew nothing of this.

Torn from the Land—an investigative project that eventually included interviews with more than one thousand people and the examination of tens of thousands of public records—didn't begin in the usual way. It didn't start with a news event; it didn't develop out of beat reporting; it didn't come from a leaked document or an anonymous tip.

Instead, it began with a friendship.

Dolores Barclay, the arts editor, and Todd Lewan, a national writer, sat near each other on the fifth floor of AP headquarters. From the start, they hit it off. They constantly brainstormed story ideas. One day, in the middle of a wide-ranging discussion about compensation payments to Holocaust-era slave laborers and slavery reparations for black Americans, their thoughts turned to just how deep the legacy of slavery ran in the United States. There were stories to be done here, stories that braided the past to the present.

Both Dolores and Todd knew from their reading that some former slaves had acquired property, started businesses, and begun to accumulate wealth after the Civil War. Had it been passed down in their families through the years? It didn't appear so. Somehow, much of it seemed to have vanished.

A little research turned up details about the Freedmen's Savings and Trust Company. Created in 1865 to help former slaves learn about finances and investments, it had failed in 1874, taking the savings of more than seventy thousand black families with it—more than $3 million. Briefly, they considered writing about that but decided it was too well known to historians.

What about the land black families had owned, they wondered. Had anyone written about that? They decided to explore the possibility quietly.

They raked through historical archives but didn't turn up much on the subject. Dolores called a cousin, a librarian and genealogist in Atlanta, who provided addresses for two black genealogy Websites. The reporters posted inquiries about family land on the sites and in a couple of black publications and got eight replies from families who thought their land had been stolen from them generations ago by white people. They called the families, who offered vague stories but no proof. Then they called a chain of experts: academics and social activists. Yes, some of them said, they'd heard such stories, too, but as far as they knew, no one had ever systematically investigated them.

> It was clear now that this was something worth investigating. It was also clear that there was a huge task ahead, mainly the identification and documentation of a large number of cases, one by one.

With that, Dolores and Todd approached Bruce DeSilva, the AP's news/features editor and were met with . . . skepticism. Bruce said he wasn't interested in a story about a handful of black families losing land. Unless this was a widespread phenomenon that has somehow been overlooked by journalists and historians, it was not worth AP's time. "We don't do history here," he said. "We do news." He told the reporters that their story had to demonstrate the impact on lives today.

Dolores and Todd asked for a couple of weeks to make their case. Bruce agreed but didn't expect anything to come of it. He figured that if land-stealing from black Americans really had been widespread, someone certainly would have written about it already. Dolores and Todd, on the other hand, thought they had a chance to succeed. They reasoned that the white people who had perpetrated the abuses would have kept quiet and black victims would have been ignored or silenced by fear, leaving the proof hidden away in the deed books in thousands of county courthouses.

From the start, the reporters knew that the project was huge and that they needed help. So they enlisted Allen G. Breed, AP southeast regional writer, and Randy Herschaft, AP investigative researcher. Eventually, another thirteen reporters of varying ethnic and racial backgrounds would contribute a day or two of interviewing or records work. But it's worth pausing for a moment to consider the backgrounds of the three people who drove the project forward.

Dolores, the daughter of a Wall Street accountant, grew up in a family well connected to New York City's financial and arts communities. The author of a couple of books, she had extensive experience as a reporter and national writer before becoming the arts editor in 1984. Todd, the son of a New Jersey engineer, had worked for eight years as an AP correspondent in Brazil, where he found race relations more comfortable than in the United States, and he had done some impressive investigative reporting as a national writer. Bruce, who had three decades of experience reporting and editing investigative sto- ries, had grown up in a New England town so parochial that he never met a black person until his senior year of high school. Now he was courting the black woman whom he would eventually marry.

Two weeks after Dolores and Todd set off to make their case, they were back, and this time they had some hard evidence. By examining land records in one Mississippi Delta county courthouse, they had confirmed the truth of several family stories about black families being swindled out of their land. In Alabama, they had talked with experts at three organizations, in- cluding the Federation of Southern Coopera- tives, who claimed to have accumulated thou- sands of uninvestigated complaints about such land takings.

It was clear now that this was something worth investigating. It was also clear that there was a huge task ahead, mainly the identification and documentation of a large number of cases, one by one. The organizations with the hoards of complaints were overwhelmed and slow in providing access to their files. It was months be- fore they provided any help, and even then it was to offer only a handful of leads.

So Dolores, Todd, and the growing team had to develop their own leads, and at first it was slow going. A few professors at black colleges

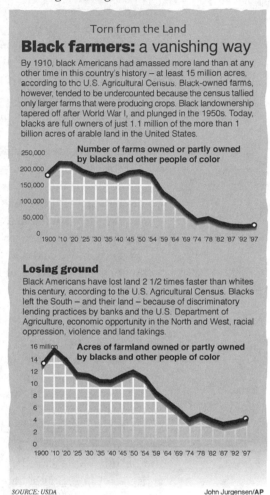

Torn from the Land

Black farmers: a vanishing way

By 1910, black Americans had amassed more land than at any other time in this country's history – at least 15 million acres, according to the U.S. Agricultural Census. Black-owned farms, however, tended to be undercounted because the census tallied only larger farms that were producing crops. Black landownership tapered off after World War I, and plunged in the 1950s. Today, blacks are full owners of just 1.1 million of the more than 1 billion acres of arable land in the United States.

Number of farms owned or partly owned by blacks and other people of color

Losing ground

Black Americans have lost land 2 1/2 times faster than whites this century, according to the U.S. Agricultural Census. Blacks left the South – and their land – because of discriminatory lending practices by banks and the U.S. Department of Agriculture, economic opportunity in the North and West, racial oppression, violence and land takings.

Acres of farmland owned or partly owned by blacks and other people of color

SOURCE: USDA John Jurgensen/AP

tried to help by placing ads in black publications, but this produced only a few tips, most of which led nowhere. But gradually cases accumulated. One family would lead reporters to another. A lawyer investigating one family's complaint would lead reporters to another lawyer and another case. And sometimes re- porters documenting one case in a county courthouse would stumble over an- other suspicious land transaction in the deed books or overhear a title searcher's remark about a questionable property sale.

Early on, the reporters realized that prosperity, usually in the form of property, had been the motivation behind many lynchings. Thus, they "followed the lynching trail," scouring local historical societies and old newspaper archives in Southern and border states for reports of violence against black property owners.

It was months before they discovered a way to find cases in clumps. They knew, of course, about the famous attacks on black neighborhoods in Rosewood, Florida, and Tulsa, Oklahoma. But by reading local histories they discovered that in the eighty years between the end of Reconstruction and the end of the Jim Crow era, white mobs had attacked scores of black communities in the South and in border states, often driving families away forever. They suspected that some of those families must have owned homes, farms, and businesses. That hunch led them to clusters of cases in such places as Pierce City, Missouri, Birmingham, Kentucky, and Ocoee, Florida.

From the beginning, the team established a high standard of proof. They would publish nothing that came from an anonymous source. Every case would have to be documented conclusively with a paper trail of deeds, land transfer records, and tax records. Ambiguous cases would be discarded.

Some families had meticulous records: original deeds, land transfers, tax receipts, even old photographs of the family home. But most could provide no more than a partial record: an old deed, a musty tax bill, or some yellowed newspaper clippings. For the most part, the reporters had to unearth the documents themselves.

Besides examining property records, some cases required a search for federal land documents, government censuses, bank records, land surveys, death records, estate papers, court transcripts, wills, oil leases, and more. Much of this records research was new to members of the team. Early on, Dolores and Todd encountered a University of Wisconsin graduate student researching an old federal land project in the Mississippi Delta. He gave them a tutorial on how to trace property ownership through grantee indexes, grantor indexes, and deed books, a skill they refined as they moved from courthouse to courthouse across the South. Later, they would teach the skill to other AP reporters called on to help with the research.

The records research was physically demanding. The property indexes weighed thirty to forty pounds and were often thick with dust and mold. At the end of each day, the reporters' muscles ached, and their sinuses were clogged. The work was also extremely time-consuming. It often took a day, and occasionally a week or more, to track the history of a single piece of property—that is, when the records could be found at all.

In some Southern counties, old property records had long ago been trucked to the landfill. The reporters found others rotting in courthouse basements, covered in rat feces. In one Mississippi county, they rescued old property books that were about to be thrown into a dumpster. Even when they found the books, they discovered that some had had pages torn from them and others had been crudely altered, perhaps to cover up land thefts.

And then there were the fires. A third of the county courthouses in Southern and in border states had been burned, some more than once, since the Civil War. Some of the fires had been set deliberately to destroy property records. The condition of the records became another avenue of investigation and meant that the full extent of the land thefts could never be discovered.

Sometimes, the reporters found creative ways to find copies of records that had been destroyed. Had the black farmer applied for a USDA loan? Perhaps a copy of his deed was on file at the agency. Had he done business with the old federal Freedman's Bureau? Perhaps copies of his land records could be found in Washington. Was his land part of an old Spanish land grant? There would be records at the National Archives or even in the state archives.

Dolores and Todd sometimes traveled together through the South, and as far as they can tell, they never attracted a second look. But when they traveled alone, they occasionally ran into trouble. While investigating cases in northern Louisiana, Todd was stopped by a group of white men who demanded to know what he was up to. In Texas, Dolores was stopped by two state troopers who interrogated her for twenty-five minutes, demanding to know what she was doing in Panola County and refusing to believe she worked for the Associated Press. Todd had similar experiences with police in Virginia and South Carolina. In Arkansas, a pickup truck with a Confederate flag tried to run Dolores's rental car into a ravine after she had spent the day gathering documents about a land snatch.

For security, the reporters always lodged outside the counties in which they were reporting, often driving an hour or two each day between courthouse and hotel.

At the courthouses, Dolores, Todd, and Allen Breed acknowledged that they were reporters when asked but did not volunteer the information. Usually, county clerks assumed they were professional title searchers or researching their family histories. One clerk, discovering that they were reporters, refused to allow them access to public records, claiming they were fragile and could not be handled.

But the story was about more than records. It was also about people. Many black families knew the story, or at least some of the story, of what had happened to their ancestral land. Those oral histories had to be collected. And the writers also needed to know how the land losses had affected these families financially and emotionally and how the effects lingered today.

Some families were eager to tell their stories, but many more were reluctant. The reporters were surprised to find that, even in cases where the land thefts took place more than a century ago, some families were fearful that they might come to harm if they told the truth. Land thefts often involved betrayals: by white judges, lawyers, lawmen, community leaders, and sometimes state and federal officials. Until now, no one had been interested in righting these wrongs or even hearing the stories. Who were these reporters, and why were they asking about these things now?

Eventually, most families agreed to share their stories, often inviting the reporters into their homes. The race of the reporters never seemed to be much of a factor. What opened doors was their genuine interest in the truth and the fact that a powerful news organization was determined to tell the story.

Many families asked if the story might lead to getting their land back. The reporters offered no false hope. Statutes of limitations meant that few of these wrongs would ever be righted, they explained, but at least they could tell the world what had happened. Some people said they decided to talk because the reporters had been honest with them.

Some of those interviewed were uneducated people, and the reporters respected their ways. Dolores and Todd visited a family in the middle of a rare January snowstorm in the Mississippi Delta. The family didn't have much and lived frugally, but they invited the reporters to stay for dinner. The reporters politely declined until they realized they were offending the family. So they stayed for a hot dinner of rice, string beans, and biscuits.

In Georgia and South Carolina, dialects made some interviews difficult. In Darien, Georgia, for example, Dolores found herself writing phonetically as she tried to make sense of the speech of an elderly black man. Finally, she put her pad down and asked him about his dialect. It was Gullah, he said, a dialect that derives in part from a West African language. Later, she had another source who understood Gullah and helped translate some words on the interview tape.

Much of the historical research had been completed when Dolores and Todd made a startling discovery: black land losses weren't just a thing of the past; they were still occurring, and in a big way, though now they were the result of legal manipulation instead of intimidation and violence.

Partition laws intended to help resolve family disputes over land passed down without wills were being used by unscrupulous land dealers to strip black Americans of family land all over the South. Suddenly, another avenue of investigation opened up.

Fortunately, academic researchers had done a lot of work on partition sales. They told the reporters how the legal manipulations worked and how much land was being taken this way. But the reporters set out to track more than a dozen individual partition sale cases to understand the process fully and to gather concrete examples. These cases were so complicated that the AP's law firm had to review the documents to be sure they were interpreted correctly.

Meanwhile, Todd and Randy Herschaft researched historical land owner-ship statistics to demonstrate that the land thefts played a role in a century-long decline in black land ownership in America. Allen unearthed a brutal land tak-ing in Maine. Although most cases occurred in the South and in border states, the case was evidence that living in the North of-fered no guarantee against land grabs. And

> The reporters were surprised to find that in cases where the land thefts had occurred more than a century ago, some families were fearful that they could come to harm if they told the truth.

Dolores looked into eminent domain cases to discover what role they may have had.

The last part of reporting involved gathering reactions. Corporations and (invariably) white owners in possession of land stolen from black people gen-erations ago universally reacted with surprise and shock. A few old white men who had stolen land from black families in the 1950s and 1960s reacted defen-sively or with hostility, as did land dealers involved in partition sales.

By now, the reporting had consumed eighteen months. Not once did senior editors at the AP express reservations about the investment in time and travel costs. From time to time, Jon Wolman, the former AP executive editor and then projects editor, would ask for an update and encourage the team to press on. There was a shared sense that this was not only an important news story but that AP was on the verge of writing a new chapter in the history of race rela-tions in America.

With the reporting nearly done, it would be another six months before the story, which eventually included three long main stories, seven sidebars, dozens of graphics and photographs, and a Web presentation with audio and video, was ready for publication.

The sheer volume of information was daunting. The reporters had a file on each of the more than two hundred cases they had investigated. Some were only an inch or so thick, but many were much larger. The most complicated case, in Texas, filled an entire three-foot-long filing cabinet. Then there were the interview tapes and the notes that consumed scores of notepads and floppy disks.

For weeks, Dolores and Todd closeted themselves to review every case, examining every note and every document, not only to understand what they had but to explore what might be missing. Might there be an undiscovered document that would change one of the stories? Every case they used had to be unassailable. Bruce felt that some people would challenge the story, leaping on any error, no matter how small, in an attempt to discredit it. In the end, about half the cases fell into the category of "almost certainly true" but not quite proven. They were thrown out.

The story had significant implications for the national debate about reparations for black Americans. It was decided to give this only a passing mention because many Americans were turned off by the reparations movement and might not read the story if they thought it was about that.

After Dolores and Todd wrote drafts, Bruce assigned his deputy, Chris Sullivan, to review them. Chris's orders: Assume everything is wrong, and challenge the reporters to prove every sentence.

Then the stories were read by AP projects editor Jon Wolman and managing editor Mike Silverman, who made suggestions about organization and urged that more historic context be added. Without it, some readers wouldn't understand why black people couldn't simply have called the police or sued when their land was stolen.

In the end, the stories appeared in hundreds of newspapers, often on front pages, in the United States and overseas. Play was particularly heavy in the South.

Afterward, there were follow-ups to write, including a long narrative about one man's search for land his family was driven from in the 1920s after oil was discovered in the area. There was also a follow-up about an Alabama family that had been unfairly stripped of its ancestral land by the state in 1964. A few months after the series appeared, the state agreed to give it back.

At this writing, at least two documentaries about stolen black land are in production as a result of the series, and the reporters continue to receive tips about other cases.

To screen the Associated Press team interview, select UNTOLD STORIES on the DVD Main Menu then "Torn from the Land."

DISCUSSION POINTS

- Editor Bruce DeSilva told his reporters that he wanted a human story, not a history lesson. How did the series accomplish the assignment?
- Is the story fair to the descendants of the white people who took the land?
- This series is grounded in the paper trail that the reporters created to prove the land theft claims. Why is this so essential to this investigation?
- This saga connects the "lynching trail" in the South with the land thefts. How does this compare with what you know about this chapter of America's history?
- What has this series taught you about how to prove if a pattern of racial or ethnic injustice exists?

SUGGESTED READINGS AND WEBSITES

Books

Leighley, Jan. E. *Strength in Numbers? The Political Mobilization of Racial and Ethnic Minorities.* Princeton: Princeton University Press, 2001.

Jan Leighley uses national survey data and showcases the state of Texas to demonstrate how racial and ethnic groups organize and participate in politics and how political power elites attempt to cultivate them.

Winbush, Raymond A. *Should America Pay? Slavery and the Raging Debate Over Reparations.* New York: Amistad/Harper Collins, 2003.

A collection of essays, based on the UN Conference on World Racism held in Durban, South Africa, in 2001, that introduces a global perspective on key issues of the reparations movements, from the displacement of Native Americans to the slave trade in the United States.

Websites

cyber.law.harvard.edu/people/ogletree

The Website of Harvard law professor Charles Ogletree Jr., a leader in the drive for reparations.

www.straightblack.com/culture/African-American-Articles/African-American-Slavery-Reparations.html

www.afrocentric.info/News/Reparations.html

Two Websites on African American culture that deal with reparations.

CHAPTER 9

STORY

RIM OF THE NEW WORLD SERIES

ANNE HULL, *THE WASHINGTON POST*

ANNE HULL

Anne Hull is a four-time Pulitzer Prize finalist and a two-time winner of the prestigious American Society of Newspaper Editors Distinguished Writing Award. Hull began her career at the *St. Petersburg Times* in Florida. She was a Nieman Fellow in 1995 at Harvard University and joined *The Washington Post* in 2000. Hull's newspaper stories have been anthologized in ASNE's Best Newspaper Writing in 1994, 2000, 2001, and 2002 and are included in college journalism curricula and textbooks.

rim of the new world

For more than eighteen months, reporter Anne Hull of The Washington Post went looking for the new America that is emerging from large-scale immigration. She found it in unique corners of a city long defined racially and ethnically in two tones: black and white. With more than two hundred thousand foreign-born people arriving in metropolitan Atlanta in the last decade of the twentieth century, Hull found this "new world" in old places.

Her four-part series, a 2003 Pulitzer Prize finalist in national reporting, had datelines ranging from a gritty Dairy Queen to a busy airport restroom as she followed the fortunes of young immigrants and others coming of age on the rim of the new world. Hull takes readers inside the sights and sounds of change.

Listen to Hull describe Cisco, one of her major characters, and get transported to a fast-food window that looks out and in at a slice of America many journalists are reluctant to portray. Hull's stories, essay, and interview show remarkable insight into the reporting, writing, and thinking tools necessary to render authentically the kinds of complex characters who populate her stories. She puts on display the potency of narrative storytelling and the great power of a piece driven as much by the voices of her sources as by the compelling facts that give the story its national heft. The chapter is a lesson on how to write about census figures without getting lost in soulless numbers. It forces readers to expand the often narrow frames into which many stories of immigrants are placed. It underscores the need for keen observation and strong interviewing skills, and highlights the value of listening until the story reveals itself.

Perhaps most provocatively, Hull attacks the fear of offending that paralyzes many reporters, causing so much writing about race and ethnicity to turn bland in the name of sensitivity. She challenges the notion that reporters should avoid stories that play to racial or ethnic stereotypes and offers up steadfast reporting as a cure for those damaging, one-dimensional portrayals.

OLD SOUTH GOES WITH THE WIND

Part I of a series

By Anne Hull
The Washington Post
Published December 8, 2002

ATLANTA—The Dairy Queen glows in the night, a beacon of Americana. But inside, chaos descends. Twelve customers are waiting at the front counter, and the drive-through lane is a snake of headlights, the voices over the speaker unrelenting.

"I want caramel in the bottom of that Mudslide, a lot of caramel, hear?"

"One chicken value meal with a Mr. Pibb and, lemme see, three value meals, and could you cut all the burgers in half?"

"Do you have supersize drinks or is the large the biggest?"

Cisco Montanez is 15 and working the window. His DQ hat is cocked on his head like a tilted ornament, his khakis circus-big. He is half Latino and half black, so he has plenty of reason to glare at the Confederate flag moving toward him on a GMC Suburban. At least one flag comes through a night.

Cisco turns his back on the flag and reaches for a plastic banana split boat. As he fills it with three puffs of vanilla ice cream, he begins to rap.

> This life hurts
> No cushion for me, no carpet laid out
> We either sell or we're getting sold

The Indian immigrants who work at Dairy Queen have no idea what Cisco is talking about. He raps all night long, breathless incantations about injustice, pistols and housing projects. The Indians are mystified by a brain that fires out couplets but won't do school work.

"He don't use it in the right way," says Ali Momin, the 22-year-old assistant manager.

Ali presses the drive-through speaker and greets the customers with his musical Indian accent. "Welcome to Dairy Queen, may I take your order, please?"

Long pause, and then a Southern drawl. "Do what now?"

This little Dairy Queen. The walls decorated with plaques of all-white T-ball teams. An employee named Miss Carol—hired back before the world

Sarah L. Voison—The Washington Post
The Dairy Queen in Stockbridge, Ga., is Indian-owned and half the crew is Indian or Pakistani.

changed—wears a "Jesus Cares" pin on her uniform while her Muslim supervisor cooks his food in a crock pot separate from DQ food. The franchise owner, an Indian, swings by in his Porsche to check on receipts.

And Cisco at the drive-through, ranting about race six miles from a tourist spot called the "Gone With the Wind Historical District."

The Dairy Queen on State Road 138 has been visited by a global awakening, all beneath a swirl-top soft-serve cone.

As Cisco says, in one of the night's chants:

Tomorrow is right now.

The Dairy Queen is 14 miles southeast of Hartsfield Atlanta International Airport, just inside Clayton County. Not long ago, Clayton County was pastures and okra stands. Then, like the rest of the suburban South, it exploded in the 1990s with a 30 percent population growth and the sound of bulldozers moving across red clay.

The proof is in the exit ramp civilizations that cling to the pilings of the interstates. Waffle House, Taco Bell, Holiday Inn Express, Quik Trip in endless repetition. But it's here in this numbing sameness, amid the heat lamps and sparkly stucco plazas, that a racial and ethnic fusion has taken hold. This is the new soul of the South.

Until the early 1990s, the three major epochs in Southern history had to do with race: the Civil War, Reconstruction and the civil rights movement. Now comes the fourth. During the past 15 years, an unprecedented wave of immigration swept over the South, transforming the meaning of race in the very place it was defined.

Immigrants from Mexico, India, South Korea, Vietnam and other countries shocked a fundamentally white and black society. This first generation poured in for work—and to survive, many of them sweated on the margins of one of the most prosperous chapters in the American economy.

Now their children are coming of age, with different expectations of what a life can be. They may live in cramped apartments with parents who speak no English and earn $7 an hour, but their own yearnings have been stoked by Niketown. They are testing every institution in their path, in schools that are unprepared to teach them, in a place that has no context for immigration and in a part of the country historically hostile to anyone not white.

Atlanta is at the front edge of this new pluralism. Some sociologists call it a mini-Los Angeles in the making. The metropolitan area, with 4.1 million people, is a mix of urbanism and suburbs that radiates out in a 20-county sprawl. The cradle of the civil rights movement, Atlanta

Sarah L. Voison—The Washington Post

Cisco leans out of the drive-through window waiting for the next customer. The Dairy Queen on State Road 138 is part of an exit ramp civilization.

represents the two-tone world of the past that is now giving way to a new society. Between 1990 and 2000, more than 256,000 foreign-born people arrived here.

A Dairy Queen hardly seems like a staging ground for the future. The store in Stockbridge looks like any other. On sunny days, the red sign creaks in the wind. Car exhaust from the road blows up on the patio tables. At night, the white-lit building glows luminous and cold.

Inside, there are wooden booths and chairs, and a freezer that holds cakes and Dilly Bars. A menu board with pictures hangs above the counter—"HOT EATS"—along with the ice cream concoctions. A silver counter and three cash registers separate the customers from the crew.

Half the crew is Indian or Pakistani. In their blue polo shirts, they work as if each sale brings a handsome commission instead of low wages in the grubby trenches of the American economy.

"How about a Blizzard Chocolate Extreme?" Farzana Khan suggests in her Urdu-inflected English. "It's full of delicious cocoa fudge. You like chocolate right, ma'am? We are selling *lots* of these."

Next customer: "Gimme a kids' chicken fingers."

Farzana presses the drive-through microphone button. "What sauce, ma'am? We have all kinds delicious," Farzana asks.

"You got *what*?"

"Honey mustard, Italian, barbecue," Farzana says.

"Okay, gimme honey mustard."

"You don't like white country gravy? It's real good, ma'am."

This zeal boggles the minds of the American employees, most of whom are the sons and daughters of the working class, still in high school, or, as a 16-year-old employee says, "I'm home-schooling myself." A few are saving for college. One is waiting to turn 18 so he can get hired at the deli at Costco.

> Cisco has a gold dental grill that goes fang-to-fang, a diamond in each fang. As for his hair, he tells the barber to use a No. 7 guard on top, then tight on the sides with a No. 3.
>
> Maintaining his appearance requires most of his $150 weekly pay from the DQ. Maintaining his persona could be more costly.

Cisco works the window. The average fast-food worker in America quits or is fired after four months, but Cisco has six months at the DQ. He is supposed to be in the eighth grade, but never went back after a suspension. But the DQ holds him. He's rarely late for work. "I like ice cream," he shrugs.

His mother is Puerto Rican. She left the Bronx with her two children when Cisco was 4 because she thought the South would be a gentler experience. Now Cisco is completely black-identified. He tells his mom to use the word sausage and not chorizo.

One evening, Cisco takes his dinner break on the DQ patio. He eats his fries and lights a cigarette, pocketing his chicken sandwich for later. From the patio table, Cisco can almost make out the skyscrapers of Atlanta. Atlanta means Lenox Square mall and the clubs of Buckhead, where rappers like Pastor Troy and the other So So Def Recording artists go to chill. Once, Jermaine Dupri came through the Dairy Queen drive-through and ordered a cone with sprinkles. "He had a big white Beamer with a peanut butter dash," Cisco remembers.

But Cisco's world is closer to the Dairy Queen. "The next exit is my exit," he says, "and the exit after that is my cousin's exit." His mother or grandmother brings him to work. He gets out of the car with his red Nautica shorts peeking out of his khakis as he does his little walk into the DQ. Sometimes, Cisco sees the owner arriving in his Infiniti. A subdued car like that just makes him shake his head in pity. "He let all that money go to waste," Cisco says.

Rizwan Momin arrived in Atlanta in 1985 from the Indian state of Gujarat. He had $310 in his pocket. His uncle had just purchased a sagging, white-owned Dairy Queen in a black neighborhood in Atlanta. Riz went to work for his uncle, mopping, sweeping, saving, scheming, wearing $3 shirts from K-Mart, sleeping on the floor, working day and night at the DQ except when he went to his second job at a laminations factory on Buford Highway, where he tended the boiler.

Seventeen years later, Riz owns nine Dairy Queens in the Atlanta metro area. He's one of the largest franchisees in the Southeast. Drives the Porsche on some days, the Infiniti SUV on others, Indian music blasting from the Bose speakers in the wood-grain console.

> "Forget the white kids with the studs in the tongue," Riz says. "Indians are gonna work for you. At the beginning, they work for minimum wage. Then little raise, little raise, slowly, slowly. Everyone live together; they are saving money, six people in household working, they bank 80 percent of their money and use 20 percent for expenses. They don't drink, no clubs, no fancy clothes. Suddenly, they have $60,000 in the bank. Then they will buy the Subway or the Blimpie."

Indians now own 60 of the 208 Dairy Queens in Georgia. Half of Riz's workforce is Indian. "Forget the white kids with the studs in the tongue," Riz says. "Indians are gonna work for you. At the beginning, they work for minimum wage. Then little raise, little raise, slowly, slowly. Everyone live together; they are saving money, six people in household working, they bank 80 percent of their money and use 20 percent for expenses. They don't drink, no clubs, no fancy clothes. Suddenly, they have $60,000 in the bank. Then they will buy the Subway or the Blimpie."

But Riz worries about the second generation. No vision. Where's the next young entrepreneur ready to climb out of the low-wage landscape? "These people just want to be the Riz," says Riz with concern. "You can't copy the Riz. You must build your own entity. The second generation wants the shortcut."

The source of his worry is his cousin, Ali Momin, 22, who is the night supervisor at the Stockbridge store. Ali could be the heir apparent if he wanted.

One Thursday afternoon, Ali is changing the grease in the deep-fryer. With his sleeves rolled up, he drains the old grease, scrubs out the stainless steel vats, rinses everything down with a hose and then pours in fresh oil. Periodically, he looks out toward the parking lot, where his 2001 silver Honda Accord is backed in so he can keep an eye on it. The CD player is loaded with Eminem and Indian techno music.

Sarah L. Voison—The Washington Post

The owner of this Diary Queen—and several others—is Rizwan Momin. He arrived in Atlanta in 1985 from the Indian state of Gujarat with $310 in his pocket and worked his way up the economic ladder. In his home, he hatches plans to open a new store, selling goods "As Seen on TV."

Ali came to Stockbridge from India when he was 16. He dropped out of Eagle's Landing High School his senior year. He wanted to hurry up and get started in the DQ pipeline.

But unlike Riz when Riz started out, Ali won't wear $3 shirts from K-Mart. His cologne is Dreamer by Versace. His savings account is zero. "Riz tells me a whole buncha times, 'Don't be wasting money,'" Ali says. "I keep that in my head for a couple of days, then it goes away."

His ambitions are vague and specific. "Be a something owner; that's all I want to do," he says.

At the Dairy Queen, they all have ambitions.

"I'm gonna be in sports and music, some kind of star," says Xavier Thurston, homegrown Georgia, his cornrows playfully tied off with pink butterfly barrettes. "I'm never gonna be a regular guy."

Xavier and Cisco exist in a fantasy galaxy called the Dirty South. The phrase was coined by a rap group to describe a Dixie-fied urbanism, lifting the

South up from its woeful place and making it the hippest and "baddest" spot in the consciousness.

Cisco pours himself into the role of a Dirty South habitué. He hangs around a recording studio in East Atlanta, hoping to be discovered. The trim on his $90 sneakers carefully accents another piece of clothing. He owns a collection of $70 silk sports jerseys, his most prized being his University of Georgia.

"Down here we got special things," he says one day, filling up the bins of pineapple topping and Heath Bar pieces. "We wear ruffle socks to match the jerseys. We don't be lacing our shoes all the way. We do it like a big X, then a big bow. We gotta have a hat. I always gotta have a hat."

Cisco has a gold dental grill that goes fang-to-fang, a diamond in each fang. As for his hair, he tells the barber to use a No. 7 guard on top, then tight on the sides with a No. 3.

Maintaining his appearance requires most of his $150 weekly pay from the DQ. Maintaining his persona could be more costly.

One afternoon, Riz the owner makes a surprise visit to the DQ. Riz starts yelling about the mess and everyone begins mopping and wiping furiously. After Riz leaves, Cisco and Xavier relax back into their usual selves. "We don't change for nobody," Xavier says.

Cisco nods. "Yeah, keep it real."

Xavier assembles a bacon cheeseburger. "My granddaddy said don't ever let no one put fear in your heart."

Americans, as seen from the drive-through window:

They are fat, skinny, haggard, pampered, with slobbering dogs in their laps, with open beers in the cup holders, with soccer schedules taped to the dash, and, one afternoon, an infant riding in a laundry basket in the back seat.

A deacon in a gold suit. A woman with a 50-pound bag of Alpo on the jump seat and a pack of Kools on the dash. A teenager with a Bad Kitty steering wheel cover and a decal of a dagger on her tinted window. She wants a Mister Misty.

Often their hands tremble with anticipation as they tear the wrappers off their milkshake straws. Some drive up with other warm fast-food bags on the seat beside them. The workers form their own stereotypes. They say the Mexicans like banana splits and black customers can be so picky that if you don't make it exactly right, they want it for free.

"I'm ready!" a customer shouts.

The driver of the car has three piercings thru his lip and eyebrows. "Only in Stockbridge," Cisco says. "They a disgrace to Atlanta." His co-worker, Karl, a black high school senior, nods in agreement. "You know that."

Sarah L. Voison—The Washington Post

Pakistani worker Faisal Khan, 14, puts a large drink on a customer's tray. "If you're gonna be somebody, then you gotta do some things you don't like," he says.

The assembly line of humanity keeps rolling forward. One man is covered in tattoos: animals, a spider web and a swastika. His female passenger is also a mural of ink. A baby is smiling from the car seat. The driver passes his money up to Cisco. Each knuckle on one hand is tattooed with a letter:

S-K-I-N.

Cisco turns away from the window. Keeping his voice low, he tells Karl, "that man got a Nazi tattoo." Karl leans over to steal a look. The customer senses Cisco and [Karl] gawking but his face registers no emotion. Cisco gives the man his ice cream cone, mocha-colored fingers wrapped around the white napkin that covers the cone, and into the outstretched knuckles that spell S-K-I-N.

As soon as the man puts the car in gear, Cisco whirls around and spits out a rap.

> I represent the South
> where the niggas stay scared.
> red mouth, nobody mouth as red as mine
> down south affiliated with that Georgia pine.

The pace quickens. Cisco hustles around in his big pants. Ali the night manager begins to shout. "Hey, drop me 15 pieces of chicken strips!" A woman pulls up in a turquoise Cougar with Mardi Gras beads dangling from the mirror. She has four orders, and four envelopes of money. "What is *taking* y'all so long?" the next car demands over the speaker.

The Dairy Queen is no meatpacking plant. But you make ice cream cones for $5.75 an hour and then come face-to-face with a shiny new Navigator at the drive-through window, a fine-looking woman behind the wheel, and all you can do is hand her the cone. There are so many reminders of what you aren't.

By the time the DQ closes at 10, the asphalt under the drive-through window is a spillage of coins, napkins, relish packets, cigarette butts and a maraschino cherry. Cisco goes out and sweeps it up, one scrawny boy with a broom and a dustpan, singing the "Welcome to Atlanta" re-mix.

The Ku Klux Klan members who used to stand at the intersections at lunch time in their pointed hoods asking for donations are gone. But now life out there is as mixed up as the Dairy Queen on a Friday night. On Tara Boulevard, Clayton County police are investigating some Latin Kings who shot up a *quinceañera*. The putt-putt golf course is now an Asian game room. Families are living in extended-stay hotels for $174 a week.

At the DQ, what signals the passage of time is the arrival of new merchandising material. After the Scooby-Doo promotion starts, a new employee named Faisal Khan joins the crew. Faisal is 14 and Pakistani. He grew up in a one-bedroom apartment next to the gas station his dad owned near the Atlanta airport. His hobby is designing Web sites. He's saving for college.

His first week at DQ, Faisal is whacked by the velocity "I want one small dip cone and one medium cone," a customer at the drive-through orders. "And make the medium kinda little 'cause it's for a girl."

"Can I have a number three without pickles, small Sprite, small Oreo Blizzard, a medium sweet tea, and that's all," says the person in a car with a Braves license plate.

Faisal falls behind. He may be an ace at school but this place is something else.

"Can you grill that hot dog for me?"

"We don't have a grill."

"Does that mean you can't grill it?"

In time, though, Faisal no longer needs to look at the diagram of how to make a Blizzard. With his first paycheck, he buys his mother clothes. He is slender and quiet, with Phase One of a moustache. He covets almost nothing, and exists in a solitary focus. "If you're gonna be somebody, then you gotta do some things you don't like," he says.

In the summer, Faisal attends Muslim day camp and works at the DQ on Friday nights. From the counter he can see the drag racers who gather in the Big K parking lot across the street. They gun their engines and smoke cigarettes before tearing out for the back roads. Faisal is at the register one Friday night when a hot rodder walks in, striding toughly and wearing a gold rope around his neck with a big diamond "R."

The mild-mannered Faisal folds his thin arms across his chest and cops enough attitude for all the playas in the Dirty South.

"S'up?" he says.

In 1998, Dairy Queen was purchased by Warren Buffett's Berkshire Hathaway Inc. With total revenue of $450 million a year, DQ is the eighth-largest restaurant chain in the United States and is expanding worldwide.

The employees at the Stockbridge store are unaware of their role in the global market. What's happening right in front of them is all they can take.

A customer is trying to scam Faisal for a reduced-price banana split. Employees are supposed to speak only English, but someone is barking Urdu over the roar of the milkshake blender. Someone else is nuking Indian food in the microwave, a forbidden practice because American customers don't like the smell of curry with their ice cream.

One of the employees takes his break in his black Cavalier in the parking lot, blasting the hardcore metal band Cast Aside the Fallen.

Farzana notices Cisco giving a customer ice water in a 32-ounce cup. She explodes. "This is not a free store!" she yells. "This cup costs the DQ money!"

Cisco struts off, muttering, "I'll put the 50 cents in." He starts to bob and the words fly out in razor rhymes.

Although they say we're free, we're not.
I act like I'm loving life but I'm not.

Employee Karl Griffin comes into the DQ in a panic. He's wearing his Hardaway silks and new pair of Jordans. Karl had planned on getting a room at the Holiday Inn Express for a party but he lost his $40. He looks everywhere for the money but can't find it. The DQ crew pitches in $38.

Riz Momin has reserved a table at Maharaja, an Indian restaurant in the Atlanta suburb of Tucker. It's his mother's 71st birthday, and he has arranged a surprise dinner. The DQ baron arrives wearing a white starched shirt with gold cuff links. His wife and two sisters—each work at one of the family-owned Dairy Queens by day, their polo shirts spattered in butterscotch and straw- berry topping—now appear in *punjabi*. Ali arrives a bit later, his new Motorola V-60 phone clipped to his belt.

Riz has just purchased his 10th Dairy Queen, adding to his string of three Orange Juliuses. As he expands his empire, some DQ operators still hang signs on their leader boards that say, "AMERICAN OWNED." At the Atlanta regional meetings of DQ operators, the Indians sit on one side of the room and the white owners on the other. "The whites don't even say 'hi' to the Indians," Riz says. "It's hard."

He has his rags-to-Armani immigrant narrative, but he still doesn't have the one thing he most wants: respect. The fast-food business launched him; now he wants more. His latest brainstorm is to open a chain of "As Seen on TV" stores. They sell products such as the Flowbee Haircutting System, Bug Wand, Bye Bye Blemish and Juice Man II. In the hours before his mother's birthday party, he scoped potential mall locations and investors. "If I open my wings wider and talk to the people, they will join me," he says.

At the Indian restaurant, the table is stacked with gifts, and there's a sheet cake from the Danish Bakery. When Riz's mom walks in, she clasps her hands to her face. The family lines up to pay homage, with Riz leading the way. He presents his mother with a small box. She opens it and her eyes fill with tears.

"Real diamonds," a sister of Riz whispers.

The 3 o'clock crew drifts in one Friday afternoon. They start refilling the vats of syrup and stacking new sheaths of cones. Cisco is missing. Lately his grandiosity has been increasing. He's gone from home for days at a time, and he talks about how deep life is at the Bowen Homes housing project in Atlanta. "You either from the 'hood or you from the sub-urbs," he'll say. "I'm 'hood till I die."

The truth is, Francisco Montanez lives on a cul-de-sac in a modest two-story house, where the dining room table is set with cloth napkins twisting out of the ice tea glasses.

The afternoon Cisco is a no-show, an Indian supervisor picks up the phone. "The Cisco is never late," she says, as she dials his grand-mother's house. "Hello, can I talk with the Cisco?" As it turns out, the schedule was changed and no one told Cisco. He materializes an hour later, carrying his blue DQ polo.

"You gotta get you a cell phone, boy," Ali says.

Cisco says, "I ain't got as much as you."

Ali orders Cisco to wipe down the storage freezer.

The first Confederate flag of the shift ar-rives. Cisco carries a bucket and a scrubby to-ward the freezer in the back, making up a rap about a place called DQ Town.

Total chaos
for these play-ahs
ATL
ATL

Sarah L. Voison—The Washington Post

The multicultural workers at the Dairy Queen often find themselves serving people whose cars, or in this case, T-shirts, are adorned with the Confederate flag. Leah St. Cyr, 20, stops by the Dairy Queen when she attends a nearby church service.

The DQ in Stockbridge keeps its employees much longer than most fast-food restaurants. Still, life moves on. Farzana stays as a $7-an-hour assistant manager, but in September, Faisal quits to focus on ninth grade and Xavier quits to focus on varsity football.

Ali is transferred to another DQ store in the Riz empire. A plan for his life? "I don't got one," he says. "I'm too lazy, for real."

Cisco gets fired for erratic work habits. He is now enrolled at Morrow High School as a ninth-grader.

Riz Momin buys two more Dairy Queens, opens two "As Seen on TV" stores and launches a costume jewelry boutique called Accessory Necessity.

Read the rest of the *Rim of the New World* series on *www.theauthenticvoice.org*

THE MAKING OF

RIM OF THE NEW WORLD

By Anne Hull
Washington Post Staff Writer

Rim of the New World, a four-day 15,000-word series in *The Washington Post,* explored immigration's epochal transformation of the American South. The underlying question—the very river beneath—was simple: what's it like for a young immigrant to come of age in a place so historically defined by white and black? The 2000 U.S. Census had provided the numerical proof that one society was dying off and another rising up: the two-tone world of the past was giving way to a mass arrival of immigrants. What did it feel like to be a young outsider, living inside this wave?

The series came about by accident. As a national reporter for *The Washington Post,* my job is to look for stories around the country. I'd noticed that several Latino teenagers in Atlanta had died in what police were describing as gang killings. Gang stories are nothing new, but Latino gangs amid the magnolias seemed fairly fresh.

I went down for a week of reporting. But after spending some time on the ground—talking with teenagers, cops, and teachers and just riding around for countless hours—a larger theme emerged. The violence and homicides were symptoms of a sense of displacement among Atlanta's young Latino immigrants, most of whom were the sons and daughters of low-wage Mexican workers who'd poured into the South in the 1980s. These kids were rebelling against their destiny as the South's new servant class. Unlike their parents, they weren't willing to clean motel rooms or lay bricks for low wages. And yet the public schools were woefully unprepared to teach them. Dropout rates were climbing. Teen pregnancy rates for Latinas were of concern to public health officials. It became clear that what police called "gang violence" was more an expression of rage, boredom, and defiance against invisibility.

What to do with all these random ruminations? How do you make sense of all that you've reported? This part of the process—the thinking—is the most underutilized phase of journalism. Liz Spayd, *The Post*'s national editor, offered lots of listening, challenging, and brainstorming. We decided that a story on Latino gang violence would be perfectly fine, but a better story would be to focus on the more ordinary life of a young immigrant living in the frontier of immigration in the South.

After many interviews and much searching—at high schools, flea markets, job fairs, social service agencies—I settled on Nallely Ortiz, a fifteen-year-old who'd come to Atlanta with her parents from Mexico in the mid-eighties.

Steve Coll, *The Post*'s former managing editor, read the Nallely story and made a bolder suggestion: why not write about the lives of other young immigrants coming of age in Atlanta, as a way to document more fully immigration's sweeping changes in the American South?

The concept presented lots of challenges. I would have to find new subjects but in ethnic communities about which I knew almost nothing. I spoke only English, an increasingly severe limitation in multicultural America. Also hindering this effort was my distance from the story: it was in Atlanta, and I lived in Washington.

Journalists parachute into an unknown community and find the necessary navigators. We call social service agencies, school principals, public health workers, immigrant and refugee agencies, any possible gateway into particular ethnic communities. It's also helpful to be less formal. Drive through communities. Eat in the local ethnic restaurants. Listen to bands. Hang out. Go online and find out when a high school is holding various club meetings or sporting events. You are basically dragging the lake here.

I settled on three subjects from three distinct communities. Amy Nguyen was a seventeen-year-old Vietnamese girl. Adama Camara was a twenty-two-year-old immigrant from Mali. The third story wasn't so much a character as it was a place—a Dairy Queen owned by an Indian immigrant. White middle-class kids had largely abandoned workplaces like Dairy Queen in favor of Starbucks or the Gap, leaving places like Dairy Queen as the low-wage province of working-class white and black kids and immigrants.

How does a reporter report on a Dairy Queen? You stand at the drive-through window and experience the Friday night slam. You count the number of Confederate flags that approach. You listen closely to the voices and dialects that come across the drive-through speaker. You jot down every bit of dialogue spoken by the employees and customers. You follow the workers home to see the difference between their public and private lives. For example, Rizwan Momin, who owned the Dairy

Dick Norling
Washington Post reporter Anne Hull discusses the story.

Queen, tooled around Atlanta in an Infiniti and wore starched dress shirts to business meetings with good-ole-boy bankers. But at home, with his tea and silk robes, he had re-created his native Gujarat, and it was important to see the two very distinct lives he was negotiating.

In the DQ story, I experienced very few ethical dilemmas. I often had trouble understanding the Indian/Pakistani accents, but the subjects were patient when I constantly asked them to repeat what they said. The same applied to a young African American teen who worked at the DQ and spoke in a patois of Black Southern colloquialisms and hip-hop slang. I often made him repeat himself so I could copy down exactly what he said. But over time my ears adjusted to all the accents and dialects. Being in this global audio stew was a good awakening for the reportorial senses and made me realize how bland most newspaper stories are when it comes to capturing authentic voices.

I believe in using exact language, which can pose a problem when someone's grammar is broken or someone is still learning English. And yet the alternative—to scrub and sanitize speech—feels untrue. The musical language of people mixing their native tongues with new English should somehow be telegraphed to the reader without embarrassing or ridiculing the subject. So, I use this music sparingly, just enough to get the flavor across.

Three of the four stories in the *Rim of the New World* series required me to hire professional interpreters. Most of my subjects spoke English, but their parents didn't. I needed the interpreter to ask the parents for permission to spend time with their children and to make clear that a story and photographs would ultimately be published on the front page of *The Washington Post*. I told the interpreter to emphasize to the parents that the decision was theirs to make. This sounds obvious, but new immigrants tend to be pleasers, and they often say yes even if they are uncertain of what they are agreeing to.

Adama Camara from Mali spoke the most limited English. I contacted a professional interpreter service used by the Georgia court system and was lucky enough to find a woman who spoke Bambara, one of Adama's native languages. But language was the least of my challenges. The premise of his story was fraught with fault lines: what is it like to have black skin in the South but not possess the historical hardships of the experience? Because of his skin color, Adama's place in the American South was loaded with foregone conclusions. Along with that was the extra tension added by his African American coworkers (Adama worked as a janitor and busboy at the Hartsfield Atlanta International Airport): they saw him as an overpleasing and naive employee who happily cleaned toilets without realizing it was the bottom of the ladder. Plus, some saw him as an immigrant taking work away from "real Americans." When Adama himself was the victim of racism by white people, he didn't get mad, mostly because he didn't understand the slight or have a lifetime of such slights stacked up inside him. I interviewed lots of Adama's coworkers about these things, prefacing my questions with, "These are sort of sticky things to talk about, can we just not worry about offending each other and talk honestly?"

No story about race or immigration can be reported in a bubble. The tension comes from interaction with the majority culture. These exchanges/clashes/collisions take place in the small moments of reporting. This involves hanging out with someone in the mundane moments of their life: riding the bus, going to the grocery store or church or a nightclub, just basically gluing yourself to their days and nights. Pretty soon, these small moments begin to accrue, and you learn it's not as much the formal interviews that begin to describe a person as the observed moments and intersections with the majority culture.

I went with Amy to an all-day Vietnamese wedding. The wedding party hired a limousine, which happened to be chauffeured by an African American. This presented an opportunity, of course. I asked the driver his views on Asian immigration in the South. His comments—poignant, humorous generalizations about Asian success in business—echoed lots of commonly held stereotypes. I later used this conversation as a way to ask Amy sensitive questions, so that the two worlds could bounce off each other.

> No story about race or immigration can be reported in a bubble. The tension comes from interaction with the majority culture. These exchanges/clashes/collisions take place in the small moments of reporting.

It's important to reveal the immigrant's own stereotypes. Nallely and her friend Saul Avina were constantly critiquing other Latino immigrants, making fun of the "new arrives." It was a sport for them to mock "FOB" (Fresh Off the Boat) Mexicans by noting their tight jeans, campesino haircuts, and nortena music. Nallely and Saul were blistering in their criticisms, and yet within this criticism was a heartbreaking attempt to announce their foothold on assimilation. It's important to include or at least consider these moments in stories because they hint at a complexity more shaded than the all-too-common portrait of the immigrant as a champion of his or her own people.

Before publication of the series, I'd asked a few trusted journalist friends of different racial/ethnic backgrounds to read the drafts and be brutally honest about where I'd gotten things wrong or been culturally insensitive. I'm neither Asian nor Hispanic and can never fully know the experience. After the stories published, I was gratified by the letters we received from young immigrant readers who said they saw their own lives in the stories. But *The Post* also received critical letters from the National Association of Hispanic Journalists and the Asian American Journalist Association for what the groups perceived as my stereotypical treatment of the subjects.

A member of NAHJ said I had reinforced a negative stereotype by profiling a Mexican American girl who became pregnant and dropped out of high school. The truth is, I began following Nallely when she was fifteen and not pregnant. In the course of my reporting, Nallely became pregnant. In so doing, she joined an alarming trend that showed young Latinas getting pregnant at higher rates than white or black teen females, particularly in the South.

Was I supposed to turn away from telling Nallely's story because it wasn't positive? I felt that my job was to explain the hows and whys of Nallely's choices, in hopes that her individual choices might explain a larger—and statistically real—picture.

AAJA said my story on Amy Nguyen had reinforced the "model minority" stereotype by writing about Asian parents who wanted their child to become a doctor. My intent was the opposite: Amy was rejecting her parents' expectations and trying to define herself on her own terms. It was an incontrovertible fact that at Amy's high school—a formerly all-white rural high school—the arrival of Asian students in the last decade had bumped up SAT score averages. Academically, Amy Nguyen was not an envelope pusher, and yet she lived under the cosmic pressure of expectation. She was also living under her parents' dreams that she go into medicine. My intent was not to profile a superachiever but to write about the bravery required to follow one's heart.

Writing about race and immigration is one of the most exciting enterprises in journalism, in part because it's freighted with hazard. Half the challenge is penetrating the public and polite dialogue. Don't shy from the truth of your reporting or language that is alive with truth. Always remember you are not the master narrator but one small storyteller of one small story. Even so, you are carrying something large and heavy and ultimately representative. Be mindful of this.

To screen the Anne Hull interview, select UNTOLD STORIES on the DVD Main Menu then "Rim of the New World."

DISCUSSION POINTS

- Anne Hull writes that "no story about race or immigration can be reported in a bubble. The tension comes from interaction with the majority culture." Discuss how her series depicts this tension.
- Hull describes using the "music" of language in her essay. Specifically, how do her language choices reach this authenticity?
- Discuss the roles that Cisco Montanez, Nallely Ortiz, Amy Nguyen, and Adama Camara play in portraying aspects of immigrant life in Atlanta.
- Anne Hull's character choices could be criticized as stereotypical. Discuss her justification for picking them against your own reaction.
- If you were assigned this story, where would you go to find a setting similar to the Dairy Queen?

SUGGESTED READINGS AND WEBSITES

Books

Bayor, Ronald. *Race and the Shaping of Twentieth Century Atlanta*. Chapel Hill: University of North Carolina Press, 1996.

Winner of a 1997 Outstanding Book Award, Gustavus Myers Center for the Study of Bigotry and Human Rights in North America, this book is a comprehensive history of Atlanta race relations, offering an analysis on the legacy of segregation in the urban environment.

Pomerantz, Gary M. *Where Peachtree Meets Sweet Auburn*. New York: Scribner, 1996.

In this biography of Atlanta and its racial conscience, Gary Pomerantz documents five generations of the white Allen and black Dobbs families, using Peachtree and Auburn streets to depict their parallel worlds.

Websites

www.npr.org/news/specials/polls/2004/immigration

The site offers a survey, conducted jointly by NPR, the Kaiser Family Foundation, and Harvard's Kennedy School of Government, of more than eleven hundred native-born Americans and nearly eight hundred immigrants regarding their attitudes toward immigrants and immigration.

www.voicesofcivilrights.org

The site offers personal accounts from people who are part of the civil rights experience. Sponsored by the AARP, the Leadership Conference on Civil Rights (LCCR), and the Library of Congress, the site enables people to share their own stories and to take a virtual bus tour of the key cities in the civil rights movement.

CHAPTER 10

STORY

THE DEATH OF LCPL GUTIERREZ

STEVE GLAUBER AND BOB SIMON

CBS NEWS, 60 MINUTES II

STEVE GLAUBER

Steve Glauber is an award-winning producer who started his career with CBS in 1978, working as a senior producer on *The Evening News with Dan Rather* and then on *48 Hours,* the newsmagazine. He began as a producer with WNET/Channel 13 in New York. He has produced more than one hundred stories for *60 Minutes* and several one-hour documentaries.

BOB SIMON

CBS correspondent Bob Simon has reported for *60 Minutes,* one of the highest-rated television news programs in history, since 1996. Simon was named CBS Middle Eastern bureau chief in 1987 and since has earned respect as one of the premier broadcast journalists in that part of the world. Simon has twice won the Overseas Press Club Award, and in 1996 he received the George Foster Peabody Award. He has been honored with numerous Emmys for his international reporting.

the death of
LCpl Gutierrez

The tale of Jose Antonio Gutierrez had been told by other journalists and was making its way into the growing narrative of American heroes when a veteran team at CBS's *60 Minutes II* picked up the story.

Packed with the kind of irony that brings emotions into unpredictable conflict, Gutierrez's story was made for television's magazine format: A young Guatemalan man slips into the United States illegally, lies about his age to get documented, joins the Marines, and is one of the first soldiers from the United States to die in Iraq. In death, he wins citizenship and instant status as a hero.

Producer Steve Glauber and correspondent Bob Simon brought Gutierrez to life through family anecdotes and the stories that followed him from an orphanage to the Southern California suburbs. The CBS team traced Gutierrez's story back to his impoverished village in Guatemala and then moved it forward to its tragic end, helping viewers to understand the simple ideals that propelled him across the border and the brief, complicated life that he found there.

Awaiting journalists in this chapter is a lesson in the complexities of immigration law and military service that don't fit comfortably into the polarized arguments frequently offered up by the media. Simon and Glauber show journalists how to take an emerging story deeper, finding the people who are able not just to illuminate Gutierrez's life but also to challenge through key sources the noble notion that his story should be cast as a tale of heroism alone.

Many of the choices Glauber and Simon made—from their decision not to interview Guatemalans on air to the provocative use of words and phrases in the piece itself—are sure to spark debate among those reviewing this chapter. The two longtime CBS pros also invite discussion about how journalists should view the primary purpose of doing such stories.

Like Jose Gutierrez himself, the chapter underscores the contradictions, imperfections, and surprises that surface when journalists plunge into matters of race and ethnicity.

"THE DEATH OF LCPL GUTIERREZ" (TRANSCRIPT)

CBS News, *60 Minutes II*
Airdate: August 20, 2003
Correspondent: Bob Simon / Producers: Steve Glauber and Yvonne Miller /
Editor: David Rubin

Bob Simon: [studio intro]	Did you know that some 38,000 Americans in uniform are not American citizens, and that at least 10 men who have been killed in Iraq were not US citizens? That sounds astonishing, but, in fact, it's nothing new. It's been like that in every war the United States has fought from Valley Forge to Vietnam. We're not just talking about immigrants. Their valor is well-documented. More than one out of every five Medal of Honor recipients has been an immigrant. But as we first reported earlier this year, the heroism and sacrifice of non-citizens was barely known until Lance Corporal Jose Gutierrez died in battle in Iraq. He came from Guatemala, and he came to the United States illegally.
Bob Simon: [on camera]	We can tell you how his story ended. He was killed in a tank battle in southern Iraq on March 21st. We can also tell you how his story began. It began here in a slum outside Guatemala City. We can't show you any pictures of Jose, though, at least not when he was a kid here. There are none. Jose was orphaned when he was six years old and became a street child. Street children in Guatemala do not get their pictures taken.
[voice-over]	This is how America will remember Jose Gutierrez, handsome and heroic. But shortly before Bruce Harris met him, he was homeless and helpless, what Latinos call "the dust of the earth."
Bruce Harris:	He was really a survivor, and that's how he made it up to the United States because he was a survivor.
Bob Simon:	Bruce Harris began running Guatemala's Casa Alianza orphanage—that's Covenant House in Spanish—shortly after Jose was taken there at the age of nine. Today Harris directs all their operations in Central America and fights for children so fiercely that Queen Elizabeth invested him into the exclusive Order of the British Empire in his native England.

produced by Steve Glauber
Yvonne Miller

The Death of
LCpl Gutierrez

Courtesy of CBS News, 60 Minutes II

Bob Simon introduces the Gutierrez segment on the 60 Minutes II set.

"Most Marines are only high school graduates. Most are working-class; many are Hispanic. When a green card holder joins the military, he can apply for citizenship after three years instead of the usual five."

—Bob Simon

Bruce Harris:	He wasn't satisfied in trying to etch out a subsistence survival in a country like Guatemala, where more than 80 percent of the people are poor.
	He wanted more. He knew there was more to life than just being poor.
Bob Simon:	So in 1997, 12 years after entering the orphanage, Jose said he was leaving for America. It was a 3,000-mile trail of tears, by foot, by tire, by train, a modern-day version of the Underground Railway *[sic]*, and the last leg over the wall. But when Jose made it to the border, he got busted. He was 22 years old, and the INS was going to turn him back. But he was saved by his baby face. He told the authorities he was only 16. Minors don't get turned back. He was allowed to stay in America and get a green card.
Bruce Harris:	Once he crossed the border, and he had to lie to get in, you know, some people say, "Well, that's not very good." I mean, it's not something that we would prefer. But he knew that to survive, if he'd said he was 21, he'd be thrown back with the tens of thousands of "wetbacks," a derogatory term used on that side of the border towards people who want to survive.
Bob Simon:	His pilgrimage continued through a series of foster homes, one after another, but once again he got lucky. He wound up in

Torrance, California, with Nora and Marcello Mosquera, both Latin American immigrants.

They not only took him in, they loved him and called him their son.

Nora Mosquera: My son told me many, many times—he said, "Mom, I don't know why God has me in this world and why I have survived so many"—I mean, he for many, many times in Guatemala and so forth, he was very close to being killed. And he used to tell me, "But I know God has me in this world because there is something special that I'm going to do. I don't know what it is." And he wanted to be an architect. "And everyone is going to remember who I am, and you're going to be very proud of me."

Bob Simon: When you think about him, I mean, here's a kid who lost both his parents when he was very young.

Nora Mosquera: Yes.

Bob Simon: He was dirt-poor, and you talk about a—him having such a positive attitude.

Nora Mosquera: Yes. You find children that when they encounter so many problems as—in their early childhood, it—they either go the right path or the wrong path. Either they make them stronger, a fighter, a soldier to get ahead and—and become someone in

Courtesy of CBS News, 60 Minutes II

U.S. Marine Lance Cpl. Jose Gutierrez

"'Mom, I don't know why God has me in this world . . . But I know God has me in this world because there is something special that I'm going to do. I don't know what it is.'"
—Jose Gutierrez

life, or they go down the wrong road. I think with Jose, all his experiences made him stronger.

Bob Simon:
[voice-over]

Jose was one of more than 20 foster children taken in by the Mosqueras, but he became a real brother to the Mosquera daughters, Lillian and Jackie.

[interview]

Did he change much in the years that he was here?

Jackie Mosquera:

He became sillier.

Bob Simon:

That must mean happier.

Lillian Mosquera:

Yeah.

Jackie Mosquera:

That's this last New Year's Eve, we—we all were just up. You know, we were dancing and just having fun. We had a great New Year's. And then we just started playing different CDs, and he loved The Beatles. So we were playing The Beatles. And then "Hey Jude" came on, and he's sitting there singing, "Hey Dude." I'm like, "Jose, it's not 'Hey Dude.' It's 'Hey Jude.'" He's like, "No, it's 'Hey Dude.'" And by the end of the song, we were all singing "Hey Dude."

Lillian Mosquera:

"Hey Dude."

Jackie Mosquera:

So . . .

Bob Simon:

Maybe it's "Hey Dude."

Lillian Mosquera:

Yeah, you know . . .

Bob Simon:
[voice-over]

Jose went to a community college, played soccer there and then dropped out last year to join the Marines. He was not an unusual recruit.

Most Marines are only high school graduates.

Bob Simon:

Most are working-class; many are Hispanic. When a green card holder joins the military, he can apply for citizenship after three years instead of the usual five. But Jose told his mother he had other reasons for joining, other reasons for wanting to go to Iraq and help topple the regime of Saddam Hussein.

Nora Mosquera:

Before he was shipped out, he told me, "I cannot stand having a regime do to women and children what this regime is doing in Iraq, and I'll give my life if I have to in order to defend those children." And that—those are the ideals of the Marines, and those were his ideals—of becoming someone, of being able to help those other children that are not as fortunate as he was.

Bob Simon: Is that what it was really all about? Giving back?

Lillian Mosquera: Primarily.

Jackie Mosquera: Yeah.

Lillian Mosquera: And, also, he wanted to achieve education—his education.

Jackie Mosquera: Yeah. I think it was both kind of coupled together. I mean, here he saw an opportunity to go to school, to fin—originally I think it was to finish his education—go in, do his time, finish his education and, also, give back.

Bob Simon:
[voice-over] He gave back, all right. He was one of the first US servicemen to die in combat in Iraq. No death of any soldier goes unmourned, but the death of a man who died for a country that was not his, that proved especially poignant to many Americans, including President Bush, who visited two wounded non-citizen soldiers and made them citizens on the spot.

President George W. Bush: You know, we've got an amazing country where it's so powerful, the values we believe, that people would be willing to risk their own life and become a citizen after being wounded. It's an amazing moment.

Bob Simon: Jose was also granted American citizenship, posthumously. And that's also when he became a hero.

Unidentified cardinal: Let us now continue our—our prayer in honor of our great brother Jose Antonio.

Bob Simon: A cardinal officiated at a funeral service in this Los Angeles suburb. There were many poor people here, many Latinos and Jose's parish priest, Gustavo Castillo.

Reverend Gustavo Castillo: Isn't it amazing that those that are not acknowledged as citizens here are the ones that are doing the fighting, risking their lives.

Bob Simon:
[interview] Now if Gutierrez had come home, probably would have gone back to study to become an architect. Instead, he got killed. He got really unlucky. Does that make him a hero?

Rev. Gustavo Castillo: He is a hero now. And it's unfortunate sometimes that that's what has to happen in order for people to be known, in order for them to accomplish something, maybe.

Bob Simon:
[voice-over] An American hero, but in Guatemala, a little more complicated. He wanted to be buried here. That's what he told his family. It was, after all, his home. The Marines came down

"And so we have a plaque for him: 'In memory of . . . who loved life, Jose Antonio Gutierrez.' It's important to be here. This is . . . this is his home."

—Bruce Harris

Courtesy of CBS News, 60 Minutes II

Bruce Harris shows Bob Simon the Jose Gutierrez memorial in Guatemala.

to give him a proper military farewell, but there were hardly any Guatemalans at the ceremony. After all, officials said, he didn't die for Guatemala. But Bruce Harris mourned him. He's the guy who lifted him off the streets nearly 25 years ago.

[interview]

Bruce, in the States now Gutierrez is treated as a hero. How has it played here in Guatemala?

Bruce Harris:

One group felt that these young Hispanic men were being sent as cannon fodder into the battlefield because, at first, many of the US Marines who were killed were Latinos, and that created a big question here. Are young Hispanic men who go up to the United States looking for a future, for an education, are they being sent to the front because they're dispensable?

Bob Simon:

You're saying that in Guatemala he was viewed more as a victim than as a hero?

Bruce Harris:

I would say a bit of both. It's always a very difficult situation. I mean, we—we've looked at how we use the terminology. Having been for years the throwaway kid, the rubbish of society, who are we now to question that he should be called a hero after living so many years as a nothing? But it's a high price to pay for a title.

Bob Simon: [voice-over]	The US government bought Gutierrez a plot in Guatemala's ritziest cemetery, probably making him the first kid from the slums ever buried here. But this is where Harris wanted him buried, in a plot reserved for Casa Alianza kids, the street children of which he was one. Another neighborhood, another kind of cemetery.
Bruce Harris:	And so we have a plaque for him: "In memory of … who loved life, Jose Antonio Gutierrez." It's important to be here. This is— this is his home. It may not be the fine manicured lawns and nice trees and suchlike, but this is where his people are. It's a beautiful poem there. It says, "Here I am, Lord, but I can't—I can't arrive unless you take me by the hand. Take me to your side because I want to know your beautiful face. Excuse my errors, but I want—I want to share your beautiful heart. I'm yours—I'm yours, Lord. Take me home."
Bob Simon: [voice-over]	And at home, in America, where he saw his future, he's finally a citizen, and he didn't have to wait three years to apply. Right now Congress is considering several proposals which will make it quicker and easier for green card holders to become Americans when they join the military.
[interview]	How did you feel about the government bestowing American citizenship on Jose after he had died?
Lillian Mosquera:	Saddened that he wasn't alive to see it. And, hopefully, by taking these examples of these kids coming home in boxes and giving it to them, hopefully this will show Congress or someone in the White House to let these immigrants that are fighting for us have the privilege to enjoy being an American citizen in their daily lives instead of coming home in body bags.
Bob Simon: [on-camera]	Jose Gutierrez was also a poet. Here's part of a poem he wrote before he joined the Marines: "I come from far away, where the angels live in misery, dress themselves with filth and eat dreams." The toughest thing about doing the Jose Gutierrez story is that we never got to meet him.
Bob Simon: [studio close]	Several weeks after we broadcast this story, the US military revealed the cause of Gutierrez's death. It was not from Iraqi guns, but friendly fire from his fellow Americans.

THE MAKING OF

THE DEATH OF LCPL GUTIERREZ

By Steve Glauber, CBS News

Four truths come to mind when reflecting on *The Death of LCpl Gutierrez* story. First, the initial story idea for most television news reporting is not original but derivative. Second, despite the lack of initial originality, the power of television to communicate that a story is remarkable. Third, a producer's personal experience determines his or her interest in pursuing a story. Finally, television news, unlike print reporting, is always a group effort.

As a producer, I am responsible for originating story ideas as well as executing the production. Good ideas are hard to find, and producers are competitive. For a job well done on an ordinary story, you get faint praise. For the same quality of work on a terrific story, you rake in awards.

The story idea on the death of Jose Gutierrez, an immigrant who joined the Marines and was subsequently sent to Iraq, began not with an original idea but with my reading an article in the *Los Angeles Times* in March 2003. Shortly after the invasion of Iraq, that newspaper reported that at least ten of the first few dozen soldiers killed in the early fighting were noncitizens, so-called green card soldiers. Marine Lance Corporal Jose Gutierrez, born in Guatemala and living in the Los Angeles area, reportedly was the first green card soldier to die in Iraq. He also was the second U.S. serviceman to die there, period.

My curiosity was immediately aroused because the potential story could provide a chance to cover an ignored population: Latin American immigrants in the United States. Television news networks increasingly shy away both from foreign stories (Iraq is not a foreign story but about Americans in a foreign location) and stories about foreigners recently arrived in America. The former topic is too costly both in money and viewership: too much money covering the story there, too few viewers watching here. The latter topic—new immigrants in America—involves people who lack power and money or, more bluntly, the sufficient political muscle to make headlines or earn enough money to buy Volvos and Viagra. Most television producers will tell you that there is a ratings turnoff when the coverage is about non–English speaking people. Hence the wonderful book title derived from quoting a reporter's question in Africa, "Does Any Nun Who Has Been Raped Speak English?"

"Jose was one of more than 20 foster children taken in by the Mosqueras, but he became a real brother to the Mosquera daughters."
—Bob Simon

Courtesy of CBS News, 6o Minutes II
The Mosquera sisters, Lillian and Jackie, discuss Jose's life in the United States.

Of more personal interest was the possibility of doing a story about the immigrant experience. I am an immigrant who escaped Europe when my parents, Jews living in Czechoslovakia near the German border, abandoned their home only weeks before the Nazi invasion of their homeland. They barely escaped arrest while fleeing through Europe and ended up in North Africa for three years before traveling steerage on a Spanish boat to the United States at the end of 1941.

Growing up in America, I was aware of being a foreigner. I watched my parents struggle. My father, a middle-aged doctor, had to study anew to pass his medical boards while learning English at the same time. My older sister, coming home the first time from college, humorously revealed to me that "not all adults have a German accent."

Today, migrant and refugee issues resonate in my soul. In New York City, where I work, taxi drivers, most of whom are immigrants, must bear my questions about their experiences. Small ethnic restaurants get my business not only because their food and prices are superior but also because I want to help them. Being an immigrant in America is tough, and I have empathy.

So the story itself—the high percentage of green card soldiers killed in Iraq—raised immediate and fascinating questions. Why would a noncitizen like Jose Gutierrez enlist in the United States armed services to risk his life for a country that was not his? Was Jose's incentive economic, the best or only alternative for a decent paying job? By chance, was he coerced to enlist in the Marines as the only alternative to going to prison? That kind of thing happened a lot in World War II.

Had he crossed the border seeking the American dream but, finding a nightmare, joined up to get away from it all? Conversely, was Jose's motivation patriotic in some way, a love of the country where he was living or at least a huge gesture of gratitude? Perhaps the impetus had nothing to do with his life in the United States but instead flowed from his sympathy with the Iraqi people suffering under the regime of President Saddam Hussein? Perhaps he felt empathy with foreign victims of Mr. Hussein, such as Kurds who were gassed or Iranians who were shot?

What did Jose's family think about the decision? Did he have a family? Did it make a difference if his family lived in the USA or in Guatemala? Was the high percentage of noncitizen deaths a statistical aberration or were there many such enlistees? Had many noncitizens enlisted in prior wars? How did they perform?

And there was potential irony. Immigrants like Jose are loathed by many Americans. Probably he had experienced prejudice personally. Certainly he

Courtesy of CBS News, 60 Minutes II
Keith Woods interviews producer Steve Glauber, and correspondent Bob Simon.

"Most television producers will tell you that there is a ratings turnoff when the coverage is about non-English-speaking people. Hence the wonderful book title derived from quoting a reporter's question in Africa, "Does Any Nun Who Has Been Raped Speak English?"

—Steve Glauber

had observed intolerance. Indeed, bigots often have called immigrants like Jose wetbacks. Now Jose was an early war casualty: an automatic hero.

Associate producer Yvonne Miller, whose mother was born in Mexico, agreed that doing a profile of Jose Gutierrez might help us pose these questions and get some answers. Why try for Jose and not the second or seventeenth noncitizen solider? Nothing profound other than "first" makes a better hook. Our interest was not to educate the viewer but to tell Jose's story.

Locating Jose's family was easy. We rode the coattails of the *Los Angeles Times,* which did a terrific story about Jose's life as we were beginning our research. The article mentioned the names of Nora and Marcello Mosquera, American citizens initially from Ecuador and now living near Los Angeles, who had taken in Jose several years earlier and treated him as a son. They were in Guatemala when Yvonne first called, but they promised to speak with us upon their return, as they wanted Jose's story told.

Turning the Story into TV

At this stage, we had a story but not a very good one. The people we had set up to interview—the Mosquera family, Jose's priest, his community college soccer coach—all could talk about Jose when he lived in Southern California, but they did not know him in Guatemala or between the time he crossed the border and the moment he entered their lives. Further, they could not speak about the reaction in Guatemala to Jose's death.

Put another way, we had a sweet cliché story about a lovely young immigrant who overcame the odds, was loved, and now was a war hero, but all this was insufficient. We had not yet answered the questions that caused us to pursue the story. Everyone would say Jose was a hero, and no one would raise the questions that I kept asking: Does dying on a battlefield make you a hero? Did people in Guatemala see him as a hero? What makes someone a true hero, and how do different people define that term? We lacked both answers and edge. We had to go to Guatemala to get answers.

The Mosquera family told us that Jose had a sister living in Guatemala. Yvonne reached her, but she could not add much to Jose's history since she had not seen her brother since he had gone into the orphanage at age nine. The orphanage was Casa Alianza, Covenant House in English. We wanted to speak with someone from the orphanage who may have known Jose. The Casa Alianza Website said Bruce Harris had been executive director of Casa Alianza since 1989. The same Website synopsized Harris's life, and he seemed fascinating. He was from England and had been a truck driver before becoming involved in children's rights and joining Casa Alianza. A fierce advocate for homeless children, Harris had been inducted into the prestigious Order of the British Empire by Queen Elizabeth. He had even been nominated for the Nobel Peace Prize. Perhaps he had known Jose.

When we finally reached Harris by telephone, he had strong memories of Jose. Then Harris revealed a startling fact that was either unknown to the Mosquera family or had not been covered by newspaper articles: Jose had immigrated illegally and then lied to Immigration and Naturalization Service authorities, telling them that he was sixteen, not twenty-two. This fact is crucial. Had Jose provided his accurate age when he was arrested at the border, he would have been sent back to Guatemala. But he looked young for his age, and the INS allowed him to enter into the country legally.

During the conversation, Harris indicated that the reaction to Jose's death in Guatemala was quite different from the responses in the United States. Instead of perceiving Jose as a hero, many Guatemalans saw him as a tool. Local anger about U.S. immigration policies and treatment of people in the country illegally, Harris said, coalesced around Jose's plight of survival in California and death in Iraq. He said Jose's funeral service was held with minimal publicity since both the Guatemala government and the U.S. embassy, which had arranged the service, knew Jose's sacrifice was less honored than questioned. Harris himself seemed eager to share his own views. In short, it struck us that Harris was the story's savior. He was in touch with the reaction of both Guatemala government officials and ordinary citizens. He had known Jose. He was acquainted with hundreds, perhaps thousands, of youths like Jose who had grown up impoverished and fled to the United States. He had his own strong opinions. Plus, he spoke perfect English, a crucial factor in communicating the story to our English-speaking audience. Harris seemed the perfect storyteller. He said he could meet us beginning the next week in Guatemala.

Bob Simon Signs On

Dan Rather, with whom I usually work, could not take on the assignment to go to Guatemala or Los Angeles. However, CBS correspondent Bob Simon—who is stationed in Tel Aviv and was in the United States for several weeks to work on other stories—said he was free to travel. More important, Bob expressed a serious interest in the story. Bob is the real deal: a distinguished foreign correspondent who covered the Vietnam War, traveled the world for CBS News, and was arrested during the Gulf War and jailed for ninety days in Iraq. Bob has interviewed the famous and the fragile, Saudi kings and Muslim mullahs as well as Cambodian peasants and African gorilla handlers. He is also known as one of the great television writers. Often, a producer will write the script when a

Courtesy of CBS News, 60 Minutes II

Casa Alianza Orphanage director Bruce Harris remembers Gutierrez.

". . . Harris was the story's savior. He was in touch with the reaction of both Guatemala and the United States. He had his own strong opinions. Plus, he spoke perfect English, a crucial factor in communicating the story to our English-speaking audience. Harris seemed the perfect storyteller."
—Steve Glauber

correspondent is busy. Working with Bob, the producer will gladly defer and watch him sit over a computer, a cigarette in his mouth and fingers flashing on the keyboard, creating not just journalism but poetry.

The actual shoot took only five days, including two days flying back and forth. That is pretty fast for a shoot, but we wanted to get this on the air as soon as possible, given the news value of the Iraq war. Bob, Yvonne, and I flew from New York City to Los Angeles on Wednesday to prepare for shooting, which took place over Thursday and Friday. We used a two-person, locally based crew to interview the Mosquera parents, their two daughters, a priest with whom Jose had worshipped, and a junior college soccer coach for whom Jose had played. By Friday evening, we were on our way to Guatemala, where we met two new crews, one that had flown in from Miami and the other from Mexico City. Three of the four crewmembers spoke Spanish, an added benefit as the Spanish of Bob and Yvonne is limited and mine is nonexistent. Harris, of course, is perfectly bilingual, but there would be times when we all separated. In addition, I wanted to be assured that we had independent translators as I needed to remain skeptical about Harris's translating accurately. After all, he had his own agendas.

On Saturday, we began with a Bob standup in the cemetery where Jose is buried. We continued the trip with Bruce Harris to Antigua, the city where Jose had lived in Caza Alianza (the site is now a fancy hotel) and a visit to the grave for its orphans. We continued the shoot with a standup in a typical slum and ended late at night with a sit-down interview between Bob and Harris. On Sunday, we flew back to New York City. On Monday, Yvonne and I worked with editor David Rubin, and we created a basic structure and selected the sound bites from the interviews. I wrote a draft of the narration, and Bob, on Tuesday, turned it from typing to writing. That evening, we screened the story for executive producer Jeff Fager, and, ignoring habit and fiddling with a word or two or suggesting huge changes, he said, "Don't change anything. We'll broadcast it tomorrow."

Why This Foreign Story Worked

If most foreign stories die when proposed and are turned off when viewed, why did this story idea get approved within CBS News and applauded by viewers and critics? *60 Minutes* attracts viewers partly because its management over the years is less interested in ratings than reporting. This follows the so-called law of reverse effort: "The more you want something, the less likely you are to get it; the less you want something, the more likely you are to see it." Jeff Fager, who took over as executive producer of *60 Minutes* from the legendary Don Hewitt, is committed to serious reporting and eager to ignore television's conventional wisdoms, including its reluctance to air foreign stories. As far as I know, management does not commission surveys of what audiences wish to see. It is not interested in teaching the public about issues. *60 Minutes* executives seek stories that interest them. They trust their guts.

The Death of LCpl Gutierrez avoided some of the viewer problems usually associated with these subjects: (1) All the characters spoke English; (2) Most of the characters were citizens; (3) The main character—Jose Gutierrez—lived in the USA and died a Marine in a U.S. war; and (4) the issues raised are domestic, not foreign.

The viewer mail was typically light. There seemed to be an equal mix of admiring letters about Jose and nasty letters accusing us of being leftist antiwar propagandists. The truth—again—is far simpler. We were not trying to influence viewers about the Iraq war or contribute to understanding of the immigrant experience but simply trying to tell a story. Personal experience and interest cause all reporters to chase certain stories, but, in the end, we are not educators but journalists telling stories about the news.

To screen the Steve Glauber and Bob Simon interview, select UNTOLD STORIES on the DVD Main Menu then "The Death of LCpl Gutierrez."

Tips from the Making of "The Death of LCpl Gutierrez"

By Steve Glauber

Translators

- When researching and shooting the story, if the reporter does not speak a foreign language perfectly, always hire an independent translator. Do not use a translator associated with the people being interviewed because there may be a conflict of interest between the interviewer and the subject or the translator may not be fully competent. Also, the translator may have a personal bias that can lead to misinterpretations.
- When the story is broadcast and an English speaker is utilized to imitate the accent and speak the words of an interviewee, always use a narrator from the same country who speaks with the same accent. An alternative: use an English speaker with no foreign accent.

Scheduling

- Assume that in most countries, things take twice as long to get done as they do in the United States. Triple that for third-world countries.

Cultural Differences

- Once you leave the USA corral, you are not in Kansas anymore. Most things are different: culture, language, body language, politics, assumptions, and so on. One thing remains the same, however: people. The basic wants and desires are the same, from the need for physical, psychological, and economic survival to feelings about love and loss and the meaning of life.

Bodyguards

- A reporter dislikes using bodyguards, as it leads to distance from the subject. But better safe than sorry. Try to be as inconspicuous about it as possible, unless the situation calls for displaying weaponry.

Crews

- At least one of the crew members should speak the local language, and, if possible, it should be the photojournalist, who can best illustrate the mood of the interviewee plus pan to a scene to which the interviewee is referring.

Fairness

- Because many disadvantaged people in foreign countries are being treated unfairly, and because American publishers and broadcasts often overlook these people, be particularly careful about fairness and balance in your reporting. Sympathy and empathy can cause emotions that overtake objectivity.

DISCUSSION POINTS

- What surprises you about the Jose Gutierrez story?
- Discuss the story elements that reach across racial, class, cultural, and geographic boundaries.
- Visually, the interview with Gutierrez's adopted family indicated a certain level of middle-class success. What other ingredients contribute to shaping this piece?
- Producer Steve Glauber frankly discusses the fear of using non-English speakers on television. Given the increase in the Spanish-speaking population in the country, what advice would you give *60 Minutes* on creating a more inclusive approach?
- Discuss Steve Glauber's assessment that journalists are not educators.

SUGGESTED READINGS AND WEBSITES

Books

Suarez-Orozco, Carola, and Marcelo M. Suarez-Orozco. *Children of Immigration.* Cambridge: Harvard University Press, 2002.

This book describes at length the great importance of education to immigrant children, who regard it as their path to survival and success in America. The book also looks into forces within and outside the family that shape immigrant children's developing senses of identity and their ambivalent relationships with their adopted country.

Ready, Timothy. *Latino Immigrant Youth: Passages from Adolescence to Adulthood.* New York: Garland, 1991.

This study examines a group of young Latinos during their rise out of the poverty in which they lived after their arrival, focusing on their experiences with education and employment and the effect of these encounters on their family and friends. The author explores educational and career development programs and the implications of immigration policy for employment.

Websites

www/fallenheroesmemorial.com/oif/profiles/gutierrezjose.html

www.corpsstories.com/memoriam-gutierrez.htm

These two Websites offer brief outlines of Gutierrez's life and in memoriam messages from friends, family, and others.

mumford1.dyndns.org/cen2000/report.html

The Lewis Mumford Center for Comparative Urban and Regional Research Website carries studies about demographic, social, and economic conditions of minorities and policies that affect them in the United States, based on data from the 2000 Census.

PART IV

Cultural Competence

CHAPTER 11

STORIES

DIVERSE AND DIVIDED & A TALE OF TWO CULTURES

ELIZABETH LLORENTE

THE RECORD OF BERGEN COUNTY, N.J.

ELIZABETH LLORENTE

Elizabeth Llorente is a senior writer at *The Record of Bergen County*, New Jersey, where for the past eleven years she has specialized in covering immigration and ethnic communities. During that time, Llorente has gained national recognition for her coverage, which includes stories on the abuse of immigrants in federal detention centers and an investigation of a driver's license black market in New Jersey that preyed heavily on immigrants.

Diverse and Divided
& A TALE OF TWO CULTURES

Elizabeth Llorente of *The Record* journeys to the center of seismic demographic shifts in two series out of Bergen County, N.J. With *Diverse and Divided* and *A Tale of Two Cultures,* the veteran reporter introduces readers to the next chapter in the country's immigration story, one in which old tensions and new opportunities roil and blossom in small-town America.

In *Diverse and Divided,* Llorente reports from inside a simmering dispute between longtime African American residents of Paterson and Latino immigrants whose swelling numbers altered the city's political landscape. *A Tale of Two Cultures,* a universal story of fear and ambition, unravels the complex conflicts that arose when white residents of Palisades Park objected to the community changes brought about by immigrants from Korea and Guatemala.

In each story, Llorente helps readers to see the common human threads that connect all stories of change. She shines a light on the often invisible lines that separate fear and bigotry, perception and reality, legitimate anger and ignorance-inspired bitterness. In each case, her patience and persistence are rewarded with stories about not just the dividing lines in communities but also the unexpected ties that belie the animosity.

Llorente's stories showcase a new way to deploy the prism through which so many journalists look at stories of immigration and other racial/ethnic change. Journalists should note how the story of the Korean community breaks from the mold of the striving, struggling immigrant population, how the racial and ethnic tensions in Paterson underscore the ways minority groups can be bigotry's victims and perpetrators at the same time.

In this chapter, Llorente shows how strong, deep, on-the-ground reporting, informed by research and bolstered by the conscious development of key sources, can take a journalist past clichés, platitudes, and shallow suspicions and into the undiscovered core of demographic change. You'll learn how to interview people about racial and ethnic issues in a way that uncovers what Llorente calls the "phantom dialogue." You'll learn how to render those ideas in a way that is fair, compelling, and interesting to a wide spectrum of people.

Journalists will be challenged in this chapter to think about some enduring craft issues: handling the quotes and sound bites of people who do not speak English well; deciding how the race and ethnicity of the audience might influence the storytelling; how to describe people when race, ethnicity, and nationality are all capable of bringing the American melting pot to a fiery boil.

DIVERSE AND DIVIDED

One City, Two Communities

By Elizabeth Llorente
The Record Staff Writer
Published January 25, 2004

From his apartment in the predominantly black 4th Ward of Paterson, Bishop Brown sees an America that increasingly pushes him to the margins.

His neighborhood feels lost—in poverty, crime, in a sense of having been forgotten amid the great swath of boarded-up windows and vacant lots.

The feeling of displacement grows deeper in Brown's neighborhood as Hispanics—who edged past blacks last year to become the largest minority group in the nation—soar in number and influence.

For the first time, Paterson has a Hispanic mayor, one who beat the first black mayor in his reelection bid. Hispanics own most of the city's small businesses. They must be getting special breaks, many in the 4th Ward believe, breaks that are denied to blacks.

Across Martin Luther King Way, from Harry Alcazar's point of view, America is a vastly different place.

He sees opportunities waiting to be seized. After all, he says, he knew no English when he came from Colombia; but he went from doing odd jobs to graduating from college and, now, working for state government. He worked hard to get everything he got, he says. Alcazar is energized by a mayor named Jose "Joey" Torres. Blacks, he says, have had their chance.

Hispanics and African-Americans are lumped together under the term "minorities." They have a lot in common: great pride, strong spiritual beliefs, a history of discrimination, inferior schools, and limited access to health care. In Paterson, they live in adjoining neighborhoods.

But between them lies a deep divide.

The neighborhoods with the highest concentration of blacks lie mainly to the north of Martin Luther King Way. Those with the most Hispanics are mostly to the south. Blacks rarely venture into the predominantly Hispanic areas because, they say, shopkeepers in those areas tend to regard them with suspicion. Hispanics say they stay away from black neighborhoods out of fear.

The boulevard named for the slain civil-rights leader traverses two vastly different perceptions of America—one, the age-old immigrant belief in the Land of Opportunity, and the other, a gnawing doubt and cynicism, laced with the knowledge that their ancestors came here against their will. It defines a

Bergen County, NJ/Danielle P. Richards
City councilwoman Vera Ames-Garnes of the Fourth Ward sitting on her stoop, which she calls "my office." Whispering to her is Celine Mann, eleven, one of fours girls she cares for.

clash among two groups who start out together in tough Paterson neighbor-hoods, on the bottom rung of the American dream—one with hope for a bright future, and the other with the frustration of living some of the worst of America's struggle with race.

In this city, where the census shows 150,000 people packed into eight square miles, blacks and Hispanics can't help but come into contact in school, on buses, in downtown shops and city offices. Yet, like strangers on a congested New York City train, they remain worlds apart even when their paths overlap.

"For business purposes, we have dealings, no problem," says Carlos Garcia, one of the city's most prominent businessmen and community leaders. "But not after hours. We go on our own way."

Occasionally, the friction heats up.

In October, a race-related argument broke out in a City Council meeting when a Hispanic councilman proposed a candidate for constable and two of his African-American colleagues opposed him. During the meeting, two of the council members—one black, the other Hispanic—got up from their seats and exchanged shoves.

At John F. Kennedy High School, administrators say black and Hispanic students get into racially charged confrontations over such things as girl-friends and slurs every day.

These tensions echo problems that marred relations between earlier generations of immigrants and blacks, who saw waves of newcomers move up and enjoy the acceptance and better living conditions that eluded their race. But the consequences are more serious today than ever. Hispanics and blacks form one third of the American population. In Paterson, the two groups constitute an overwhelming majority.

As the population of Hispanics increases, often in cities that have been home to solid black communities, the tensions seen in Paterson are playing themselves out across the country. Blacks and Hispanics have clashed in Miami, Manhattan, and Southern California, as well as traditionally black areas in the South, where many new immigrants from Latin America are settling.

> The two-way avenue is filled with dilapidated buildings. Yet, few immigrants see the neighborhood as grim. Stacked against what they saw in their homelands—children begging in the streets for food and money, starving dogs roaming through neighborhoods, supermarket shelves nearly bare—21st Avenue is glorious.

Paterson, the birthplace of the Industrial Revolution, has long been a first stop for immigrants. Europeans came in droves to work in the city's textile mills. When blacks moved north after World War II, many settled in Paterson. In 1990, Hispanics surpassed blacks in Paterson to become the largest minority group. Today, the city reflects a current of change that is sweeping America and holds important lessons for race relations throughout the country.

"If blacks and Hispanics are at each other's throats, race relations in this country will only get more complicated; it'll get worse," says Ron Gross, a 71-year-old civil-rights activist and lifelong Paterson resident. "That will be bad for everyone."

Life on 21st Avenue

Twenty-First Avenue, a generation ago the domain of Italian business owners, is now unmistakably Hispanic.

The strip, which lies a mile south of Martin Luther King Way, crackles with entrepreneurship. Immigrants from Spanish-speaking countries as varied as Peru, Cuba, the Dominican Republic, Colombia, and Ecuador own and run real estate offices, travel agencies, money-wiring firms, pharmacies, beauty salons, bodegas, fast-food eateries, and white-tablecloth restaurants that play soft background boleros.

Awnings bear the colors of flags from the owners' homelands. Spanish is the main language.

The two-way avenue is filled with dilapidated buildings. Yet, few immigrants see the neighborhood as grim. Stacked against what they saw in their homelands —children begging in the streets for food and money, starving dogs roaming through neighborhoods, supermarket shelves nearly bare—21st Avenue is glorious.

Like the immigrants before them, Hispanics view 21st Avenue as the American dream in technicolor.

In his 12 years in the United States, Ricardo Diaz has worked in laundromats, factories, and newspaper delivery. And during that time the Peruvian immigrant has been stung by prejudice: A Clifton man hurled slurs at him one day when Diaz delivered his newspaper late. Some employers have demeaned him. His marriage has crumbled.

Now 48, Diaz is still struggling. Sitting in a Cuban restaurant on 21st Avenue, he says he works on his English when he gets time away from his 60-hour-per-week job at a laundry service firm. He hopes to take a course in medical radiology and earn enough to buy a small home.

"I've had setbacks, but I was not discouraged," he says. "It's gone well here. I'm still happy to be in this country."

Down the avenue, in Carlos Garcia's real-estate office, an 18-foot sign proclaims: "The most important tool for success is the belief that you can succeed. You never know what you can do until you try."

Many of the shopkeepers speak of coming to the United States with little money, and taking odd jobs in the early years. They cut lawns, waited tables, hoisted buckets of cement, baby-sat children who taught them simple words in English and introduced them to Babar and "The Itsy Bitsy Spider." They dreamed of owning the kinds of homes they scrubbed.

Puerto Ricans were the first Hispanics to settle in the Silk City, says Paterson business administrator Eli M. Burgos, whose parents came to the U.S. mainland in 1951. He remembers how lucky Puerto Ricans felt to land factory work, no matter what the working conditions.

Burgos, an energetic, diminutive man who speaks in staccato sentences, is part of a group of Puerto Ricans who grew up together. Many in the group, which included the future mayor, Joey Torres, dreamed of the day when Hispanics would be a force in the city.

Step by step, many of them rose up the political ladder.

"For a lot of people, the work here was better than 12 hours a day of cutting sugar cane in Puerto Rico, or working in pastures with cows and horses," Burgos says.

Some scraped together nearly all their savings and started businesses.

Census figures for Paterson show that Hispanic-owned businesses have soared. Between 1992 and 1997, the latest figures available, the number of Hispanic businesses rose from 893 to 1,222. In that same period, sales rose from $66 million to $128.3 million, and the annual payroll increased from $3.9 million to $26.3 million. City officials say that now most small businesses are Hispanic-owned.

"Latin Americans, and a lot of other immigrants, like Arabs, are very business-oriented," says Burgos, breaking into his easy smile. "If there's a little table, they'll set something up there and sell it."

Elsa Mantilla didn't have a little table. But she did have a shopping cart. Mantilla, who came to the United States from the Dominican Republic in 1972 with less than $100 in her pocket, sold perfume, costume jewelry, and lingerie door-to-door. Hers is the story of many immigrant shopkeepers who peddle their goods from the back of a van, the trunk of a car, or a basement apartment.

Years later, Mantilla opened a small store on 21st Avenue.

"I was a novelty," says Mantilla. "The only other Hispanic business around was a bodega owned by a Cuban. But I felt accepted by the Italians."

Today, Mantilla, who sports stylish, short-cut hair and fitted blazers, owns a busy boutique at a larger location on the same strip. Her husband, an Ecuadorean native, and three adult children work alongside her.

Mantilla, 49, and other Hispanic merchants say African-Americans rarely enter their businesses.

And when they do venture into an Hispanic-owned store, they are not warmly welcomed, she acknowledges.

"A lot of people say they watch blacks closely when they come into their stores," Mantilla says.

The suspicion toward blacks gnaws at Rafael Cuellar, a Cuban-American whose family operated a supermarket in Paterson for many years.

"It's silly and racist on our part," says Cuellar, 34, whose family now owns a supermarket in Passaic. "It's wrong, it's not giving people a chance. A lot of people who treat African-Americans that way never grew up with them. I grew up with them, I went to school with them. They're 20 percent of our customers, and they're some of our best customers."

Back in her shop, Mantilla is checking RSVP cards for a breakfast she has organized for the coming weekend. The ticket money, she explains, will be used for academic scholarships for Hispanic students.

"We have to do things for our community, no one else does it for us," Mantilla says.

Being Passed By

Hispanics are etching their imprint in Paterson well beyond their enclaves.

Most of those who live along MLK Way itself are black. But there are signs of Hispanic culture everywhere along the drag, which is also known as Broadway. A bright blue Barnert Hospital sidewalk directory reads "Bienvenido." Up a few streets, a huge billboard promoting an African-American dentist's practice proclaims: "Se Habla Español." Farther down the boulevard, near the heart of the 4th Ward, a supermarket window boasts "Fiesta Goya."

A few blocks away on Rosa Parks Boulevard, Carnie Bragg Jr. sits in the office of his funeral home, one of the oldest black businesses in Paterson. A portly man with a quick wit, Bragg lives over the funeral home, just like his father before him.

Drug dealers dawdle outside the squat building, even during the day, as kids with Disney-themed backpacks walk home from school. Despite that, the funeral director stays put.

"Life for the African-American community here hasn't changed much from when I was young," Bragg says. "We were poor then, and we're poor now."

Statistics from the Census Bureau bear him out. In Paterson, blacks have the highest poverty rate—26 percent. The Hispanic rate is 21 percent, with whites at 16 percent.

Bragg, an elegant dresser who exudes a corporate boardroom air, has seen other groups arrive in Paterson, create a middle-class life for themselves, then leave. "This whole neighborhood was Jewish when my family moved in," he says. "We were received fine, but they started moving out."

He sees Hispanics following in the footsteps of earlier ethnic groups while blacks remain behind.

He loves his community; speaking with pride about its rich history, its spirituality, and all that it has endured.

But he says: "Look, we can't blame things on immigrants. Immigrants do jobs blacks won't do. It's not just Hispanics. You have a lot of West Indies immigrants who work very hard; they have two and three jobs. I get [American-born blacks] coming to me who have no skills and they want a job that pays $15 an hour."

One block north of Bragg, Vera Ames-Garnes, the longtime city councilwoman representing the 4th Ward, holds court on her cramped porch, which she only half-jokingly calls "my office."

Bergen County, NJ/Danielle P. Richards
Elsa Mantilla, left, sharing a laugh with customer Ana Rodriguez in her shop on 21st Avenue in Paterson, New Jersey. Both women are from the Dominican Republic.

She is more den mother than politician. She wears her gray-flecked black shoulder-length hair in braids. She says "ain't" and tells it like it is. On this day, she sports a T-shirt that says: "The Only Time You Look Down On A Sister Is When You're Helping Her Up."

From the porch, Ames, who is 56, sees the best and the worst of inner-city black life. She knows the people here won't go to City Hall. So they go to "Miss Vera." They tell her when something goes wrong in their life. And they tell her when something goes right.

A young man drives by in a pickup truck, honks, and shouts: "Hi Miss Vera."

Like most of the people who pass by Ames' modest, multilevel home, the young man has a remarkable life story that the councilwoman knows in fine detail.

As usual, it involves something terribly sad.

"He was in jail, for drugs," Ames says. "But he's got a job now. He's clean."

He is a reminder that there is hope.

Bergen County, NJ/Danielle P. Richards

Harry Alcazar, 30, a Columbian immigrant, sees Paterson as an opportunity to be seized. "This is a Hispanic city," he says. "Hispanics rule."

A young woman passes by along the vacant lot across the street. She tells Ames she wants work. Does she know of a job? Ames says Kmart and the new Ikea are hiring.

"But I've got a record," the woman shouts.

She is a reminder of the struggles.

Ames looks toward the corner where her street meets Rosa Parks Boulevard, and finds more reminders of the struggles. She can see part of the blocks-long row of businesses there. At one time, the businesses were owned mostly by blacks, she says. A black grocery store is a bodega now, a black laundromat is Hispanic-owned, a black restaurant became a Hispanic-owned poultry place.

The black merchants closed their shops, either to retire to the South, where many of Paterson's black families hail from, or to end the stress of having to cope with the drug dealers who scared their customers away.

Census figures show an increase in the number of black-owned businesses between 1992 and 1997. But the data include all blacks, including black immigrants, who have been moving into New Jersey in large numbers. At the same time, though, payroll for black businesses in Paterson declined 42 percent for black firms, while it skyrocketed by 575 percent for Hispanic ones.

Ames and other Paterson residents say they don't need government data. They see what's happened to black businesses with their own eyes.

"This is our main economic thoroughfare," Ames says of the strip along Rosa Parks, where drug dealing still is a problem.

"Three of the businesses are black, two are Muslim, and seven are Hispanic. Some people say they're afraid of us, but they're not afraid of us economically, are they?" Ames says. "Everybody makes money off the black community, except the black community."

Struggle for City Hall

Until two decades ago, African-Americans were the city's largest minority group, and many Latinos voted for them.

"We knew we couldn't get elected, so we supported black candidates because they were the ones most likely to address our issues," Burgos says.

The fledgling alliance unsettled some white political stalwarts, who tried to drive a wedge between the two groups, both camps agree.

"They went to the Hispanics and told them that blacks were trying to stop us from progressing," says Idida Rodriguez, a consultant who worked on Torres' campaign. "And they went to blacks and told them Hispanics wanted to take over the city."

Still, blacks reached important milestones, winning seats on the City Council, and appointments to boards and commissions.

For Latinos, the political world was tougher to crack. Latino leaders, including some in power now, say that when they sought help from blacks, more often than not, it did not come.

In 1997, "after we waited so, so long," as resident Ron Gross puts it, Paterson elected its first black mayor. The man who'd ripped through the barrier was Marty Barnes, who struck many as bright, charming, destined for great things—perhaps national office.

But the historic tenure lasted only one term, and ended in disgrace.

Barnes pleaded guilty to accepting bribes from companies doing business with the city. He was sentenced last year to 37 months in a federal prison.

At the same time, the Hispanic population continued to grow, in numbers and influence. Through an unabating wave of immigration and high birth rates, they became the largest minority group and, eventually, the majority. They elected Torres mayor.

Harry Alcazar, the Colombian immigrant, was thrilled.

"This is a Hispanic city," says Alcazar, who is 30. "Hispanics rule."

Many blacks speak highly of Torres. Still, they say, it's painful to see the first black mayor end up in prison.

Bishop Brown, the 4th Ward resident, once felt the same sort of pride as Harry Alcazar. When African-Americans had a majority on the City Council and a black man in the wood-paneled office of the mayor, he felt like "I just got my space," he says.

Now, Brown, 29, says, "I feel my space is being invaded."

"Their resentment is a matter of people who've suffered as much as they have, when they get something, they're going to fight to keep it," says Jose Morales, a longtime Paterson resident and pro-Latino activist.

"But they fall into the same trap of most people who take power, they don't want to share it," he says. "The oppressed becomes an oppressor. When Hispanics say 'minority,' they mean Hispanics, blacks, Asians, everybody. But when blacks say 'minority,' we learned that they really mean blacks, and only blacks."

The tensions extend to the city leaders. One of the most public expressions of the friction was the October scuffle between council members Juan Torres, who is Hispanic, and Anthony Davis, who is black.

> "The oppressed becomes an oppressor. When Hispanics say 'minority,' they mean Hispanics, blacks, Asians, everybody. But when blacks say 'minority,' we learned that they really mean blacks, and only blacks."
>
> —José Morales

Ames, who sided with Davis, says with exasperation that Juan Torres can be divisive.

Torres says he is sensitive to African-American issues as well as Hispanic ones, but that's more than he can say for some blacks on the council.

"Blacks have five votes on the council. They're the majority," he said. "We should work together. Blacks and Hispanics have common problems and common needs. But they [blacks] try to pass whatever ordinance or resolution is in their favor."

Bias Runs Both Ways

The tension between blacks and Hispanics stays beneath the surface, lurking in the everyday side glance, in the extra degrees of body space between people who look different, in the eyes that see an illegal alien in every Hispanic and a mugger in every passing black male.

Sometimes, the friction rears its head. When it does, it shocks.

Marilee Jackson recalls a time when she overheard the owner of a bodega tell a visitor from Africa that he liked foreign-born blacks, but not American-born ones.

"I was surprised, and I was angry," says Jackson, a lifelong city resident and director of Paterson's Department of Community Development. "I was going to buy something, but then I made a conscious decision not to exchange money with the store's owner."

Jackson, a gregarious woman with curly, close-cropped hair who stands 6-foot-1 and loves large hoop earrings, says she could have tried to explain to the bodega owner that blacks and Hispanics share a great deal in common—slavery and being colonized, for starters.

"Hispanics were dropped to cut canes, and we were dropped to pick cotton," she says, "that's all. We're alike in many ways. But I thought 'What's the point?'"

Bergen County, NJ/Danielle P. Richards

"Blacks are kept down in this country," says Cleashon Poindexter, eighteen, who uses the rap name "Trigga."

Assimilation by Hispanics, many blacks say, seems to mean adopting the larger society's prejudices against them.

"People buy into the racism here," says Jackson, who gives her age as "more than 50." "You have ethnic groups that think they can assimilate with white Americans, and so we allow ourselves to be separated because of race."

The accusations of discrimination, though, go both ways.

Gus Penarando, a community leader, saw a group of black youths vandalize a park sign this summer that bore the name of Mayor Torres.

"I was so angry, very angry," Penarando says. "There wasn't really anything I could do. I watched them, and I thought 'Why, what is the point of all that?'"

"They pointed to the sign, to the name," Penarando, 34, says. "They hit it, they kicked it. I found it discarded about a block down. That sign used to say Mayor Marty Barnes, and it was never touched."

A few weeks ago, Elsa Mantilla says, an encounter in her shop with an African-American woman who was searching for a wedding gown ended in a heated exchange.

As Mantilla and the bride-to-be finished what Mantilla described as a pleasant conversation, the woman who accompanied her warned the friend not to believe that the dress would be ready on time.

"She said to the other woman, right in front of me, 'You can't believe those Hispanics.' I let her know I didn't care for it," Mantilla says.

Those who bridge the divide sometimes find themselves in a rough spot.

Alicia Williams, 18, says her mother strongly disliked Puerto Ricans. But that didn't stop her from falling in love with Justin Rosado, 19.

"I probably would have felt like my mother about Hispanics if I hadn't met Justin and gotten to know Hispanics," says Williams, who is black.

She became pregnant toward the end of 2002.

"I really heard about it from my mother," Williams says. "She said 'Why do you have a baby with that Puerto Rican?' She thinks they're lower than us."

Her mother and Justin's disowned them. They were forced to sleep in his car.

All the hostility toward their relationship brought them closer together.

"I like to think that there are other people who think like Alicia and I do about race, which is: It doesn't matter," says Rosado, wearing a shirt with "No Justice" written on it. "And then there are other people who try to feel superior to another group so they're not in the lowest spot. But really, we're all just struggling in life."

> Extended families living under one roof are common. If only one parent lives at home, or both parents are away working long hours, often a grandmother or other relative comes from overseas to supervise the young.

While some young people are forging cross-racial bonds, others are perpetuating the friction.

In the city high schools, racial and ethnic groups have claimed certain corridors and cafeteria tables as their turf. Fights break out over racial and ethnic slurs.

"We've had a lot of conflicts," says Zaida Padilla, the school district's ombudswoman. "But the students are reflecting the friction that exists in the community."

Struggles at Home

Look at their faces. World-weary. Lost in thought.

Look at their eyes. Sometimes defiant. Often dispirited.

Most young blacks in Paterson are growing up in broken homes: only a third of the black families with children are headed by married couples, according to the 2000 census. Single women head 58 percent and single men head another 9 percent.

The young pastor of St. Luke Baptist Church, the Rev. Kenneth D. R. Clayton, a lanky bespectacled man, has taken the role of father of several children in his church who come from troubled homes. He attends their parent-teacher conferences, goes to their recitals, and makes sure they keep up with their school work. One of his prized possessions, which he has framed and displayed in his office, is a letter from six siblings thanking him for caring.

"Before, in the Forties and Fifties, when we faced blatant racism, we still thought that we could overcome," Clayton says. "The difference was that in those times, we had a strong family structure, parents at home to instill love of yourself. The breakdown of the family has been one of our problems."

Gangs and drug dealers fill the void, he says. "They become the surrogate family."

Two married parents head 58 percent of Hispanic families with children in Paterson, while 32 percent live with a single mother, and almost 11 percent with a single father.

Make no mistake: Hispanic kids are also falling prey to drug dealing and gangs.

But there are safety nets. Extended families living under one roof are common. If only one parent lives at home, or both parents are away working long hours, often a grandmother or other relative comes from overseas to supervise the young.

The immigrant enclaves hold out a strong sense of possibilities. Here is an immigrant-owned business that is flourishing. There is a poor villager from Latin America who now is earning enough to drive a sturdy car and send money back to his homeland.

Blacks who grow up with a parent at home often find themselves going it alone.

"So many [black] young people have mothers and fathers on drugs," Ames says. "The kids have to handle the problems and be the mother and the father of the family."

Bergen County, NJ/Danielle P. Richards

The Reverend Kenneth Clayton recognizes achievement of his young congregants during church service in Paterson.

Carrying the weight of such burdens, some, like Dina Earl, have remarkable gumption.

The single mother, 37, walks purposefully toward the multifamily house where she lives across the street from Ames. Her almond-shaped brown eyes burn with hope, even as she stands in front of the door, tired and harried.

> Some blacks, including several prominent national leaders, are convinced that AIDS, drug epidemics, and long prison sentences for minor offenses are part of a government conspiracy to eliminate them.

Her mother is battling a drug addiction. Her father, who is deceased, also was hooked on drugs.

She is determined to give her three children the kind of home life she craved. But the path often twists and dead-ends; it's so exhausting, sometimes, to keep hope alive.

No matter how many times she has walked up the front steps and crossed the narrow porch to the door of the home, her insides twist in disgust.

The uneven wooden floors of the porch groan and creak. The worn siding is cracked, the dirty white paint is peeling. The ceiling bulges downward, looking as if a collapse is imminent.

Earl wakes up at the crack of dawn to collect the mice in the traps around her apartment before the children wake up.

"I don't want the children to see that," Earl says. "Just because we're poor doesn't mean we should live like this."

A single mother, Earl is determined to find a better life. She is taking classes at Passaic County Community College ("I'm getting great grades") and hopes to someday attend Montclair State University.

"Sometimes, I go into the bathroom, shut the door so the kids don't see me, and I just cry," Earl says. "But then I say no, I can't give up, I've got to do better so my kids don't have to live like this."

She is conflicted about Hispanics.

On one hand, she finds common ground with them when, for instance, she and Hispanic single mothers share stories of hardship while waiting for the wash at the local laundromat. On the other hand, she says she has been denied work in the city because she is not Hispanic.

"They say they want someone who is bilingual," Earl says. "We know what that means. It means Hispanic. There are lot of opportunities for them to learn English, but not for people like me to learn Spanish."

Malik Myles, 18, was an orphan by the time he was 10. His father died when he was very young. His mother, who he says was a crack addict, died in 1995. His grandmother raised him.

In a barely audible voice, Myles speaks matter-of-factly about his difficult home life. There were times he'd be so distressed by his mother, he says, that he'd refuse to open the apartment door for her.

He ended up like so many—selling drugs, and landing in jail about a half dozen times.

"I was impatient, I wanted money," he says. "I couldn't wait for a check from a regular job. You can make $1,000 a day selling drugs. If you get busted, you have enough lawyer money."

He finished his last jail sentence in March.

He has five siblings—three are locked up on drug-related charges, Myles said.

"I don't feel shocked that they're in jail," he says evenly.

Myles dreams of being a big-time rapper. Many young men in his neighborhood hang their hopes for a better life on becoming rap stars.

A lot of his friends feel threatened by the growing influence of Hispanics. But he doesn't.

"Too many of us blacks put ourselves down," he says. "No one takes your opportunity away. If they take an opportunity, and you didn't, it wasn't yours, it belongs to them."

Feeling Victimized

To lift spirits, especially of the young, Paterson's black leaders often invoke the mention of the teachers, ministers, union leaders, and physicians who have emerged from their community, usually against staggering odds.

Some became legends, such as Norman Therkield Cotton, who grew up in poverty in North Carolina in the late 1800s and became a doctor known for his kindness to the indigent. Or George Jiggett, a Virginia native who started a transportation business out of his home that expanded from one taxi to an entire fleet. Or Larry Doby, who was the first African-American to play American League baseball, and the second to play major league ball.

Paterson is also home to any number of successful blacks—people who have managed to navigate a route beyond the city's intractable problems.

The examples of triumph inspire some. But they fail to stir other blacks—including young men, pastors, community leaders—who feel life in this country is designed to keep them down.

The legacy of slavery and decades of institutionalized racism, they say, continue to have an impact. It is why, they believe, they languish while other groups move on.

They note that slave labor helped build the country and enrich the government and corporations, while denying blacks compensation for their work.

The disparity in wealth and quality of life between blacks and whites, they say, was perpetuated by government policies long after slaves were freed. They say legalized racism such as Jim Crow laws, which allowed segregation between blacks and whites, laid the groundwork for other discriminatory legislation that erased gains by blacks.

Some blacks, including several prominent national leaders, are convinced that AIDS, drug epidemics, and long prison sentences for minor offenses are part of a government conspiracy to eliminate them. Such theories, long dismissed by authorities, have nevertheless circulated in black communities for years.

"Some things, like AIDS, were meant to wipe out blacks, but they got out of hand, I think," Kevin Thomas says during a break from rehearsals for Kid Fella, a play he wrote, produced, and directed for a youth theater group.

Cleashon Poindexter, the lead in Thomas' play, purses his lips as he listens to Thomas speak. They are sitting in a circle at the Hispanic Multi-purpose Youth Drop-in Center, which has lent them space for their rehearsals.

"Blacks are kept down in this country," Poindexter, 18, says. "You go for jobs and you don't get hired, no matter how qualified you are."

Marcia Hinds, 16, decides she can't sit by idly for another second.

"Don't blame immigrants, blame the employers," Hinds, who is black, snaps at Poindexter as their eyes lock. "Why aren't you doing something to change it? Go to school, get educated. I'm so tired of people saying, 'It's because I'm black.'"

Perhaps, Poindexter tells Hinds, she doesn't understand how blacks like him feel because her skin is lighter than his.

"Sit in the sun all summer and turn darker, and just see how you're treated."

"The other day, a white kid called me a [slur] when I was walking down the street. I wanted to kick him," Poindexter says. "You get tired, so we have to take care of things our way, the street way. Police bother me and my friends because they're racists. All those things make me feel [bad] about this country."

Thomas nods: "Blacks are always at the bottom."

And that view generates resentment of Hispanics.

"They should leave the United States, all of them," Poindexter says.

Susan McKay, 23 who plays keyboard in Kid Fella, says: "I don't want to sound racist, but we need to take care of the people already here before we take more people in."

Hours later, a Peruvian dance group uses the same room.

"This is a beautiful country," says Lucy Figueroa, the mother of one of the children in the group.

They find it hard to understand how native-born Americans—whatever their race—cannot succeed if immigrants can.

"We immigrants are not given things in this country," Figueroa says as others nod in agreement. "I did housekeeping and baby-sitting and studied English. My husband worked as a gardener from 7 a.m. until 6 p.m., then he went to school to learn about home repair at a school in Wayne."

The owners of the homes she cleaned in affluent suburbs in Bergen County told her she could make her dreams come true in America. She clung to their words, replaying them in her head.

"A woman from Emerson told me to work toward my goal, no matter how long it takes. Now I'm a nurse's assistant, and I'd love to go to college to keep learning."

> Racial and ethnic misunderstandings are further deepened, Thomas says, by newer communities who were not witness to the civil-rights struggles.

"Blacks blame racism," says Mary Mendoza, another Hispanic mother. "We ourselves can get immersed in racism and being the victim if we let it happen. We can foment racism if we're convinced we'll never be accepted. This idea of race as a barrier is something we create in our heads."

"How Dare You?"

Thomas, like many blacks, fumes over such assertions.

Racial and ethnic misunderstandings are further deepened, Thomas says, by newer communities who were not witness to the civil-rights struggles.

Kelly Moss recounts the time a woman of both Hispanic and West Indian descent asked her why blacks "allowed" themselves to be slaves.

"I think Latinos care," says Moss, who is black and works as a part-time receptionist at the Hispanic Multi-purpose Youth Drop-In Center. "I think they just don't understand our history."

But down the hall from the reception area where Moss works, Thomas is less forgiving.

"It's frustrating to have immigrants look down on us, too," he says. "You feel like 'How dare you?'"

Across MLK Way, in the 1st Ward, Ron Gross says: "People tell blacks to pull themselves up by the bootstraps, but we don't have any boots."

Other blacks, however, say that their community must get more aggressive about improving their lot, and focus less on obstacles—real or imagined—put in their path.

The Rev. Michael McDuffie, who heads a ministry of 50 members, says blacks must recognize that they have many more choices in their lives than they have been willing to acknowledge.

"Some blacks say, 'I sell drugs because the white man don't give me jobs,'" McDuffie says. "No, you're selling drugs to that black man because of greed. The white man isn't making you do it."

During summers, McDuffie and a group of volunteers take to the most troubled areas of Paterson and, through catchy prayer songs and dance, try to reach out to drug dealers, prostitutes, and gang members. Many respond, often in tears, as they fall into McDuffie's arms and join in prayer.

Pastors have seen children who struggled academically begin to earn A's after they have held annual ceremonies that recognize such students before the congregation.

From the outset, blacks say, immigrants and blacks start from different places.

"People who save and save to come to America have one ambition, to come for a better life," Marilee Jackson says. "That person will do whatever it takes to get that better life. They'll make sacrifices to get that American dream. They'll take hard jobs, they'll live together with other relatives, older relatives will help out in taking care of children so that other relatives can work. Then they make enough money to buy a house."

Touching on a divisive issue among blacks, Jackson says: "I think African-Americans take things for granted. We think we are entitled because we helped build this country. And to a certain extent, we are entitled, but America doesn't see it that way. We don't take advantage of education. Many of us are still thinking we deserve 40 acres and a mule."

Friction on Parade

A flashpoint of contention between blacks and Hispanics in Paterson is, ironically, an event that normally conjures up images of cheer: the parade.

In this city, the parade has become the most prominent display of the huge Hispanic presence. It is a raucous, spectacular showcase of pride, momentum, and revelry that is repeated many times over each year as Paterson's numerous Latin American and Caribbean immigrants celebrate their national roots, and pay homage to their patron saints.

It is the kind of big-time show of cultural pride that does not take place in the black neighborhoods to the north of MLK Way.

Each parade event draws—easily—tens of thousands of spectators.

On a sun-kissed late summer Sunday, the sidewalks of Market Street are jammed for blocks with people who have turned out for the annual Dominican parade.

For about two hours, the crowd cheers as the floats glide by, some with bands playing the pulsating beat of Dominican music, some with beauty queens, and a few representing other Spanish-speaking nations in a show of solidarity with one of the city's fastest growing Hispanic groups.

> "We don't understand that people bring their cultures with them. What most other cultures have that we don't is that celebration of their history and ethnicity."
>
> —Marilee Jackson

Emcee Raffy Medina Garcia looks out from the makeshift stage in front of City Hall and smiles. The display of Dominican pride—reflected in the posters that say "Viva La Republica Dominicana" and the thousands of Dominican flags—flows down Market Street as far as the eye can see.

He tells the crowd that Dominicans are becoming a force in town. He cites the Dominican domination of the bodega businesses in Paterson, and their ballooning presence in the schools.

"We are pervading all areas of Paterson," he says to cheers.

Kelly Moss remembers watching the Puerto Rican Day Parade as a child.

It was like nothing she'd ever seen in her community.

Men played bongo drums, moving their hands so fast they seemed a blur. Women shook the maracas. They all seemed to feel so lucky to be Puerto Rican.

"I'd love to see the blacks have an African-American parade with floats," Moss says. "We should have that. I'd love to wave a flag."

But some blacks complain about the parades.

Several years ago, some residents from the 1st Ward, another predominantly black area, asked the city to deny a permit for the Puerto Rican Day Parade, contending that the event, which took place in their section, was too disruptive.

Puerto Ricans denounced the move as racist.

"Slavery worked to the degree that we lost our culture," says Marilee Jackson. "We don't understand that people bring their cultures with them. What most other cultures have that we don't is that celebration of their history and ethnicity.

"But I still couldn't believe that we tried to rain on someone's parade."

Copyright © 2004 North Jersey Media Group Inc.

Read the rest of the *Diverse and Divided* series on *www.theauthenticvoice.org*

A TALE OF TWO CULTURES

Palisades Park Grapples with Change

By Elizabeth Llorente
The Record Staff Writer
Published August 23, 1998

Susan and Roger Brauer fell for each other watching "Anne of the Thousand Days" at the Park Lane Theater. Colleen Blackmore never missed the rock bands that played in the National Bank parking lot.

Whether they were buying a London broil at Introna's, the latest fashions at Warjac's, or a ham and mozzarella calzone at Palisades Pizza, they always ran into friends.

Broad Avenue was more than Palisades Park's main drag. For generations of borough residents, it was a way of life. It's where they learned of births and deaths, comings and goings.

But in the 1980s, the recession and competition from malls forced many of those shops to close. The Park Lane Theater, so popular that it drew crowds from out of town, also saw its last hurrah. It was boarded up in 1986, a hulking shell scarred with graffiti and rimmed by empty beer bottles.

Then came immigrants from Korea, who looked at the struggling avenue and saw a path to the American dream.

Suddenly, Keum Ho Restaurant thrived where Gino's eatery once stood. Korean businesses moved into spots that once housed Introna's, the Gascony bowling shop, and Palisades Pizza. The number of Korean shops soared, from a handful in the late 1980s, to 95 percent of the 200-store commercial district today. Even the old Park Lane is a mini-mall of Asian shops.

Now, it's the Korean newcomers who are making memories on Broad Avenue—running into friends while buying kimchi or miso paste, and catching up on each other's lives and the latest news from Seoul.

"This is like Korea," says Jeong Kim, a borough resident for 10 years and co-owner of Keum Ho, Palisades Park's first Korean restaurant. "Broad Avenue is Korean."

And that's not sitting well with some old-time borough residents. Broad Avenue—once an outdoor "Cheers" for natives of Palisades Park—has become a symbol of a deep-rooted tension. The tension, heightened by a conflict between Korean merchants and town officials that has reached Superior Court, extends beyond the main street and into schools and everyday life.

Longtime residents acknowledge that Koreans recharged the dying local economy. But they say Koreans are balkanizing their one-square-mile town of 15,000 into factions that can neither relate to nor communicate with each other.

"I feel like a stranger in my own town," says Brauer, president of the Palisades Park Homeowners Association. "I work in Manhattan. I want to come home to a grassy town with families on the front porch. Now it's people who don't want to adjust to our culture."

Courtesy of ABC News, Nightline
Rodeo Plaza illustrates the changing look of the shops.

As the borough grapples with its transformation, the situation illustrates a familiar, oft-repeated, and uniquely American challenge: how to absorb the immigrant groups that account for 60 percent of U.S. population growth.

Koreans at first downplayed the criticism as a natural ambivalence about immigrants and thought it would soon pass. Now they are growing exasperated.

Many blame the divisions on cultural misunderstandings, and ignorance about the hardships of starting anew in a foreign country. Most concede that their community is insular, but they say that earlier waves of immigrants were that way, too. The huge tasks of building new lives and raising families, many say, leave little time for mastering a language and culture that bear little resemblance to theirs. Others see racism, and even envy over a well-educated immigrant group prospering in a largely working-class town.

"We've hit rock bottom," says Jason Kim, long one of the borough's most optimistic voices about bringing together Koreans and non-Koreans. "This country sells the American dream around the world. Immigrants listen and come here to cultivate it. Then they are blamed for not paying attention to other things. Koreans don't understand this."

The foreign-born population in New Jersey, as well as nationwide, is reaching levels not seen since the turn of the century. In New Jersey, 15.4 percent of residents are foreign-born—fourth behind California, New York, and Florida. Latin America and Asia are the primary sources of newcomers to New Jersey—the nation's most diverse state—and the rest of the country.

Other North Jersey towns have received new immigrants—particularly Asians, the fastest-growing group—with some ambivalence. But seldom have the cultural clashes become as deep and enduring as in Palisades Park. For in this tiny, quite ordinary town, immigration came quickly and dramatically—from Asia, South America, even the tribal jungles of Guatemala.

In the span of a 10-hour plane ride, the Koreans catapulted from a military dictatorship to a democracy. When they arrived, they put away degrees in law, medicine, and engineering to peddle kimchi, bean curd, and manicures. They left a culture that stressed conformity for one that trumpets individualism. They traded a nation whose shopkeepers are expected to be reserved, Koreans say, for one that expects them to offer friendly chit-chat.

Of all Palisades Park's newest settlers, Koreans arrived in the largest numbers and in the biggest way.

They form the largest contingent in an Asian population that comprises 30 percent of the town's population and nearly 40 percent of the school district. They immediately made their mark on Broad Avenue, the town's heart. And they occupied the highest rungs of the economic ladder.

All these changes—less jolting in more transient or affluent towns, such as Fort Lee and Closter—occurred in less than 10 years.

"It's weird," says former Mayor Susan McGinley Spohn, an advertising executive and lifelong resident. "This isn't a city. It's just a small borough. And yet the country's main immigration and English-only issues have come to our doorstep. It was almost too much for a part-time mayor, and certainly a town as small as Palisades Park, to handle—local, national, and international issues."

To be sure, there are islands of hope. Many residents have had positive encounters—sometimes even formed friendships—across the cultural divide. It happens while Koreans and non-Koreans are watering their lawns and exchanging smiles. Or when their children—who, adults note, always seem to surmount linguistic and cultural barriers—bring sets of parents together.

"It shows it's possible," Brauer says.

Population projections for 2050 show America as nearly half white non-Hispanic, 26 percent Hispanic, 14 percent black, and 8 percent Asian. In New Jersey, such demographic changes will likely occur sooner.

> "They don't carry American sizes. They don't have anyone who can speak English. Sometimes they're abrupt. The message you get is they don't want Americans in their store."
>
> —Colleen Blackmore

Palisades Park's struggle to make a community out of groups divided by language and culture underscores a call by President Clinton and other leaders for a commitment to the integration of immigrants. Unless communities help immigrants assimilate—and immigrants make stronger efforts to learn English and understand American culture—ethnic divisions could escalate as diversity increases, the bipartisan U.S. Commission on Immigration Reform warned.

"It is literally a matter of who we are as a nation and who we become as a people," wrote Barbara Jordan, who headed the advisory immigration commission before her death in 1996. "E Pluribus Unum. Out of many one. One people. The American people."

Day to day in Palisades Park, the split between Koreans and other residents expresses itself quietly, almost matter-of-factly. Mayor Sandy Farber calls it "a cordial strain."

Korean shoppers abound on Broad Avenue, which is alive with the aromas of Asian cuisine and neon Korean lettering on store windows.

In other parts of New Jersey, Korean merchants have picked up some English to conduct business. On Latino Bergenline Avenue, just a few miles away in Hudson County, Korean merchants say "Hola" and quote prices in Spanish.

But none of that has been necessary in Palisades Park, where a large Korean customer base has kept cash registers ringing.

"I reach out to people who aren't Korean in my other restaurant, like putting more variety in the menu," says Jeong Kim, referring to the second Keum Ho restaurant she opened in Edison. There, non-Koreans seem more interested in patronizing her restaurant than in Palisades Park, she says. "In Palisades Park, my customers are [mostly] Korean."

Broad Avenue is the fulcrum of something larger: a parallel universe that re-creates American traditions in Korean style. Koreans call it

Courtesy of ABC News, Nightline
Sushi takeout begins bright and early.

"Koreatown." It boasts child-care centers, churches, sports games, a Korean class mother for every non-Korean one, and a parent-school group set up by and for Koreans.

But the borough's fastest-growing group is all but invisible in most townwide activities. Faces at meetings of the Homeowners Association, the PTA, and Borough Council tend to be uniformly white.

Farber says he has promised to enunciate slowly or provide interpreters at council meetings if the Koreans would only attend. The Koreans' insularity has been an issue with Farber as far back as 1991. That was when, as the borough's Little League coach, he unsuccessfully invited Koreans who had their children in Korean leagues to consider the town's team.

"This is their town, too," says Farber, whose 1996 mayoral campaign promised a more harmonious Palisades Park. "They live here. They buy expensive homes here. With as many Koreans as there are in Palisades Park, there should be at least two or three at any town meeting. I say to them, 'Come see how this town, this country, works.' But they don't participate."

Koreans say cultural barriers, overlaid with the everyday demands of work and raising families, keep many immigrants from community involvement. "There's nothing insidious about it," says Jason Kim. "If people insist on seeing it as insidious, it'll just widen the divisions."

In turn, many non-Koreans avoid Broad Avenue.

The main thoroughfare, they say, has transformed from their memory-filled main street to a place that is culturally and linguistically forbidding.

> "Some people might say I'm a racist. I'm not. I don't want to see Korean lettering all over our downtown. I don't understand Korean. What's wrong with our PTA, our sports teams? It seems to me they don't give a damn about this town, about Americans, about this country."
>
> —Colleen Blackmore

"When I was a teenager, I'd gather with other kids behind a bank parking lot," recalls Colleen Blackmore, 40, an office worker who has lived in the borough all her life. "Bands would play in the parking lot. We'd have the best time."

Now she feels out of place. "I've tried," she says. "They don't carry American sizes. They don't have anyone who can speak English. Sometimes they're abrupt. The message you get is they don't want Americans in their store."

Farber has taken unusually assertive steps to, in his words, "make Americans feel comfortable" in the heart of town. His administration requested businesses to post signs and take out local newspaper ads showing Korean and American flags with the message: "We welcome all customers."

Korean merchants say they are not snubbing others. Many merchants and their employees know little or no English, they explain, and dread coming face-to-face with people who speak it. Carpet store owner Charles Park recalled the day an American customer complained to him that employees of another Korean shop wouldn't open the door to let her in.

"Apparently, they were afraid of not speaking English right, of putting themselves in an embarrassing, shameful situation if they say the wrong words to an American," says Park, 58. "So they didn't open the door."

In sidewalk chats, council meetings, and letters to the editor, native residents are calling on Koreans to be less isolated. In increasingly bitter tones, they say they want Koreans to learn English and adopt American customs.

"As an American, I consider it obnoxious," Blackmore says. "Some people might say I'm a racist. I'm not. I don't want to see Korean lettering all over our downtown. I don't understand Korean. What's wrong with our PTA, our sports teams? It seems to me they don't give a damn about this town, about Americans, about this country."

Koreans have made overtures, using acts of friendly persuasion to turn around the negativity. They have donated thousands of dollars to the public library, set up academic scholarships, risen early on Saturdays to pick up trash on Broad Avenue, planted trees in the business district. They have serenaded the mayor with the Star-Spangled Banner at virtually all their functions, including their annual church-sponsored Christmas party and Chamber of Commerce gatherings.

Farber calls it "gratifying." He says it moves him to hear immigrants sing the national anthem. Still, he says, it's not enough. "I'd trade the money they give and all the symbolic gestures for something functional."

For the second year in a row, the mostly Korean borough Chamber of Commerce last month held a picnic for the town. Titled "Harmony for Palisades Park," it was instead a bittersweet event. Koreans and non-Koreans sat largely separated. The mayor and several invited residents' groups boycotted it.

Says Changwon Lee, the chamber's president, "It's ridiculous. The mayor said he would attend, and we announced it. For that day, we should have put our problems to one side, for the town and for unity."

Farber says he refused to go once he learned that he had been maligned as "anti-Korean," among other things, at a Chamber of Commerce meeting.

"I can't just go and stand next to people who say horrible things about me," he says, "and pretend it didn't happen."

Over the years, the resentment has led to worrisome incidents.

Shortly after Koreans began to establish a presence on Broad Avenue in the late 1980s, some of their store windows were broken or pelted with eggs.

More recently, a resident scratched two 10-inch-long gashes into a contractor's pickup truck because, police said she told them, she didn't like Asians and wanted "to teach them a lesson for parking in front of her house." The truck, it turned out, was not owned by an Asian.

Courtesy of ABC News, Nightline
Korean businessmen at a Palisades Park Chamber of Commerce meeting.

What has hardened the division between Koreans and non-Koreans is the nasty, lingering fight between Korean merchants and the two most recent borough administrations. Citing quality of life, Spohn and Farber enforced ordinances that hit Koreans the hardest—addressing everything from building codes to parking meter hours to demands that signs be translated into English.

One of the most controversial ordinances requires five all-night Korean restaurants—including Keum Ho—to close at 3 a.m. Merchants have sued, alleging discrimination and saying their customers work long days and can patronize their businesses only very late. The case is pending in Superior Court and is likely to go to trial in January.

Particularly disturbing to Koreans—even the sizable number of those who don't support all-night hours—was the town's allowing the only "American-style" diner to operate 24 hours a day.

Michael Kimm, a Hackensack attorney who has represented Koreans in lawsuits against the ordinances, says the enforcement is anti-Korean: "It's divisive politics to harden residents against Koreans. Koreans are politically expedient. A lot aren't citizens and can't vote. But Koreans invested a lot of money in Palisades Park. They took a desolate, dying downtown and revitalized it. It's as much their town as it is everyone else's."

Borough officials deny discrimination. They say they want to protect residents from noise and disorderly conduct blamed on drinking at the karaoke clubs and, to a lesser extent, all-night restaurants. "We've had numerous complaints about people who leave these places being rowdy," Farber said.

Tensions even have gripped the high school, which is just 37 percent white, and where administrators express concern about self-imposed segregation among students. At a spring panel on race relations, Korean and white students repeatedly snapped at each other. When the moderator asked the panelists for their vision of the future of race relations in town, all the students responded with pessimism.

Jee Ae Yook, 18, who served on the high school panel, lamented in an interview that the town could not enjoy its diversity. She feels estranged from whites, and pressured by her Korean friends not to mix. So she has put off hopes of experiencing ethnic harmony until college. "I like the different races, I want to be with them," says Yook, who came from Korea six years ago. "But there's hardly mixing in the school."

Palisades Park's Koreans uprooted themselves, traversing multiple time zones and thousands of miles. For the immigrants, the change was staggering.

"Coming to America is much bigger culture shock for Asians than for many other immigrants," says Jason Kim, the borough's first Korean-American school board member. "Latin Americans at least come from the same hemisphere."

Kim and other bicultural Koreans call themselves the "1.5 generation"—they were born in Korea but came to the United States young enough to learn English and assimilate. Many find themselves explaining one community's culture to the other.

For example, they explain that the linguistic and cultural barriers belie the real efforts many Koreans make to verse themselves in English and Americana. The problem is that those efforts often end in frustration. Those who arrived in the United States as adults often work at least six long days a week. That schedule, combined with family obligations, leaves many immigrants little time to sort out the basic complexities of English, they say.

Courtesy of ABC News, Nightline

Immigrants from Guatemala wait on a Palisades Park corner for casual labor jobs.

"People are basically asking them to be exceptional," says Danny Han, assistant pastor of the First Presbyterian Church.

Some, like Kyung Cho, who has studied English at every opportunity since arriving more than 20 years ago, concede that they still feel uncertain about the language. "I read several newspapers with a dictionary next to me," says Cho, 55, who occasionally stops to ask whether she has made herself understood.

"I still have to keep working at it. It's a hard language for Koreans."

The public library is full of signs of immigrants' efforts. Most of the 20 bilingual English-Korean books—including "The Adventures of Tom Sawyer" and the autobiography of Benjamin Franklin—got so worn that only about five remain usable, says head librarian Ana Chelariu, a Romanian immigrant.

In a room downstairs from the Korean collection, Han J. Kang, 68, struggles to keep up with the day's English class, where most of the students are Korean housewives. The teacher, Rosemary Postel, constantly reassures Kang, telling him not to be frustrated.

But later, in an interview, Kang shares his sense of futility.

"Fifteen years ago, when I came to America, my dream was to learn English," Kang says haltingly, his tone dejected. "I try for 15 years, but I can't. My wife just wants to watch Korean TV, read Korean newspapers. We need to learn English, but it is too late for me."

Then there are the cultural barriers, much harder to chip away. The bicultural Koreans note that their elders and Americans hold contradictory views of community involvement and social etiquette.

Koreans who came as adults were reared in a culture of strict protocol. While small talk is valued as sociable in the United States, it is frowned upon as unpolished in Korea, Koreans say. The immigrants also were shaped in Korea at a time when people were suspicious of government and there was little civilian access. Life in Korea was confined largely to the extended family and close neighbors.

"Many older Koreans don't even know they're permitted to go to town meetings," Han, 34, says.

And finally, Asian immigrants—with an annual median income that is $10,000 more than whites'—brought an upscale air to town, which many Koreans and non-Koreans see as a factor in the complex conflict.

"There's some . . . envy . . . sure," said Eddie "Babs" Babkewicz, a 79-year-old retired subway conductor who moved to Palisades Park about 18 years ago. "God bless the Koreans, I guess. They drive their big fancy cars and have their nice homes and their own businesses. They came with money. Not like my parents; they worked in factories. I looked for work in the Depression."

To be sure, some Koreans bluntly say their priority is not soaking up English idioms and Americana—it's their own futures.

Jeong Kim came to the United States nearly 20 years ago and took some college courses, but she still struggles with English. Despite living in Palisades Park for more than a decade, she knows little about community events.

Each week, her world pivots around 90 hours of hard work at Keum Ho.

"I just work, sleep, work, sleep," says Kim, one of the merchants who is suing the town for alleged anti-Korean discrimination. "People have to realize my generation is preoccupied with surviving, working, right now. We will not be able to concentrate on English and town activities for many years. Our kids, and maybe relatives who come later to join us, they'll be more able to do it.

"It was the same thing with other immigrants, like Italians, Irish, who were the first ones here," says Kim, whose American-born daughters are more fluent in English than in Korean. "They stayed together with other people from their countries. They worked hard to make it in America."

Amid the din of disharmony, one important thing gets lost: the regret—on both sides—about prickly relations and a wish that the town come together.

"I basically like and respect Koreans very much," Farber says. "It would be easier, in a way, if there were bad things I could say about them as people. But there aren't. They're quiet, lovely people.

"I want them to stay in this town. I don't want them to leave. Palisades Park would be in trouble if they did."

Jason Kim's voice grows wistful when he speaks of the tensions.

"We want to be good neighbors to the whole town," Kim says. "If we're doing something wrong, tell us, and give us time to adjust. Sometimes there's been too much enforcement, instead of communication.

"Consider that we may not understand the rules, and explain, instead of shutting down a youth program or creating an ordinance that is going to have a big effect on Koreans."

Residents like Brauer believe the immigrants could surmount the obstacles if they tried. "They've got a great work ethic," Brauer says. "But maybe they should work less if it means the town is paying a price. There's also our ethic of adjusting to your new country, participating in your hometown."

The 1.5 generation is trying to build bridges. For instance, before the Korean parent group, Kim notes, the PTA did little to include Korean parents.

"The district was disenfranchising the parents of 40 percent of our student body," says Kim, the first Korean-American in Bergen County to run for public office. "Now they're in the system, and learning, in the language they understand, about how to participate. . . ."

Warren Leiden, a former member of the Commission on Immigration Reform, says Palisades Park's Korean network can be the groundwork for ethnic harmony.

"That means you have leaders in place—in business, in church—who can work with town officials and the broader community leaders," Leiden says. "In places where [the commission] found ethnic harmony, we found that leaders meet on a regular basis to the point where it trickles to the grass roots. And they made concerted efforts to cool the hotheads in each of their communities."

In some municipalities with large immigrant influxes, efforts by political and immigrant leaders to improve relations have been crucial to keeping tensions low.

In Closter, for example, Mayor Steve Harz studied Korean to better serve that burgeoning community. He also established a cultural awareness committee. Fort Lee officials maintain close contact with Korean merchants and the Korean press. Koreans and officials in both towns, where Koreans comprise about 18 percent of the population, say the outreach helps lessen ethnic polarization.

Many say that's easier said than done in Palisades Park. A borough politician privately concedes: "The truth is that if you do anything to accommodate the Koreans, you anger a lot of the older white residents in this town."

And bicultural Korean-Americans who have persisted in trying to defuse tensions say they constantly meet with apathy and resistance among leaders in both communities. But enough people in the borough seem willing to keep trying.

Brauer is considering making more assertive efforts to recruit Korean members into the Homeowners Association. Korean residents have been teaching Korean at the local library, and students include non-Koreans from the borough.

And two weeks ago, Peter Suh, a real estate broker, became the first Korean-American candidate to seek a council seat in the borough. Suh, who is running under the slogan "Harmony, Equality, Fellowship," says one of his main priorities would be to resolve the ethnic conflicts.

In a state and country that are rapidly changing, Americans and newcomers have little choice but to move forward together, Koreans and non-Koreans say.

"We came a long way to make this our home," says Kyung Cho, a volunteer for the American Cancer Society. "This is where we'll live the rest of our lives. It's where we'll be buried."

Read the rest of the *Tale of Two Cultures* series on *www.theauthenticvoice.org*

THE MAKING OF

DIVERSE AND DIVIDED
& A TALE OF TWO CULTURES

By Elizabeth Llorente
The Record Staff Writer

In the most basic sense, *Diverse and Divided* and *A Tale of Two Cultures* chronicle the transformation of two very different places.

The transformation came hand in hand with the arrival, and then meteoric growth, of immigrant groups in quiet Palisades Park, New Jersey, and in Paterson, the state's third largest city. Korean and Guatemalan immigrants settled in large numbers in Palisades Park, unwittingly rocking a town that had for generations been home almost exclusively to white people of Irish and Italian descent.

Paterson, known as the cradle of the industrial revolution, long had a Puerto Rican community, but it was overshadowed by far larger non-Hispanic white and African American populations. But by 1990, as the Koreans and Guatemalans were building their communities in Palisades Park, enough Latino immigrants had moved into Paterson to make them the majority.

Tensions arose in both places. Long-time non-Hispanic white residents of Palisades Park publicly took issue with the "eyesore" created by the Guatemalan day laborers who stood in the center of town waiting for contractors to hire them and, later, with the "Koreanization" of the borough's main commercial strip, where Korean businessmen owned 95 percent of the two hundred concerns by the mid-1990s.

In Paterson, the tensions were deep and strong, if less publicly expressed. Black people, who felt that they were finally gaining power with the election of several African Americans to city boards and committees—and then the mayoralty—expressed resentment toward the Hispanic population, which became the new establishment, both economically and politically.

Each series presented its own challenges. One of the main difficulties in *A Tale of Two Cultures* was this: How do you tell what was essentially an American story of fear without producing something that felt like yet another cliché anti-immigrant story?

In *Diverse and Divided,* a main challenge was telling the story of tensions between two communities of racial and ethnic minorities when neither side was especially eager to air their feelings about the other publicly. How do I produce a story on a subject that makes many readers uncomfortable? How do I tell this story in a way that will engage even people who would rather avoid stories about race and ethnicity and leave them with a sense of the subject's complexity?

Somewhere in the process of reporting both projects, three things became clear:

- These stories had to capture vividly the perceptions that each group had of the other.
- Those perceptions had to be put into context.
- Those perceptions needed to be balanced against the reality.

I had to immerse myself in my subjects' world. I had to present each person as a full, complex character. Readers don't have to like the characters, but they must care about them, feel interested in them. When we report on tensions responsibly and honestly, we will rarely turn out stories that have either saints or sinners, because there is both saint and sinner in every one of us.

Diverse and Divided

In 2003, Census officials announced that Hispanics had surpassed black people as the largest minority group in the United States—an important demographic shift that had been anticipated, but not quite so soon. Much of the media presented the development as a horse race.

Many of the stories followed a predictable pattern: they raised the specter of a minority-minority cat fight. But away from reporters' notebooks and news cameras, both communities voiced other sentiments. Many African Americans worried aloud about losing the focus on their issues—though still far from ideal—that had been so long in coming. Some expressed the same kind of anti-immigrant fear and resentment long associated with non-Hispanic white people. Many Hispanics viewed African Americans' accounts of everyday racism as "paranoia" and a baseless default to victimhood. And many admitted harboring stereotypes about African Americans.

The picture the media had painted—one of a brewing war between two communities—was more than myth. But most journalists had failed to see the deeper and broader story because they had not looked for it. They had been content to do what we too often attempt to do: pass off a story as fair and balanced because it begins by hurling a charge and concludes by refuting that charge.

After a decade of writing about ethnic and race relations and a lifetime of picking up on the tensions and hearing the comments people made in hushed tones, I knew there was a different story behind the one everyone was writing.

I had to be realistic, though. We were not going to get the real story about the tensions in a day or two. Black and Hispanic people were not going to bare their suspicions, fears, and dislike of each other in a twenty-minute interview on a city sidewalk. No one would. Still, I had enough confirmation of the tensions to include a paragraph or two about them in daily stories.

I told the editors what I sensed to be the real story. I gave them examples of the resentment and hostilities that I'd heard expressed

Yann Nicolas

Reporter Elizabeth Llorente discusses her stories in an interview with Keith Woods.

from members of both communities over the years. I told the editors I believed relations between the two groups would be one of the most important facets of race relations in the United States in the coming decades. I thought we had to get our arms around it now.

I stressed that such a story needed a commitment of time. We could not cut corners on a topic that was so frighteningly easy to get wrong but harder to do right. The editors agreed. From the beginning, they committed to publishing whatever story developed, no matter how potentially upsetting it might be for readers. We would not fear backlash if we knew that our story was accurate and fair. "If we don't report what we find, even things that might be hard to read, then why do this at all?" asked my editor, Susan DeSantis.

Execution

The first important decision was how to approach this story. Would we focus broadly, reaching out to people in various locations? Or would we find one place, one city or neighborhood, that seemed to capture the most significant elements of this story? An editor suggested we go to Paterson, which for years had been experiencing the ramifications of a profound demographic shift. Paterson was ideal because its Hispanic population was diverse, including many of the same groups that were taking on national importance in the Hispanic community.

I made dozens of calls to black and Hispanic organizations in Paterson explaining the story and getting their views on the state of relations between the two communities. They pointed out the most promising spots where I could get a good feel for the groups. I hit the streets of Paterson nearly every day for about three months and rarely came to the newsroom. I went to social affairs in black and Hispanic neighborhoods. I spoke at length with the pastors of black churches, who introduced me from altars to the congregations and explained the story I was researching.

I attended Hispanic parades to get a feel for the ethnic pride that burned so strong in the different Latino communities. I wanted to be able to show readers the pride by describing the many ways in which spectators displayed their native flags: on hats, on shirts, on their babies and pets. I wanted to listen for any comments made by community leaders in these parades about how Hispanics were moving up, becoming more influential, a power to be reckoned with. This is where they felt comfortable flexing their muscle, and I wanted to be there, to put the reader there, too.

In the black churches, pastors often spoke to their congregations about how they should push forward, not let others intimidate them. This was a golden listening post; this is where they felt safe, where they could express feelings that might be judged harshly by outsiders but here were received with support and

Courtesy of ABC News, Nightline
Palisades Park students march in a holiday parade.

understanding. This is where they didn't worry; this is where a reporter needed to be.

I visited African American chat rooms and message boards on the Internet and found several postings about Hispanics and the demographic shift. I spent more time in black listening posts because I had more to learn about the black community. Still, I approached Hispanic neighborhoods and interviews with the notion that I could not assume anything.

Several people in Paterson and in my newsroom said that my story-in-progress reminded them of the Spike Lee film *Do the Right Thing,* which looked at the impact of a growing immigrant population in a black neighborhood. So I rented the movie and found it inspiring as well as affirming of much of what I had found in my reporting.

Challenges

One of the biggest challenges was getting people in both communities to speak candidly and comfortably. I wanted people to tell me what they truly felt, not what they thought they should say. I asked open-ended questions about the people and about the city's diversity.

Most people responded cautiously at first. Their answers were more pastel than bold. They'd say of one another "Diversity is good" and "I don't have a problem with them." But the brevity and woodenness of the comments left little doubt they were holding back.

Sometimes I'd switch to small talk, changing the topic to their dog, their garden, or their grandchildren. If I saw them relax, I'd get back to the interview. Usually, that tactic drew more candid, thoughtful responses that seemed less like sound bites and more like thinking aloud.

Many interviews lasted well past two hours, some as long as five or six, however long it took for them to relax. Once they let their guard down, most people spoke eagerly, raising points I had not thought to explore. For many, the chance to discuss and analyze feelings they had shared with only a few people, or with no one, brought satisfaction and self-awareness.

Some of the young African Americans, who expressed the most hostility toward Hispanics, were among the sources that opened up the most after I had gained their trust. When they'd see me in the neighborhood, they'd call out my name and wave or cross the street to greet me. They'd squeeze my hand and hug me. Did they know, or care, that I was Hispanic? I don't think so. Not one of the dozens of African Americans I interviewed ever asked about my ethnicity or my last name.

I was surprised when some people condemned the racism within their own communities. Some leaders and ordinary residents spoke in strong terms about how the black community had to push itself forward and focus less on the problems that others create for them.

And yet, while such experiences validated the need for this story, there were always people to make me wonder anew about the undertaking. Some asked: "Do you really want to open that can of worms?" Others asked: "Why wade into such a touchy subject that will surely anger everybody?" Isn't that what bigots who don't like either of these groups would love to read?

I defended the need for the story, telling the naysayers that letting fear or intimidation affect our news decisions would not serve any good purpose. But privately I'd replay their questions and challenges. In the end, the warnings and concerns just made me doubly determined to present a story from a variety of perspectives.

Impact

E-mails poured in after *Diverse and Divided* appeared in the paper. People in Paterson thanked me for the story, saying they were glad to see a paper tackle a subject that rarely had been explored in such depth. "Somebody had to say it like it is," said Councilwoman Vera Ames, a beloved figure in the black community.

"I'm glad someone finally had the guts to tell the story about what is happening in Paterson," said another member of the city council, Tom Rooney, who is white.

An influential New Jersey political insider newsletter praised the project and the space that *The Record* devoted to it. The newsletter described *Diverse and Divided* as a must-read for understanding race relations between black and Hispanic people. The project sparked discussions about race relations in classrooms, diners, and living rooms around the state.

A Tale of Two Cultures

A Tale of Two Cultures is a two-part series that looks at one small, working-class town's reaction to the simultaneous influx—in ten short years—of well-educated, prosperous Korean immigrants and poor Guatemalan day laborers who were in the country illegally.

The Record and other newspapers published dozens of stories about the anger in Palisades Park over the growing number of day laborers who crowded the street corners each day, hoping contractors would pick them up for work. For about a year, the day laborers remained the key topic of discussion in Palisades Park. Longtime residents expressed fear, wondered how the men had picked "our town," and vowed to run them out. But no story penetrated the world of the Guatemalans or explained why they'd come to the United States, and Palisades Park in particular.

Gradually, the resentment about the changing town shifted to the Korean community. Again, *The Record* and other newspapers published numerous stories about tensions, quoting the familiar Korean community leaders as well as town officials and gadflies. Longtime residents, most of them white people, complained that the Koreans seemed to reject assimilation and that they were "taking over."

The details of those complaints differed, in many respects, from their criticism of the Guatemalans. But a thick, common thread ran through the tensions with both groups. White residents felt displaced. As with *Diverse and Divided,* we were missing the real story, which was about the fear of change. And as journalists too often do, we had walked away from the Guatemalan story once the protests ceased.

We needed to go beyond "he said, she said" stories that simply repeated old clichés. As we did in *Diverse and Divided,* we wanted to provide a window and a mirror; a window looking in on one community and its feelings and a mirror reflecting another group's long-held views that usually go ignored or rationalized.

I spent months visiting Korean and white residents at their workplaces, homes, picnics, and classes. I spent several weeks with the Guatemalan day laborers, sitting in on their English classes and standing with them on the corners while they waited for work. I read about Korean/non-Korean conflicts in other parts of the United States. For inspiration in writing the Guatemalan story, I reread parts of Upton Sinclair's *The Jungle* and Oscar Handlin's *The Uprooted*.

Challenges

Members of the Guatemalan community were extremely reluctant to speak for a variety of reasons. They were here illegally. Many were illiterate and felt no connection to print media, particularly an English-language newspaper. There were linguistic and cultural barriers. Being a Cuban American offered me no advantage whatsoever. The day laborers spoke rudimentary Spanish, at best, since most spoke Mayan dialects. As people who hailed from the jungles of Guatemala, they saw me as a city slicker.

No one, not the Guatemalans, town officials, or church and immigration advocates, truly understood why the protests had stopped. As people explored their feelings in interviews, we pieced together the attitudes and comments to find the reasons.

Korean people who were approached politely turned down interviews, saying they didn't want to make waves. Several pointed us to a handful of frequently quoted Korean community leaders. Racism, a word that appeared in many of our previous stories, proved to mean different things to different people. To many Korean immigrants, racism was the chilly looks they received from white people. It was also institutionalized in the town ordinances that seemed to target them. To many white people, racism was the Ku Klux Klan or membership in an Aryan society. It resided inside people with crew cuts and swastika tattoos. It wasn't inside loving grandfathers, Little League coaches, good husbands—people like them.

In the newsroom, some editors were nervous about the story. They worried that Palisades Park readers would complain that their town was being portrayed as racist. They worried about publishing some of the comments that white residents made about Koreans. One editor pushed for headlines and pictures that would not reflect racial and cultural conflict.

Impact

After the series, town officials and Koreans formed a committee to review ethnic relations. Palisades Park hired its first Korean police officer. And in the most unexpected move, the Korean community reached out to the Guatemalan workers, bringing coffee and bagels to them on the street corners on the weekends and inviting them to their church for prayer and English classes.

Bergen County officials began drafting a list of recommendations on how the town could improve human relations. Asian groups in other states used the stories to discuss race relations in their communities.

In the newsroom, editors who had been nervous saw the stories in a different light. Yes, the paper received a couple of letters from white people complaining that the story should have criticized Koreans more. But the onslaught of angry letters and calls the editors feared never materialized.

Lessons

The positive reaction to the stories showed some of the editors that readers appreciate a truthful and accurate story. Even Palisades Park residents who lamented the negative headlines their town generated praised the stories as honest and responsible.

The lesson is that sometimes we don't give readers enough credit. Despite the cynicism that readers often express about the press, they still expect to find the truth in our reports. Ethnic and racial minority groups want coverage of the difficult issues they face, as long as they're covered responsibly. The failure to cover immigrants in more nuanced ways can only exacerbate stereotypes, hinder cross-cultural understanding, and undermine our credibility with all readers.

To screen the Elizabeth Llorente interview, select CULTURAL COMPETENCE on the DVD Main Menu then "Diverse and Divided" and "A Tale of Two Cultures."

DISCUSSION POINTS

DISCUSS

- Outline what Elizabeth Llorente teaches you about how to use the U.S. Census to find unique stories.
- Discuss what the Palisades and Paterson stories tell you about immigration.
- *A Tale of Two Cultures* uses a variety of perspectives to create a picture of what is happening to Palisades Park. Explain how those multiple perspectives produce a complete story.
- Why is the viewpoint of the white residents in Palisades especially critical to the telling of *A Tale of Two Cultures?*
- In the Paterson City *Diverse and Divided* series, Llorente must reach out beyond her own cultural history to understand the different tensions at play. Discuss how the series fosters a broader community awareness about cultural differences.
- Llorente speaks with authority in *Diverse and Divided*, more so than in the Palisades story. Discuss the journalistic growth that would allow her to come to her conclusions.

SUGGESTED READINGS AND WEBSITES

SEARCH

Books

Jacoby, Tamar, ed. *Reinventing the Melting Pot: The New Immigrants and What It Means to Be American.* New York: Basic, 2004.

> *This is a collection of leading authors, journalists, and scholars presenting a contrasting range of opinions about and solutions for addressing today's multicultural America.*

Wilson II, Clint C., Felix Gutierrez, and Lena Chao. *Racism, Sexism, and the Media: The Rise of Class Communication in Multicultural America.* 3rd ed. Thousand Oaks, Calif.: Sage Publications, 2003.

A Free and Responsible Press. Hutchins Commission Report. Chicago: University of Chicago Press, 1947.

> *Written by Robert Maynard Hutchins and a dozen other preeminent national leaders, the U.S. Commission on Freedom of the Press's 1947 report is a landmark in the history of press criticism.*

Websites

www.census.gov

U.S. Census statistics.

www.wnjpin.state.nj.us/OneStopCareerCenter/LaborMarketInformation/lmi25/sf1/b
er/sf155770.pdf

How diverse is Palisades Park, New Jersey? U.S. Census data from 2000 indicates that 52 percent of the borough's more than seventeen thousand residents are minorities. New Jersey is home to the country's fifth-highest Asian population, with the number of its Asian residents nearly doubling between 1900 and 2000.

CHAPTER 12

STORY

ABOUT RACE SERIES
THE RAPE OF NANKING

EMERALD YEH, KRON-TV, SAN FRANCISCO

EMERALD YEH

Emerald Yeh is a veteran television journalist in the
San Francisco Bay area who has made herself a student
of the cultural nuances of that city. A former consumer
reporter for KRON-TV—she left in 2002 to become a
freelancer—Yeh is a winner of nine Emmys for stories
she produced over her twenty-two-year career.

The Rape of Nanking

Television journalist Emerald Yeh's story *The Rape of Nanking* reaches across generations and ethnic groups to show how a World War II atrocity reverberates well into modern times.

Yeh used the most routine of pegs—a touring photo exhibit—to launch into a story about an event some call the "forgotten Holocaust." In short order, she pulled together interviews and documentary footage, giving the story additional heft by connecting it to the publication of the late Iris Chang's best-selling book *The Rape of Nanking*.

Yeh then told the story through the eyes of a young American couple—one of Chinese, the other of Japanese heritage—adding powerful images and emotion to propel the story beyond a history lesson. She lobbied successfully for extra time to do the story—six times the usual length—and won a spot for it in KRON-TV's acclaimed series *About Race*.

This chapter will help journalists understand not just one piece of the past but the larger issue of how old, deep, hurtful events fuel current-day animosities around the world. It provides a window to the simple ways journalists, using key anniversaries or other common news pegs, can tell important stories about such longstanding ethnic and racial divisions. Yeh's insights into how ethnicity influences news judgment—she is a Chinese American—provide strong fodder for discussing the role diversity plays in everything from story selection to balance and fairness to word choice.

The chapter raises questions about how vigilant journalists should be in mitigating the incendiary effects of revisiting racial and ethnic atrocities and other historical events sure to open old wounds.

"THE RAPE OF NANKING" (TRANSCRIPT)

KRON TV, *About Race* Series
Airdate: September 4, 1998
Reporter and Producer: Emerald Yeh / Editor: Sharon Chee

Susan Shaw:
[studio intro]

Tonight in *About Race: The Rape of Nanking,* a war atrocity of such savagery that even a Nazi party member who witnessed it was so horrified he appealed to Hitler for help.

Today, much of the world has forgotten about it. Yet that event is being felt even decades later, an ocean away, here in the Bay Area.

Emerald Yeh has tonight's special report *"About Race."* And we warn you: some of the pictures you are about to see are very disturbing.

Emerald Yeh:
[voice-over]

A young couple—seeming to have so much in common . . . But race threatens to divide them. She's Chinese American. He's Japanese American.

Helen Wong:

My parents . . . first thing they said . . . "Well, why would you want to go out with him? He's Japanese. Don't you know what they did to our people?"

[percussive beat over photo of man about to be beheaded]

They go—"I don't understand how you can even associate with people like that."

[percussive beat over photo of bayoneting]

I go—"But he has nothing to do with it. His family has been in America for three generations."

[several percussive beats over photo of bodies in mass grave with Japanese soldier standing over]

Emerald Yeh:

Helen Wong and Kenji Taguma of San Francisco are generations and a continent removed from what happened 60 years ago. Both were born and raised in America. But Helen's parents carry painful memories from their childhoods in China.

Helen Wong:

I was probably 13 or so. That's when my mother started talking about how her grandfather was killed . . . Sorry [choking back a sob]

Courtesy of KRON-TV

Exhibit documents of Japanese soldiers' atrocities in Nanking.

"It is one of the most brutal chapters in history. The Japanese killed 15 to 30 million Chinese . . . One episode so chilling that it's referred to as the Rape of Nanking."

—Emerald Yeh

Emerald Yeh:	Both Helen's grandfathers were among family members murdered in the Japanese rampage across China during World War II.
Helen Wong:	The day that they were fleeing the country, they paid their last respects at a Buddhist temple. And while my grandfather was doing his prayers, they saw the Japanese soldiers come and kill him on the spot. I actually felt that it happened to me. I can actually picture myself in that situation and just seeing my own father being killed.
Emerald Yeh:	It is one of the most brutal chapters in history. The Japanese killed 15 to 30 million Chinese. The horror of those numbers is exceeded only by how the Japanese killed . . . One episode so chilling that it's referred to as the Rape of Nanking.
Iris Chang:	There were beheading contests to see how many heads could be lopped off. They actually held competitions that were recorded by the Japanese newspapers at the time, like sporting events.
Emerald Yeh:	Iris Chang . . . Author of *The Rape of Nanking*.

Iris Chang: Often ripping out body parts when people were still alive, cannibalizing them, hanging victims by their tongues, sometimes disemboweling victims after rape. Not only was murder turned into a sport but rape itself became a sport. The Japanese army would sometimes force fathers to rape their own daughters, and sons their own mothers, forcing family members also to watch. Those who refused were usually killed on the spot.

> "I actually felt that it happened to me. I can actually picture myself in that situation and just seeing my own father being killed."
>
> —Helen Wong

For people to be capable of such acts and to revel in it was terrifying for me.

Japanese soldier 1:   There was a woman holding a child on her right arm and
[translation]   another on her left. We stabbed and killed them all three, like potatoes in a skewer.

Emerald Yeh: Some were buried or burned alive. Others died in biological experiments. Tens of thousands of women were raped and mutilated.

Japanese soldier 2:   I think in this way, Japanese soldiers committed so many rapes
[translation]   that probably no virgins were left.

Emerald Yeh: Within six weeks, two to three hundred thousand Chinese were killed in this manner, one by one.

Iris Chang: Three hundred thousand people is actually greater than the combined death toll for Hiroshima and Nagasaki.

Emerald Yeh: The Nanking massacre was no secret. It was reported in foreign newspapers and repelled the world. But after the war, it became an inconvenient memory for postwar relations and was swept under the rug of diplomacy. China and Japan had become trading partners and the U.S. was aligned with Japan in the fight against communism.

The governments moved on. But the rift between the Chinese and Japanese people continued . . . a rift of lingering hatred that reached across the seas and seeped down the generations.

Helen Wong: And she goes, "No, you can't see him. You know, they're evil people."

Emerald Yeh: Kenji's family was in America during the war and had nothing

Courtesy of KRON-TV

"Kenji's family was in America during the war and had nothing to do with the massacre in China. But still he and Helen kept their relationship a secret from Helen's parents."

—Emerald Yeh

Kenji Taguma holds Helen Wong's hand as she discusses the trauma the Rape of Nanking still represents for Chinese people.

	to do with the massacre in China. But still he and Helen kept their relationship a secret from Helen's parents.
Kenji Taguma:	And I would be hiding in the closets whenever there was a chance that her mother would come down . . .
Helen Wong:	That broke my heart because you know, I was in a dilemma. I didn't know what to do at that point.
Emerald Yeh:	Two Americans . . . wearing the faces of enemies from another land and another time, paying the price for an ancient wrong.
Kenji Taguma:	It is very understandable that that hatred is still there. And from what I understand, there are a lot of Chinese immigrants who lived through that experience who still prohibit their daughters or sons from dating Japanese Americans.
Dr. Clifford Uyeda:	When we were small, the Chinese and Japanese community did not get along very well.
Emerald Yeh:	Dr. Clifford Uyeda grew up in Tacoma, Washington. He is a past president of the Japanese American Citizens League. With the revived interest in the Rape of Nanking—a photo exhibit on national tour is currently on display at Treasure Island—Dr. Uyeda says Japanese Americans must join the

movement to make Japan atone for what happened and make reparations. To this day, the Japanese government has not fully acknowledged or apologized for the Rape of Nanking.

Dr. Uyeda: Oh, I think it's a shame and a disgrace.

Emerald Yeh: A disgrace, he says, that takes a toll on all people of Chinese and Japanese ancestry in Asia and America.

Dr. Uyeda: People in Japan would have to realize that they cannot remain silent on this issue. They have to speak out. Otherwise I think it reflects on the entire Japanese people. . . .

Kenji Taguma: I had a very strong pride in my Japanese roots. I think seeing what happened caused a lot of shame . . . that not only people of my ethnic heritage could do this . . . but that they had not, they had not paid any reparations. They had not apologized in a decent manner. That was most shaming.

Emerald Yeh: While the Japanese government remains largely silent, apologies are being made by some Japanese individuals, even a few soldiers who had massacred.

Japanese soldier 2: I want to speak out about this . . . because I want to make up for what I've done. I am 77 years old and I have reflected upon my guilt.

Emerald Yeh: Simple words but a powerful tonic that begins to heal the hate and bridge racial differences. Sixty years after the Rape of Nanking, relationships—one by one—are still finding ways to cross that bridge from hate to healing.

Helen and Kenji have been dating for four years now. During that time her parents have come to accept and love him . . . and that's a beginning too.

Helen Wong: There is hope for the two cultures to start to understand each other a little better and to forgive about what happened.

Kenji Taguma: But never forget.

Emerald Yeh: (studio close) An ironic footnote: some of the former Japanese soldiers tried to come to the U.S. for the opening of photo exhibits so they could confess and apologize. But the U.S. government barred them from entering the country because they are considered war criminals, literally turning them away at the airports.

The photo exhibit will be shown on Treasure Island through the rest of this month, Fridays, Saturdays and Sundays at the old Navy Museum.

Meanwhile, in Japan, a group of some 200 Japanese lawyers have [sic] filed suits against the Japanese government seeking reparations for Chinese survivors of the Japanese atrocities.

And finally, I want to thank the makers of the documentary *"In the Name of the Emperor"* for the use of some footage, including those interviews with the former Japanese soldiers.

Copyright © 1998 KRON-TV, San Francisco

THE MAKING OF

THE RAPE OF NANKING

By Emerald Yeh
KRON-TV, San Francisco

When victorious Japanese troops first marched into Nanking, China's capital, in December 1937, the city had a population about the size of today's San Francisco. Within six weeks, more than half the city's inhabitants had been beheaded, disemboweled, or buried or burned alive. They were raped and mutilated, then killed.

Despite its breathtaking brutality, the Rape of Nanking quickly receded into history. Decades of denial have been partly responsible for causing hatred of the Japanese people to be passed down to generations of Chinese children.

Fast-forward sixty years to the United States, where a young couple's budding relationship opens up the decades-old wound. Helen Wong's mother, who'd seen her own father killed by Japanese soldiers, is horrified to learn that her daughter is dating a young man of Japanese ancestry. The San Francisco couple's struggle to be together in spite of parental objections is emblematic of the bitter resentments that continue to taint relations between the Chinese and Japanese communities on personal, political, and national levels.

I knew I had a strong story when Lillian Sing, a Superior Court judge and long-time activist in the local Asian community, brought the idea to me. Like many people of Chinese ancestry born after the war, Judge Sing knew about a historical incident called the Rape of Nanking, but she didn't know the specifics or scope of it. She did know that the repercussions and resentment had seeped down through the generations.

Inspired by a newly released book on the subject, Judge Sing thought the world should know more about this chapter of history. She was sure that getting redress from the Japanese government for Chinese victims would be a vital step toward helping today's generation of Chinese and Japanese to start relations afresh. Knowing that television is a medium that reaches the masses and can give voice to issues in a powerful fashion with a lasting imprint, Judge Sing contacted me. She also told me

> "History is our safeguard against a repeat of these atrocities. Remembrance is our only hope. If we don't dredge up the past, we can't heal. History and education are our best weapons if we're to have an open dialogue and move forward."
>
> —Iris Chang

how I could reach Helen Wong and her fiancé, Kenji Taguma, the couple whose dilemma would provide a poignant contemporary twist to the story.

A Convenient Convergence

Fueling the timeliness of this story was the publication of *The Rape of Nanking,* a best-seller by a local Bay Area author, the late Iris Chang, as well as the arrival of a photo exhibit, *The Forgotten Holocaust in Asia and the Pacific, 1931–1945,* that was on national tour and on exhibit at San Francisco's Treasure Island.

Courtesy of KRON-TV

Helen Wong and Kenji Taguma examine a display about the Rape of Nanking.

As a reporter assigned to another beat, consumer affairs, I couldn't have asked for a more convenient convergence of events and people. After recognizing the richness and value of this story, I needed to sell its merits to news management before I could proceed. I also needed to get a photographer freed up from the daily demands of the newsroom to shoot the interviews.

I handled both matters in tandem, knowing that if I could compress the interviews and b-roll shoots into one or two days, thereby not straining the newsroom's resources too greatly, it would be easier to get the green light from management. I knew all too well that sometimes the best story ideas get shot down simply because there's no photographer available.

I contacted Helen Chang, Kenji Taguma, and Iris Chang and tentatively set up their interviews on the same afternoon at the Forgotten Holocaust photo exhibit. That would also enable us to get shots of the photos on display to help us tell the story visually.

It wasn't difficult to get clearance to do the story from our assistant news director. She immediately saw this as a unique way to present a story about modern Japanese-Chinese relations. It also helped that I had quite a bit of experience at KRON reporting on stories with a strong human component and high emotional impact.

Because I already had daily consumer reporting and news anchoring responsibilities, this project would largely be done on my own time. I mention this not as proof of heroics but as an example of the extra time and effort reporters often have to expend to pursue a story they believe in if it doesn't fit into their assignment or beat.

More significant in the ready acceptance of this self-assigned, extracurricular story was the racial environment in our newsroom and in the Bay Area. People of Asian descent make up 15 percent of the region's population and 30 percent of San Francisco's. This story would resonate with a significant portion of our audience. Our newsroom staff was also ethnically diverse. In fact, the white assistant news director who approved the story is married to a Japanese American. I have found this to be true: the more diverse a newsroom staff, the more diverse its coverage.

The internal timing was also fortuitous. By coincidence, KRON was just undertaking its groundbreaking project, *About Race*. Craig Franklin, the producer and photographer of this daunting project, readily saw that the Rape of Nanking story would help amplify our coverage on race matters in an unusual way. In presenting a story about the Japanese-Chinese conflict, we had a layer of race reporting that went beyond the more conventional black community versus white community viewpoint. That appealed to Franklin (his wife, coincidentally, is Japanese-born). I asked him to be the photographer on the story because I wanted his particular intelligence and sensitivity alongside me.

Placing Blame Delicately

At the outset, I knew there was a delicate issue to be dealt with: how to tell our story about the cruel and bestial mass slaughter without inflaming a round of indiscriminate Japan bashing. I was aware of what had happened to people of Japanese ancestry in the United States during World War II and the later trade wars. Many Americans failed to distinguish between the Japanese living in Japan and those who were American citizens.

Japanese Americans suffered for this in several ways. They were stripped of their possessions and sent to internment camps, perceived as enemies in their own country when they had nothing to do with the bombing of Pearl Harbor. Years later, Japanese Americans were scapegoats for the woes of the U.S. auto industry.

In one extreme case, murderers didn't distinguish between Japanese and Chinese. It involved the beating death of Vincent Chin, a twenty-seven-year-old Chinese American. He was killed in 1982 by two unemployed auto workers in Detroit who thought Chin was Japa-

> From Helen Wong: I wanted her conflicted emotions about what happened to her grandfather and how this tragedy from the past posed a threat to a love relationship and her future happiness.
>
> From Kenji Taguma: I wanted to tap into his awareness and revulsion regarding what the Japanese army did as well as his feelings about being discriminated against because of his ethnic ties to an event that happened before he was born.

nese and used a baseball bat to beat him into a coma, from which he never awoke. Shortly before the attack, the men had blamed the loss of their jobs on Japanese car manufacturers.

Against such a social and racial backdrop, it needed to be clear in my story that the killers in 1937 were members of the Japanese National Army and that it was the Japanese government that refused to acknowledge and atone for the atrocities officially. I did not want a backlash of any sort against Japanese Americans as a result of my story.

As it turned out, Judge Sing had already recognized the importance of involving Japanese Americans in her quest. Not only were Japanese Americans revolted by what happened to the Chinese in the Rape of Nanking, they were attuned to the importance of restitution as a means of repairing great emotional damage, having fought successfully for redress for the internment of Japanese Americans during World War II.

One of the Japanese Americans at the forefront of the Rape of Nanking Redress Coalition, an organization founded by Judge Sing, was Dr. Clifford Uyeda, an elderly pediatrician who was the former national head of the Japanese American Citizens League, a principal organization in the fight for Japanese reparations. Having him as part of our story would be highly effective in conveying that this was not simply a Chinese versus Japanese conflict. As author Iris Chang was to tell me, this was, more than anything else, a human rights issue of interest and concern to anyone with a conscience.

I contacted Dr. Uyeda and asked if he could be available for an interview the same afternoon as Helen Wong, Kenji Taguma, and Iris Chang. He was. It was going to be a long afternoon of interviews for Craig Franklin and me!

A Personal Investment

Where was I emotionally in this story? Being a Chinese American, I had a similar experience to Lillian Sing's, Clifford Uyeda's, and Iris Chang's. I knew something awful had happened called the Rape of Nanking. I grew up knowing there was some historical animosity between Japanese and Chinese, and I was aware of the common sentiment among many Chinese parents that if their children didn't marry Chinese, they'd rather they marry almost any ethnicity but Japanese. I grew up having many Japanese American friends, but there were times when I couldn't help sense an unspoken divide between us.

Still, I felt sensitized to the other issues at hand. After all, I was an American-born journalist with Chinese heritage who grew up in Hawaii, where Japanese make up the dominant ethnic group. And I was a reporter who had covered a multitude of stories with racial and ethnic overtones, including injustices dealt to Japanese Americans. So I hoped to handle this story with proper responsibility and awareness. I felt that just as those hundreds of thousands of Chinese people were in the wrong place at the wrong time in history when they were exterminated and forgotten, I happened to be in the right place at the right time to help bring this travesty out of obscurity, at least in the Western world, without fueling the existing animosity.

In preparation for my interviews, I read Iris Chang's book as well as another book on the Rape of Nanking. Through our newsroom's access to a variety of news publications, I also pulled up background material that included articles about Japanese revisionists who say accounts of the Rape of Nanking were fabricated or greatly exaggerated.

At the same time, I sketched out what I wanted to elicit from each of my four interview subjects and prepared my line of questioning accordingly:

From Helen Wong: I wanted her conflicted emotions about what happened to her grandfather and how this tragedy from the past posed a threat to a love relationship and her future happiness.

From Kenji Taguma: I wanted to tap into his awareness and revulsion regarding what the Japanese army did as well as his feelings about being discriminated against because of his ethnic ties to an event that happened before he was born.

From Iris Chang: I needed her authoritative description of what occurred in 1937 and beyond. I also wanted to ask her about those in Japan who called her account of the Rape of Nanking inaccurate.

From Clifford Uyeda: I wanted to learn why a Japanese American was taking such an active role in challenging the Japanese government for its inaction on this issue.

From all of them: I wanted to understand why they felt compelled to take on an issue much of the world has forgotten about.

The Soul of the Story

Within the first minute of Helen Wong's interview, as she started to describe how her mother had seen her own father being killed, Helen was overcome with emotion and could not speak. During that moment of silence, as Helen fought to regain her composure, I felt I was witnessing the unspeakable loss the Rape of Nanking had brought upon one family. I tried to imagine that loss multiplied by more than three hundred thousand.

I was also trying to imagine what it was like to witness that loss as it happened, considering it still provoked such profound emotions sixty years later in a woman who was not even alive then. It was a difficult moment for all of us.

"It needed to be clear in my story that the killers in 1937 were members of the Japanese National Army and that it was the Japanese government that refused to acknowledge and atone for the atrocities officially. I did not want a backlash of any sort against Japanese Americans as a result of my story."

—Emerald Yeh

Craig Franklin

Reporter Emerald Yeh deconstructs the "Rape of Nanking" story.

We did not stop the interview, but let the camera roll. I think we collectively felt that Helen's struggle with her emotions was bringing history back to life.

That difficult silence, which only lasted a few seconds, would become a key moment in a television story that only had minutes to transmit the impact and import of a historic event. I believe that every television story has its own soul, and as I listened to the voices and words of the four principal characters during their interviews, that soul became clear and gave me guidance on how to shape the story.

When I returned to the newsroom, I began to structure the piece even as I continued the research. But there was one more voice I needed, a crucial one: the Japanese soldiers who did the killing. They would authenticate the atrocities in an undeniable way. And because some of these aging soldiers were now confessing and apologizing for their cruel acts, their words would demonstrate the healing power of atonement.

In my research, I found that filmmakers Nancy Tong and Christine Choy had done a documentary called *In the Name of the Emperor*. Tong and Choy had also produced the moving documentary *Who Killed Vincent Chin?* They gladly agreed to let me use wartime footage and interviews of Japanese soldiers from their film. The documentary turned out to be a gold mine. It contained confessions to specific horrors by several soldiers and an actual apology from one of them.

Cutting Distractions, Keeping Focus

In putting the piece together, I reluctantly cut out a lot of interesting information, and there were some things I deliberately chose to keep out of my script. I would have liked to have reported on the wider scope of Japanese wartime atrocities against the Koreans and Filipinos and discussed how those enmities still continue. I wished that I could have in-

cluded Iris Chang's eloquently stated motives for writing her book, more on Judge Sing, and a segment on the significance of Japanese American activists being allies in the push for Chinese redress.

I chose to leave out the criticisms and dismissal of Iris Chang's book by Japanese conservatives and revisionists. I felt it would subvert the greater truth of the story and add a distracting voice to a piece that needed to have a singular focus. More than anything else, I wanted the brutal and unnecessary loss of so many lives to count for something so that they wouldn't re-

Courtesy of KRON-TV

Helen Wong and Kenji Taguma stroll along a San Francisco street.

main nameless corpses buried by ignorance, denials, and deliberate oversight.

While I did not have room to include Iris Chang's reason for writing her book, it served as an undercurrent as I wrote the script. She said, "History is our safeguard against a repeat of these atrocities. Remembrance is our only hope. If we don't dredge up the past, we can't heal. History and education are our best weapons if we're to have an open dialogue and move forward."

The story that aired was seven-and-a-half minutes long. In the end, it was much more than a story about what Japanese soldiers did to Chinese victims. No nationality or ethnicity has exclusivity on atrocity. On the surface, my story is about race and how differences in race—indeed, differences within a race—can cause such deep and lasting injuries and rifts. But it is really a story that transcends race. It's about how we can let differences between us bring out the worst in us, but it offers hope that these differences can also bring out the best in us.

To screen the Emerald Yeh interview, select CULTURAL COMPETENCE on the DVD Main Menu then "The Rape of Nanking."

DISCUSSION POINTS

- One of the ethical issues raised by this chapter is the use of horrific images of the Nanking atrocities. What concerns do you have about showing such incendiary images in a community with significant ethnic divisions?
- Discuss Emerald Yeh's decision to leave out the voices of the Japanese who were critical of the book *The Rape of Nanking*.
- Discuss the genesis of the Rape of Nanking story and the research Yeh conducts to verify whether the wounds from this story are still relevant.
- Yeh sets out specific goals for the interviews. Does she achieve the outcome she wants?
- Explain how the use of good research and archival material was essential to this story.
- This could have been a routine daily assignment to cover a photo exhibit. How does Yeh use the opportunity to turn it into more?

SUGGESTED READINGS AND WEBSITES

Books

Chang, Iris. *The Rape of Nanking.* New York: Basic, 1997.

> *The Rape of Nanking recounts the horrible events under Japanese occupation in the late 1930s, when Nanking served as a kind of laboratory in which Japanese soldiers were taught to slaughter unarmed, unresisting civilians, as they would later do throughout Asia.*

Hicks, George L. *The Comfort Women: Japan's Brutal Regime of Enforced Prostitution in the Second World War.* New York: Norton, 1997.

> *This book describes how more than one hundred thousand women across Asia were victims of enforced prostitution by the Japanese Imperial Forces during World War II. Hicks's book is the only history in English that deals with this enslavement of women.*

Brook, Timothy. *Documents on the Rape of Nanking.* Ann Arbor: University of Michigan Press, 1999.

> *These contemporary records and judgments furnish an intimate, firsthand account of the Rape of Nanking.*

Websites

www.princeton.edu/~nanking

> *This Website is a collection of Nanking massacre photos taken by Japanese soldiers themselves as souvenirs.*

www.centurychina.com/wiihist/njmassac

> *This Website contains detailed descriptions of the Nanking massacre, 1937–1938.*

www.chinajapan.org

> *The Website serves as a home to Sino-Japanese studies, a forum for East Asian history, and links to related resources.*

CHAPTER 13

STORY

THE OTHER PRO SOCCER

GABRIEL ESCOBAR, *THE WASHINGTON POST*

GABRIEL ESCOBAR

Gabriel Escobar is a nationally recognized writer, reporter, and former editor at *The Washington Post*. Before joining *The Post* he worked at the *Queens Tribune, The Hartford Courant,* and *The Philadelphia Daily News.*

He joined *The Post* in 1990, where he covered police affairs, the local immigrant community, and did a tour as the paper's bureau chief in South America. Upon his return, he worked on the paper's regional projects team and then joined the national desk, covering immigration. He was named city editor in September 1999 and served until December 2005. He is now the associate director of the Pew Hispanic Center.

THE OTHER | Pro Soccer

Gabriel Escobar takes a routine "Sunday style" feature story about a suburban soccer league and turns it into a multidimensional exposition. Rather than falling back on a predictable portrait of new arrivals playing soccer, Escobar searches behind the scenes to find a thriving business on the field as well as on the sidelines.

He builds critical relationships with sources, tells a story even his sources didn't know, and reveals difficult truths about them. The result is a three-dimensional view of a community that rises above more ordinary storytelling that relies on extremes, where the message is often unbelievably upbeat or unfairly indicting.

The chapter offers lessons in writing with authority, reporting cultural mores, and finding hidden stories that are in plain view. There is a lesson here in working sources and figuring out how to pull together a compelling, coherent story from bits and pieces of facts and interviews.

It also lends insight into the challenges all reporters face when they have some form of membership in the community they cover. Escobar, an immigrant from Colombia, shares a language, culture and life experience with many of the people in the story. His decisions and thought processes offer an example of how journalists can maneuver through complex matters of language and loyalty to honor their primary obligation to truth telling.

Escobar pushes journalists to recognize that hard-hitting stories may win awards but not friends. He serves up provocative commentary on the reporter's obligation to sources, journalism's obligation to tell more of these stories and his own newspaper's reliance upon him to report the difficult truths about Latinos.

Use this chapter as a starting point for examining how local or regional newspapers and news broadcasts translate immigrant communities for readers, listeners and viewers. Use Escobar's writing and insights to find your own path toward cultural competence.

IN AREA'S LATINO LEAGUES, PART OF THE GAME IS PROFIT, AND THE BEST PLAYERS ARE PAID

By Gabriel Escobar,
The Washington Post Staff Writer
Published November 29, 1998

"The Scorpion," as the kid is known on the soccer field, was a hot commodity all season long. Coaches from rival Latino amateur teams around Washington, eager to snare the marquee goalkeeper, cornered him and waved cash. A lot was at stake, and money was moving. "You want to play with us?" they whispered to Melvin Barrera, tall, quick, built to keep the ball out of the net. "We'll pay you much more!"

Tempting, but Barrera declined, again and again. He is loyal to a team that took him in when he was only 13, taught him the game and paved his way to a professional soccer contract in El Salvador, an enormous leap for an immigrant who landed in Mount Pleasant with little in 1984 and now plays his dream game for a living. The boy who grew up with the vibrant Latino soccer leagues in the Washington area is now a 22-year-old man who in his offseason has the luxury of paying an old debt to old coaches by not charging for his valuable services.

There are more than 450 Latino soccer teams in the metropolitan area, and on any weekend day from spring to fall, more than 7,000 players take the field, Barrera not the only star in this galaxy of athletes but perhaps the brightest local product. The soccer spectacle has become the most visible manifestation of the Latino community at play, a sporting pageant staged every weekend on all the green space local governments can provide.

Behind the colorful production is a growing, cash-only business with few rules, a handful of impresarios, many bitter rivalries, no oversight and lots of talent, raw as well as accomplished. As Barrera's popularity attests, the competition has become so acute that some of the top teams now recruit and pay current and former professional players from Central America to boost their chances.

The most successful coaches and league presidents earned their soccer credentials in the cutthroat leagues in Central America

"People don't mind paying five dollars to come see what they like most, which is soccer," said Jose Arnando Chevez, a fan from Arlington.

and have imported some of the practices to suburbia, including establishing soccer clubs that rely on the financial support of a loyal fan base, most often

Susan Biddle, The Washington Post
Melvin Barrera, a marquee player from El Salvador, before the Taca Cup, which pitted Barrera's team, Mogotillo, against Alianza, a team of Honduran immigrants.

immigrants from the same town or region. The result is that small soccer empires are being built a crumpled dollar at a time.

Word of the lucrative game here has spread to those professional ranks, and Central American players now supplement their relatively modest incomes by becoming journeymen in the Washington area.

The result is an unusually competitive and unregulated enterprise, in many ways the only home-grown industry for Latinos that directly affects most members of the community. Whether anyone is making money from this iconoclastic brand of soccer is unclear, but what is undisputed is that these leagues, like Barrera himself, are now amateur in name only.

"I was always opposed to paying anyone, but I am aware, I know and have seen, that some people do it as a business," said Gloria Granillo, the respected director of the Washington office for Grupo Taca, the Central American airline that sponsors the region's most successful tournament, the Taca Cup. "Is it semiprofessional?" Granillo asked, echoing the question most often asked about the Latino soccer leagues. "I don't know."

That the question is even raised is important. Leagues have existed for decades and in many ways mirror the growth of the Latino community, expanding from modest beginnings in Northwest Washington and following the migration into the suburbs, where most of the more than 30 leagues are now based. The soccer boom of the last few years is described as unprecedented by longtime participants, fueled by the community's maturity and its relative affluence, particularly in the Latino business sector that sponsors leagues and teams.

One result is that the Latino soccer scene is attracting interest from outsiders. For the first time, D.C. United, the most successful franchise in professional soccer in the United States, this year sent representatives to games. The most prominent backer is Budweiser, which this summer gave $10,000 to the organizers of the Taca Cup, an enormous donation to a tournament that only two years ago held its celebration on the second floor of the airline's downtown office.

The six-day event in July and August drew several thousand fans to the auxiliary soccer field at Robert F. Kennedy Memorial Stadium and sold more than $16,000 in tickets, by far the best showing since it was launched in Northern Virginia in the early 1990s. Kappa, the sportswear company, this year for the first time requested a written contract from Granillo, fearing rival Adidas would muscle its way into the event.

The potential payoff for sponsors is exposing their products to fans who are loyal to teams. And for fans, the draw is a chance to see the game they grew up with played well, by people just like themselves. "People don't mind paying five dollars to come to see what they like most, which is soccer," said Jose Armando Chevez, a fan from Arlington.

Knowledgeable fans like Chevez relish the chance to see top talent up close, recognizing that some of these players, obscure athletes playing in obscure leagues, have what it takes. "You can see that they handle the ball well. If a [coach] came here and chose the best players in each team," Chevez said, echoing the assessment of others who follow the Latino leagues, "you could have a team that could beat any team" in professional soccer.

The Price of Playing

All of those factors, particularly the underwriting by Budweiser, have made the leagues fiercely competitive, both on and off the field, as club presidents recognize the game's potential. Leagues are set up to benefit organizers, or presidents, who charge teams enrollment fees that range from $500 to $1,500. The

John McDonnell, The Washington Post

Franklin Ramirez, 5, sits with his father's team, Centenario, during opening ceremonies for the Taca Cup.

presidents pay for referees, medical insurance and, in some cases, field rentals.

The cost of fielding a team is conservatively estimated at $3,000 by the Bolivian league, one of the most financially stable, which means that the Latino soccer scene is a $1.4 million-a-year enterprise if only the known leagues are counted. The sum does not include other revenue enhancers, which are impossible to quantify and which range from exclusive food concessions to cash fines levied on players for game penalties.

Hispanic-owned restaurants often sponsor teams and benefit directly because teams host fund-raisers on the premises and celebrate victories late into the evening. The Taca Cup spent $23,000 on, among other things, renting the field, hiring security guards, advertising the event in the Latino media and paying for an internationally sanctioned referee from Guatemala to officiate the championship match Aug. 1.

People stare at Herbert Mayorga, discreetly but with good reason. In a parking lot at RFK Stadium crammed with beat-up imports—the dented and faded fleet of new immigrants—Mayorga parks one of those buffed four-wheel-drive vehicles so coveted south of the border. As he struts toward his stable of elite players, the envy from the men left standing on the sidelines is palpable.

Mayorga has made it big in two worlds that matter: business and soccer. His company, M. & R. Partnership Contractors of Silver Spring, has helped put up hundreds of houses, and on any given day, this immigrant from El Salvador can be spotted scaling some subdivision-in-progress.

For years, Mayorga's team, El Salvador of Maryland, has been the power-house in Latino soccer. Over lunch at a suburban Chinese restaurant, he explains how. For the first time, a prominent mover in the soccer scene says publicly what soccer impresarios throughout the region only whisper: The good teams are good

> "The good players, all the good players," Mayorga said bluntly, "have to be paid."

because they pay salaries. And Mayorga pays a lot. In 1997, he spent $40,000—he jokes that he could have bought a new BMW—in direct salaries to all of his players.

Where team presidents used to provide a good player with "incentives"—paying for car repairs was a favorite—the best athletes are now demanding written contracts. Mayorga refused to take that step this year, and seven players jumped to other teams. That cost him. A team that had won the Taca Cup two years in a row did not make it to the finals.

"The good players, all the good players," Mayorga said bluntly, "have to be paid."

For team owners such as Mayorga, who underwrite teams out of love for the sport and have no stake in leagues, the aim is not to lose too much money. Unfortunately, the better his team does, the more he spends. Last year, winning the cup cost him an additional $8,000 because he had to pick up expenses for his team's victory lap to El Salvador and Guatemala, where it played professional teams. For Mayorga, the payoff is a different kind of currency—a soccer reputation—which goes a long way here.

At this year's cup, three of the four finalists had paid athletes on their roster. The most interesting of those was Mogotillo, Barrera's team, a two-time runner-up in the cup and a very successful franchise. Its support comes from about 4,000 Salvadorans, avid followers who, like Barrera, hail from the town that gives the team its name and who contribute at each match. A club official goes through the crowd, collecting money and jotting down the amount of contributions.

This year, the team's board of directors decided to boost the roster with pros from El Salvador. They called Barrera, who moved to Mount Pleasant from El Salvador when he was 8.

Barrera was tutored by two coaches on Mogotillo, Victor "The Gun" Coreas and Amadeo "The Tractor" Machado, who persuaded a professional team in El Salvador to take a look at the young prospect. He was invited for a month-long tryout and not only made the team but also was selected for the country's national squad, fulfilling a dream.

"I always wanted to play in a team, back in my country, to see how I was," Barrera said.

With Barrera in El Salvador, recruiting for Mogotillo's efforts here was easy. Felipe Martinez, the president of the team, called him. "'We need two players,'" Martinez recalled saying, "and he said, 'I'll find them for you.'" It was that easy. The two recruits earned about $70 per game plus airfare and expenses and played in the cup along with Barrera. The result is a very talented squad. "Our team," Martinez boasted, "has the ability to play any professional team in Central America."

The cup finals Aug. 1 pitted Mogotillo against an upstart team made up of players from Honduras: Alianza, which won on penalty kicks. Most of the members of that team played organized soccer in their native country—14 of the 20 players began in what is known as the "mosquito league," the little-league equivalent. "They know each other's soccer potential, and that has been an enormous help," said Porfirio Benavides, one of the managers.

The entire team has now migrated to Washington, including four who came this year. Alianza, which takes its name from a municipality in Honduras, holds picnics and other events to raise money, like Mogotillo drawing from immigrants. The team does not pay salaries. Players, however, have all their soccer needs taken care of. Benavides recently spent $2,400 on cleats alone.

The Latino leagues all describe themselves as nonprofit. Assessing how much money most teams or leagues produce—or how much a championship playoff generates, for that matter—is difficult because, with a few notable exceptions, this is an underground economy without ledgers—cash only and tax free. The Bolivian soccer league, one of the few that makes its finances public and uses a professional accountant, had gross revenue of $28,588 in 1997 and a net profit of $6,795—evidence that money can be made.

The Bolivian league and a handful of others are managed by boards of directors, but most operate like little fiefdoms. "In our league, no one is an owner," said Carlos Claros, who stepped down as president of the Bolivian league this year. "That is not the case in most others."

The King of the Cup

Elias Polio is assessing his critics from his perch at a restaurant on Columbia Pike—La Columbia, as the community calls this east-west thoroughfare that cuts through Northern Virginia. Polio is 40, portly and invariably polite. He fits into a particular immigrant mold—the savvy organizer who for years has seen the untapped business potential in the booming Latino community. Now, 22 years after he landed in Washington, Polio is comfortably sitting in what amounts to the owner's box of local soccer as the president of the area's dominant league and of the Taca Cup.

> Assessing how much money most teams or leagues produce—or how much a championship playoff generates, for that matter—is difficult because, with a few notable exceptions, this is an underground economy without ledgers—cash only and tax free.

Over the last months, as word spread that someone was reporting on the soccer scene, Polio's critics have come forth. Rumors that Latinos lost $500,000 when Polio's "informal" business of shipping money and packages to El Salvador folded in 1990 are not true. The sum was closer to $200,000, Polio volunteered, noting that the lamentable episode was investigated by the U.S. attorney's office in the District and that no charges were filed. (A spokesman for the U.S. attorney's office said no record of an investigation shows up.)

"He is the owner, and he determines everything," said Conrado Aguilar, the president of the Alexandria league and one of the many foes who question Polio's domination of the Taca Cup and, by extension, the soccer scene. Aguilar is a founding pillar of the soccer community, among the first to move the game to

John McDonnell, The Washington Post

Rafael Billatoro, of the team Mogotillo, played in the opening game for this year's Taca Cup. The team's support comes from about 4,000 immigrants from El Salvador.

John McDonnell, The Washington Post

Laura Polio prepares tortillas for sale at the Taca Cup. As president of the cup, Elias Polio has the right to the food concession at games.

the suburbs, but his league has lately lost teams, and prestige, to Polio and his star-laden International League of Virginia. "Everything that goes in and out, he controls," Aguilar said. "The question is, how does Elias spend the money?"

Fausto Fonseca, who founded the Taca Cup in 1992 only to lose it in a dispute with the airline, doesn't attack Polio directly but makes the same point. "In the last few years," said Fonseca, now president of the resurrected Arlington league, the Taca Cup has "been changed and turned into personal gain."

Polio's primary foe these days is Antonio Gonzales, the president of the Prince George's Soccer League and of the rival, and foundering, Pilsner Cup. Gonzales is convinced Polio undermined his tournament last year and eventually doomed it—a charge Polio denies.

Worse yet, Mayorga and his high-paying El Salvador of Maryland fled Gonzales' league two years ago and signed up with Polio's.

To all of this Polio shakes his head, pleads poverty and says his critics are consumed by envy. He notes that Fonseca, Aguilar, Gonzales and others have tried over the years to create a soccer federation and a regional tournament, but their efforts failed, doomed by internal squabbles and vicious recriminations. "We have a habit of eating one another," is how Polio describes the mutual antagonism.

Nothing, apparently, whets this appetite as much as money. Even critics grant that Polio has a good point. "He has been able to do something that sparks jealousy: He is making money from soccer," said Luis del Aguila, a veteran of the Latino soccer leagues and the treasurer of Metropolitan D.C.–Virginia Soccer Association, an umbrella group for the region's soccer leagues. "The Taca Cup is good, and it has the potential to be more. And I agree with Elias that you will never satisfy all the Latino teams that exist in the area. That is impossible."

Polio says the cup over the last two years has done better than ever, though he maintains it still doesn't make any money. The tournament, which is free to participating teams, is run by three people: Granillo, who represents the Taca Group, and Polio and his partner, Oscar Burgos, the sports director for Radio America, which also sponsors the cup. This year, in response to questions over the cup's finances, organizers said any future profits would go to a home for the elderly in El Salvador.

Polio, by virtue of being president of the cup, owns the popular food concession and does not allow competitors. It's unclear how much the concession generates—Polio's own estimates varied widely, ranging from a daily take of several hundred dollars to about $2,000. He concedes that the only profit he makes comes from the food, but he points out that other league presidents have similar arrangements, either as owners of concessions or by taking a cut from food sales.

Polio said the arrangement is fair because he is not paid for organizing the event and both he and his family work a long day every Saturday during the cup. "If I spend all my time there, why can't I do that?" he asked.

The work is hard, and the days are long. Well before the teams showed on game day, Polio and company set up. Smoke curled up from the grills, which were protected from the elements by a blue awning anchored to one of Polio's old, dented vans. Well past sunset, Polio and crew cleaned up after the crowd, knowing that a messy field would cost them a fine from the stadium authority.

Polio is a nervous host. There is a lot to do, too many things can go wrong, too many people are watching, too many are waiting to make money on the field. "As you can see," Polio said, echoing the lament of the immigrant laborer, "we sweat for our money."

Copyright © 1998 The Washington Post Company

THE MAKING OF

THE OTHER PRO SOCCER

By Gabriel Escobar
Washington Post Staff Writer

Perpetually arriving, never quite here. That is the unhappy condition of Latinos, as often portrayed by the media. Look long and hard, and you will—eventually—find some depth in the coverage. But, for the most part, this enormous and very diverse people tends to appear one-dimensional, interchangeable, and, of course, always arriving.

One feature story in particular has, to me, come to illustrate this phenomenon. It is not the piece on Cinco de Mayo, not the annual Hispanic festival, not the Three Kings, not any of the other predictable stories that the media often fall back on when it is compelled to portray Latinos on short notice. This is about soccer. Even before the sport became what it is today, the media (and newspapers in particular) could be counted on to deliver a feature story that depicted Latinos enjoying the sport.

In Flushing Meadows Park in Queens, in the suburban fields of Virginia and Maryland, in rural areas integrated by the labor demands of chicken and meat processing, every Saturday and Sunday bring forth this sporting spectacle. And the media, often accused of focusing on the negative, gravitate to this happy event.

But was there a story behind the soft feature? For years, I had seen the soccer games as an excellent reporting laboratory for those following the relatively new Latino community in the Washington area. There was a handful of places where you could find these immigrants in large numbers: at certain worksites (hotels, restaurants, construction sites), at church (Catholic parishes were good, but Pentecostal gatherings were often better), at immigration offices (waiting rooms, when the public was allowed), and at soccer fields on weekends. Of all these, the soccer scene was the best because it was the only place where the community was at rest. You did not have to spend a lot of time on the field before you realized that soccer was not just a game, and certainly not just good, safe, and predictable ethnic color for a newspaper's weekend display.

The Spanish-language weeklies, from the ones that folded soon after they hit the streets to the established paper run by the Catholic Church, all paid attention to these soccer leagues and routinely ran the standings, often on the same page as the listings for the professional leagues back home in Central America. When you talked to the reporters who covered the leagues, conversation always turned to the latest intrigue. Money was being made, and reputations were at stake. Even the ladies who cooked late into the night on Fridays and sold pupusas out of coolers were operators.

Was this a story? Was it worth doing? And, if so, how should it be done?

First, the Cautionary Tales

Embarking on a story of this nature has its perils. You are practically assured of angering some people, and if you happen to be a Hispanic reporter, the barbs will be sharper. One of the consequences of exploring how immigrant communities work is that, from time to time, the portrait that emerges will not be entirely positive. It may not be entirely negative, either.

But keep in mind that nuance born out of in-depth reporting in immigrant communities may bring professional accolades but not many friends among those you are writing about and, in the process, occasionally exposing. These stories are a way to shed light on the complex process of assimilation, and, executed well, they will add texture and dimension. But they will not always be greeted with applause. While activists within these communities frequently complain that the media seldom go beyond the superficial feature (and they have a point because the perennial stories tend to sound the same), it is another thing entirely when the attention becomes probing and, in the process, reveals something that someone will construe as negative.

A case in point: Several years ago, I suggested to a colleague who covered transportation that he examine why so many Latino immigrants were getting killed while crossing streets in suburban Washington. His analysis proved something irrefutable: immigrants were far more likely to die than any other group. Several theories were offered, and one of the most perceptive was that these immigrants had settled in neighborhoods built and designed for commuters. By necessity or by circumstance, they were pedestrians in places ill suited for walking. When the story ran, the paper received numerous complaints from Latino activists and others who said the reporters had stooped to a new low: accusing immigrants of being so ignorant that they did not understand something as elementary as crossing the street. Instead of pressing local communities to improve pedestrian access and educate the public, the reaction to the story removed any impetus to address what clearly was a serious safety issue.

The soccer story was sensitive from the beginning. Soccer appeared to be a business, at least in some cases. Yet the perception, on the part of local parks and recreation officials, was that these leagues were no different from those that promoted softball, baseball, or any other sport: organizations that had come together to advance an activity and certainly not money-making enterprises. Some of these Latino leagues were run by men who had reached out to local park officials and had in turn been embraced by them. They had learned the permit process, organized teams, and earned the trust of county park officials who had often been at a loss when dealing with immigrant groups. But it appeared that some of these individual clubs paid their best talent, in cash or in kind. If that was the case, then their playing on public fields ran counter to the policies of park and recreation officials, who, in almost all cases, granted permits on the assumption that no money exchanged hands.

There were risks to exposing this as a business. I knew, from covering the immigrant community in the early 1990s, that certain kinds of stories provoked a strong reaction. I had written about the local Hispanic festival, which suffered from disorganization and conflict. I had written about the problems of

a Latino economic development corporation, which had had limited success. I had explored the network of healers who set up shop in Latino neighborhoods, advertised their cures on local Spanish language television, and, while media executives gladly accepted their advertising dollars, perpetrated medical fraud. The result in each case was anger and resentment on the part of some Latino community leaders or, in the case of the healers, from the local media that were airing these ads.

The soccer story had the same potential. Soccer was a sport, organized at the lowest level. It was a pastime. Why do the story if it

Former *Washington Post* City Editor Gabriel Escobar poses outside the newspaper's headquarters.

would spark a negative response? If a community seldom appears in the pages of the newspaper, how fair is it to write a story that is bound to be critical?

These are legitimate questions, and perhaps they are not asked often enough. But in the end, not examining the soccer leagues out of concern that the resulting story would offend seemed the worst possible option. This was a homegrown business. There were serious issues worth exploring. Players, for one, were injured on the field, and none of these teams had insurance, though that was a requirement of at least some leagues. Yes, the story was worth doing.

But I went in conscious of the dangers, mainly because I had made mistakes before.

Can Journalists Be Allies?

My first daily newspaper job, in the mid-1980s, had landed me in West New York, N.J., a colorful and then hardscrabble town on the other side of the Lincoln Tunnel from New York City. Like neighboring Union City, West New York had a considerable Latino population.

Several fires in apartment buildings had forced the temporary evacuation of poor residents, almost all of them Latino. Hoboken, the waterfront town south of West New York, had gentrified years earlier, and the displacement of poor tenants was still fresh in the minds of many in the county. I fell into the story with little background on the issue and only several months' experience in daily journalism.

Being fluent in Spanish was a major asset. Tenants, who were unaccustomed to dealing with a reporter who spoke their language, embraced me because of the stories and the attention that ensued. I did not realize until it was too late that the people I was covering saw an ally in me. To them, I was on their side, and the bond was sealed by my ability to talk to them in Spanish. What I saw as a very effective tool employed in the act of reporting, they saw as some manifestation of cultural solidarity (even though they were Cuban and Puerto Rican and I was Colombian).

The stories were predictable enough; I covered the protests, followed the cases in court, kept the issue in the newspaper. When a group of tenants in one of the buildings was facing eviction, I was there when they decided they were going to resist, by force if necessary, an eviction planned for later that day. The leaders of the resistance sent teenagers up to the roof of the building and told them to arm themselves with rocks and eggs, presumably to rain down on the cops who would be conducting the eviction. The clash was brief but ugly, and it was all caught by the newspaper's photographer, who had been prepositioned to capture the drama. The story the next day detailed the planning on the part of the tenants, down to the deployment of the teenagers on the roof. I thought the story was complete, dramatic, and visual. The photos were especially strong. The tenants in the building saw it as betrayal. Relations never recovered.

I realized that I had failed in either maintaining a distance from the subjects I was covering or allowing a level of intimacy to develop. I had not been conscious that either of these was occurring, which is perhaps worse than knowing they were and not doing anything about them. The lesson was clear:

The ability to speak Spanish with the people I was writing about presented its own challenges. It was part of my job, paradoxically, to maintain some distance even as language brought us closer. Just as critical, however, was recognizing that cultural perceptions often trumped the ability to communicate in the language of the subjects being covered.

Cultural Assumptions

The cultural challenge is a phenomenon that many reporters and editors know little about, but it is something I have studied closely over the years, mainly through my own reporting. It crops up in unusual ways. Just days into my first trip to El Salvador, I was struck by how the women I was interviewing always responded in the affirmative, no matter the question. I finally asked a priest about this, and his answer revealed how little I knew about the people I

> The ability to speak Spanish with the people I was writing about presented its own challenges. It was part of my job, paradoxically, to maintain some distance even as language brought us closer.

was interviewing and how much I had presumed about them. He said that the poor, particularly the women, looked at me and saw not someone who spoke to them in their language but someone who looked and spoke like a landowner. The very language skills I thought were instrumental in breaking down barriers were, in fact, creating them. And, worse yet, I was unaware of what was happening. I have thought about this incident often. One lesson, of course, is that reporters who do not have the language skills will not face this obstacle. They will face many others, to be sure, but the presumptions and assumptions made by the women in El Salvador will not apply.

Since that encounter, I have been conscious of how this cultural factor can influence reporting, in other subtle but equally important ways. Someone who does not understand the language, and perhaps works through a translator, will be presumed to know nothing about anything in the lives of his subjects. The reporter who does speak the language sometimes suffers from the opposite: an assumption on the part of those being interviewed that he or she knows far more, simply because of the cultural connection.

The soccer story, challenging as it was, represented the best chance to use all that I had learned in covering immigrant communities, particularly Latinos who were relatively recent arrivals. Unlike many other stories, where the reporting evolves as you go along, this allowed some level of planning. I was not under a tight deadline. And I had all those lessons learned.

Soccer, I discovered, defined certain people. If you arrived in Washington in the 1980s, when the first great wave settled, you were likely a man, likely alone, and likely with little to do but work in the construction boom of the time. The one exception was soccer. The name of the enterprising person has been lost to history (or there is some dispute as to who it was), but sometime in the early 1980s, one of these men started a league and laid claim to a field in the Washington neighborhoods where Latinos had settled. The first wave of migration was followed by a second one that moved from Washington to the suburbs of Northern Virginia. The soccer scene was fractured, and Washington lost its stature as the Northern Virginians grew at a greater pace.

There were plenty of historians around, men who had run teams or leagues and remembered how migration continued to feed talent to the teams. They were easy to find. Sportswriters for the Spanish-language weeklies identified them, and the newspaper listings said when and where their teams were playing. These were the first critical sources. They were still in the game, as it were, but by the mid- to late 1990s they had been replaced by more aggressive impresarios. The dream had always been to organize some regional league, to impose order on the general chaos that defined these games, and, most important, to organize a competition that would crown a winner every year.

By luck, my timing was excellent. Just a few years earlier, one man had managed to succeed where others had failed. He had convinced several major advertisers, including Budweiser and a Central American airline, to sponsor an annual cup. Those left out, including several of the pioneers in the area soccer scene, were happy to share what they knew.

Clear Guidelines

I set some guidelines for myself. The most important was to convey, from the onset, that I was from *The Washington Post* and that the newspaper was doing a serious story about how the leagues, and this annual competition, worked. This sounds arrogant and obnoxious. But I decided that I could not afford to have the people I was interviewing assume anything else. My interviews tended to be formal, in the sense that I made appointments, visited subjects in their offices, and always wore a coat and a tie. I often treated conversations on soccer fields as just that, informal exchanges that would be followed by more formal appointments. I asked for records, I spoke to players, and quickly word got around that *The Washington Post* was taking on the leagues.

The leagues had intrigue, but they also had a level of professionalism I had not expected. Some of the major movers had experience in running leagues before they migrated. The president of the Bolivian league was especially impressive. He had made a commitment to be as open as possible with the league's operations, particularly its finances, and he noted that almost all the others were secretive groups that shared nothing with their memberships. He produced books that had been audited by a local accountant and that demonstrated, down to the penny, that these leagues made money.

The story's success hinged on getting two things: an on-the-record admission from some team owner that he paid a salary to his players and proof that the money and talent available in these leagues were drawing professional players from Central America. The first was the greater challenge, because I could see no reason why anyone would admit to paying players.

There was one owner whose team was said to be far better than all the others, in great part because he paid his players. We had been introduced once, but although I saw him on the soccer fields several times I had avoided talking to him because I did not quite know how to approach the subject. In the end, I decided to use the formal interview approach. It took some time, but he finally agreed to meet me at one of his construction sites in suburban Maryland. This was a man who had accomplished much and was proud to tell his tale (the latter being the journalistic key). But no matter how much he had managed to achieve through his business, the success on the soccer field was what crowned him in his community. We had lunch at a Chinese restaurant, and in the course of the meal he explained, meticulously, how he managed to field such a great squad year after year. Money was the root of his soccer success.

At the end of the interview, I told him that he had confirmed, for the record, what others had hinted at. And then I told him, again, that this would appear in the newspaper. Perhaps it was the confidence of the immigrant who succeeds after great hardship or perhaps it was the ego of the soccer impresario, but either way he said it did not matter if word got out that he paid his players.

There is a much longer story in this subject. I only went several levels deeper than the perennial feature story. I never explored the then-small circuit of professional soccer players from Central America who would market their talents from Long Island to Virginia, supplementing their comparatively modest soccer salaries in their home countries with $150-a-game fees in suburbia. Few leagues had insurance (though many collected fees from players), and serious injuries on the field left players unable to play and, worse, unable to work. The role of the Spanish-language radio was also worth exploring because it was a central player in the soccer scene.

The story ran and the result was . . . silence, or close to it. None of the league officials said a word. No elected official expressed interest. Some parks and recreation officials called in league presidents and warned that paying salaries to players could cost them the use of the field.

Should something have happened? These were professional leagues, unlicensed and uninsured enterprises. There were tax issues, at the very least.

Clearly the use of public fields for a private enterprise was a problem. But who would go after a pastime? What elected official would take this on as a mission? What would be gained? Did it really matter, in the end?

I set out to tell a story about a homegrown business, because this is what it was. It was a way to show how complex assimilation can be, and how strangers among us can thrive and build enterprises entirely outside of the "public" view. The other aim—and indeed the motivating force—was to put to bed that tired Sunday feature on Latinos playing soccer in suburbia.

To screen the Gabriel Escobar interview, select CULTURAL COMPETENCE on the DVD Main Menu then "The Other Pro Soccer."

DISCUSSION POINTS

- Why is learning about the history of soccer in the Washington, D.C., community so important to understanding the history of immigration in the area?
- How does reporter Gabriel Escobar use the powers of observation in providing details, like naming the type of car a person drives, to enhance the story's authority?
- Escobar's interview strategy was to follow informal conversations with formal interviews. What does that strategy teach?
- Escobar talks about the implicit trust that comes from speaking a language. Discuss the positive and negative aspects of that in his reporting career.
- Discuss story ideas that move beyond the "perpetually arriving" framework Escobar describes.
- What are the pros and cons of reporting on your own racial or ethnic group?

SUGGESTED READINGS AND WEBSITES

Books

Foer, Franklin. *How Soccer Explains the World: An Unlikely Theory of Globalization.* New York: HarperCollins, 2004.

In Europe, South America, and elsewhere, soccer is not merely a pastime but often an expression of the social, economic, political, and racial composition of the communities that host both the teams and their throngs of enthusiastic fans. How Soccer Explains the World is an eye-opening chronicle of how a beautiful sport and its fanatical followers can illuminate the fault lines of a society.

Suarez-Orozco, Marcelo M., and Mariela Paez, *Latinos: Remaking America.* Berkeley: University of California Press, 2002.

Latinos are the fastest-growing ethnic group in the United States and will constitute a quarter of the country's population by midcentury. The process of Latinization, the result of globalization and the biggest migration flow in the history of the Americas, is indeed reshaping the character of the country. This landmark book brings together some of the leading scholars now studying the social, cultural, racial, economic, and political changes wrought by the experiences, travails, and fortunes of the Latino population.

Gracia, Jorge J. E., and Pablo De Greiff. *Hispanics/Latinos in America: Ethnicity, Race and Rights.* New York: Routledge, 2000.

By the middle of the twenty-first century, Hispanics are expected to outnumber all other minority groups combined, and their values, views, and rights will play an increasingly important role in American society. But Hispanics are far from being ho-

mogeneous, differing in origin, race, language, religion, political affiliation, customs, physical appearance, economic status, education, and taste. This diversity raises important questions about their identity and their rights.

Oboler, Suzanne, and Deena Gonzalez, eds. *The Oxford Encyclopedia of Latinos and Latinas in the United States.* 4th ed. Oxford: Oxford University Press, 2005.

The encyclopedia draws together the diverse historical and contemporary experiences in the United States of Latinos and Latinas from Mexico, Puerto Rico, Cuba, the Dominican Republic, Central America, South America, Europe, Asia, and the Middle East. It contains over nine hundred articles written by academics, scholars, writers, artists, and journalists that address such broad topics as identity, art, politics, religion, education, health, and history

Websites

archive.tri-cityherald.com/newmajority/hispanics.html

This Website shows that U.S. Hispanics rank as the fifth-largest Hispanic population in the world, behind Mexico, Spain, Colombia, and Argentina.

pewhispanic.org

Demographic facts about Hispanics in the United States and national surveys of Latinos.

muse.jhu.edu/journals/hahr

The Website of the Hispanic American Historical Review.

www.nahj.org/home/home.shtml

The Website of the National Association of Hispanic Journalists.

CONTRIBUTORS

These biographies provide a brief snapshot of the careers of the *Let's Do It Better!* award winners who participated by deconstructing their work in the text essays and during the interviews on the accompanying DVD.

CHAPTER ONE: *TUG OF WAR*

Allie Shah is a reporter at the *Star Tribune,* Minnesota's largest newspaper. Before joining the *Star Tribune* in 1997, she worked as a correspondent for *The Philadelphia Inquirer* and as an intern for *The Chicago Tribune*. Shah and photographer Rita Reed won the Minnesota Society of Professional Journalists award for best feature writing and the South Asian Journalists Association prize for best newspaper story by a South Asian journalist for "Tug of War". Shah has been a visiting faculty member at the University of Iowa's School of Journalism and at the Poynter Institute for Media Studies. The daughter of Pakistani immigrants, Shah grew up in Des Moines, Iowa.

CHAPTER TWO: *ABOUT RACE* SERIES

Craig Franklin is a three-time winner of the prestigious George Foster Peabody Award for excellence in television news, once for the 1999 *About Race* series, which also won the first three of Columbia University's *Let's Do It Better!* awards. Franklin was honored with the workshop's first Television Career Achievement Award in 2002 and has written a number of essays for the program about the need for improved news content on race. Now a producer at CBS5 in San Francisco, Franklin is a frequent speaker at universities and professional conferences on his KRON-TV experiences.

Karyne Holmes, an Emmy-winning editor at KRON-TV in San Francisco, was the principal editor on the *About Race* project. She shared in the station's George Foster Peabody Award for Best Documentary, the national Pew Center Batten Prize for civic journalism, the Northern California Radio-Television News Directors Association Award, and the Northern California Society of Professional Journalists Award for In-Depth Reporting. Before the series, Holmes won several Emmy awards, including one for coproducing and editing the documentary *How We Played the Game,* which portrays four heroes of the Negro Baseball Leagues: Jackie Robinson, Hank Aaron, Buck O'Neil, and Rube Foster.

Pam Moore is an anchor at *KRON 4 News* in San Francisco. From 1994 to 1997, she served as host of *Health Matters,* a half-hour health awareness program. Moore's work on the *About Race* series garnered a number of awards, including a prestigious George Foster Peabody Award, the Pew Center Batten Prize for Civic Journalism, an In-Depth Reporting Award from the Northern California Chapter of the Society of Professional Journalists, top honors from the Black Filmmakers Hall of Fame and Best Documentary Award from the California Associated Press Television Radio Association. Moore received the Associated Press Television-Radio Association award for Best Investigative Reporting in 2001 for *Mercury Rising.*

Pete Wilson is an anchor of *ABC7 News at 6* in San Francisco. Wilson, who joined *ABC7* News in January 2002, has been a top-rated anchorman in the Bay Area for twenty-three years and a major market anchor and radio talk show host for over thirty years. He and Pam Moore reported and anchored much of the *About Race* series. Wilson began his broadcast career doing news on a tiny country-western station in Milwaukee, Wisconsin, while he attended graduate school. He has won numerous honors, including Associated Press awards and a half-dozen Emmys and has shared two coveted Peabody awards, including the one for *About Race*. He won his first Peabody for best breaking news coverage, working for *ABC7* during the Loma Prieta earthquake coverage in 1989.

CHAPTER THREE: *BEST OF FRIENDS, WORLDS APART*

Mirta Ojito, an author and freelance journalist, teaches immigration reporting at the Columbia University Graduate School of Journalism, where she was the outstanding Mid-Career Program graduate in 2001. She left *The New York Times* in 2002 to write her widely acclaimed memoir *Finding Mañana: A Memoir of a Cuban Exodus,* the story of her journey from Cuba to Miami during the Mariel boat lift. "Best of Friends, Worlds Apart," which defines the racial and economic landscape of Miami through the friendship of two Cuban immigrants, was part of the *Times*'s 2001 Pulitzer Prize–winning series *How Race Is Lived in America.*

CHAPTER FOUR: *THE FAMILY SECRET*

Alice Irene Pifer is director of professional education at Columbia University's Graduate School of Journalism as well as an adjunct professor. Before joining the school in 2003, Pifer was a producer at ABC News for twenty years with the newsmagazine *20/20*. She began her career at CBS News and has won numerous awards, among them two Emmys, for her reporting on a wide range of topics including race, health, science, human rights, and social issues. Her 2000 story "The Family Secret" was honored by the National Association of Black Journalists. Pifer has been a visiting faculty member at The Poynter Institute's "Writing about Race" workshop and was a Nieman Fellow at Harvard University in 1995–96.

Lynn Sherr is an award-winning correspondent with ABC News. Since 1977, Sherr has covered a wide range of stories, specializing in women's issues and social change, as well as the space program. She is a graduate of Wellesley College, where she serves as a trustee and was honored with the Alumnae Achievement Award for her distinguished career. She is the author of *Failure Is Impossible: Susan B. Anthony in Her Own Words* and coauthor of *Susan B. Anthony Slept Here: A Guide to American Women's Landmarks,* and ten editions of The Women's Calendar. Her most recent book, *Tall Blondes,* offered a perceptive and highly praised look at one of wildlife's most endearing but little-understood animals: giraffes.

CHAPTER FIVE: *THE COLOR LINE AND THE BUS LINE*

Ted Koppel served as ABC's *Nightline* anchor since the broadcast was introduced in March 1980. Until he stepped down in November 2005, Koppel served as the show's managing editor and principal on-air reporter and interviewer. During a distinguished thirty-seven-year career, Koppel earned thirty-seven Emmy Awards, six George Foster Peabody Awards, ten duPont-Columbia Awards, including the first Gold Baton Award in 1985 for a weeklong series originating from South Africa, nine Overseas Press Club Awards, two George Polk Awards, and two Sigma Delta Chi Awards. Koppel also was recognized with the first Goldsmith Lifetime Achievement Award for Excellence in Journalism by the Joan Shorenstein Barone Center on the Press, Politics and Public Policy at Harvard University; the Fred Friendly First Amendment Award from Quinnipiac College; and the Gabriel Personal Achievement Award from the National Catholic Association of Broadcasters and Communicators. *Nightline* was recognized in 2002 with a Peabody Award for Broadcast Journalism, citing over twenty years of excellence in long-form news presentations. Koppel is an inductee in the Broadcast Hall of Fame. He joined the Discovery Channel as managing editor in January 2006.

Eric Wray is an award-winning editor/producer at *Nightline,* where he has worked almost since its inception in 1980. He grew up in Queens, New York, graduating in 1975 with a degree in communications and mass media from the City College of New York. In 1977, he joined the television and radio staffs of WXKG in Binghamton, New York, and two years later he was working at WJLA, an ABC affiliate in Washington. He joined the ABC network in early 1980. Wray initiated the "The Color Line and the Bus Line" story, which became the linchpin for the first week of stories of the broadcast's acclaimed *America in Black and White* series. Among Wray's many honors are two Emmys, three Emmy nominations, and the 1985 NAACP Image Award for his work on a weeklong series in South Africa; he also shared in the first duPont Gold Baton award for excellence in television journalism in 1985.

Tom Bettag served as the senior executive producer of *Nightline* and, since July 2002, as senior executive producer of *This Week with George Stephanopoulos.* Bettag, who joined ABC in May 1991, helped *Nightline* develop into television's premier source for in-depth news, investigative journalism, and on-air interviews. He left ABC News in November 2005 and will work with Ted Koppel at the Discovery Channel. Before starting at ABC, Bettag spent twenty-two years at CBS News, where his achievements included overseeing *The CBS Evening News with Dan Rather* as executive producer. A graduate of the Columbia University Graduate School of Journalism, Bettag was a Fulbright Scholar in 1977 and is the recipient of six Alfred I. duPont–Columbia University Silver Batons, three Overseas Press Club Awards, and fifteen Emmys.

CHAPTER SIX: *BROKEN TRUST*

Jodi Rave is a national reporter and columnist who covers Native American issues for fifty-eight newspapers in twenty-two states for Lee Enterprises newspapers. Rave started working out of the *Missoulian* newspaper in Missoula, Montana, after completing a 2004 Nieman fellowship at Harvard University. She won the 2002 Thomas C. Sorensen Award for distinguished Nebraska journalism for the *Broken Trust* series, written when she was assigned to Lee's *Lincoln Journal Star* in Nebraska. Rave is a member of the visiting faculty at The Poynter Institute, where she writes a monthly column as part of Poynter's "Journalism with a Difference" feature for www.poynter.org.

CHAPTER SEVEN: *ASIAN-AMERICAN*

John Donvan has worked for more than two decades as a *Nightline* correspondent, chief White House reporter, chief Moscow correspondent, Amman bureau chief, and reporter in Jerusalem. Donvan, who has been acclaimed by the *Chicago Sun Times* as one of "ten war stars" for his reporting from Iraq, began his career with ABC Radio in 1980. He moved to television news two years later as a reporter covering the West Bank and the rest of the Arab world. He joined CNN's London bureau in 1985, reporting on Europe, the Middle East, and Africa. Donvan rejoined ABC in 1988, covering a variety of assignments before moving to *Nightline* in 1998. He has won two Emmy Awards, several Overseas Press Club Awards, and two Cine Golden Eagle awards. He has been honored by the National Association of Black Journalists, the Committee of 100, and the Media Action Network for Asian-Americans.

CHAPTER EIGHT: *TORN FROM THE LAND*

Dolores Barclay is the arts editor of the Associated Press. She joined AP in 1971 as a reporter, covering city hall, federal and criminal courts, and the police beat for the New York bureau. As a national writer, she was part of AP's special Caribbean team assembled to cover the U.S. invasion of Grenada. She became the arts and entertainment editor in 1984. When the arts and entertainment coverage was split into two beats in 1999, Barclay became arts editor and began to build AP's coverage of art, architecture, and design. She took a leave from editing to work on *Torn from the Land,* which was awarded the Aronson Prize for Social Justice Journalism, the APME Enterprise Award, and the Griot Award of the New York Association of Black Journalists. Barclay is the author or coauthor of five books, including *A Girl Needs Cash,* an investment guide for women, published in 1998.

Todd Lewan has been a correspondent with the Associated Press since 1988 and worked as an editor on AP's international desk and as a national features writer. He is the author of *The Last Run: A True Story of Rescue and Redemption of the Alaska Seas.* In 2001, he shared the Aronson Prize for Social Justice Journalism, the APME Enterprise Award, and the Griot Award of the New York Association of Black Journalists for the *Torn from the Land* series with Dolores Barclay and Allen G. Breed.

Bruce DeSilva is the writing coach for the Associated Press, responsible for training AP staff worldwide. Previously, he directed the AP's News/Features Department, which specializes in national enterprise reporting including investigations, explanatory journalism, and narrative storytelling. He also worked as an editor and writer at the *Hartford Courant* and the *Providence Journal.* Stories edited by DeSilva have won numerous national awards including the Ernie Pyle, James Aronson, Unity, National Headliners, and American Society of Newspaper Editors awards, two Polk Awards, two Livingston Awards, and the Batten Medal. He has worked as a consultant on writing and editing at more than forty newspapers, and he is a frequent speaker at professional conferences.

CHAPTER NINE: *RIM OF THE NEW WORLD*

Anne Hull is a four-time Pulitzer Prize finalist and a two-time winner of the prestigious American Society of Newspaper Editors Distinguished Writing Award, including her 2002 award for Outstanding Writing on Diversity. Hull began her career at the *St. Petersburg Times* in Florida. She was a Nieman Fellow in 1995 at Harvard University and joined *The Washington Post* in 2000. Hull's newspaper stories have been anthologized in ASNE's Best Newspaper Writing in 1994, 2000, 2001, and 2002 and are included in college journalism curricula and textbooks. She attended Florida State University.

CHAPTER TEN: *THE DEATH OF LCPL GUTIERREZ*

Steve Glauber is an award-winning producer who started his career with CBS in 1978, working as a senior producer on *The Evening News with Dan Rather* and then on *48 Hours,* the newsmagazine. Born in 1938 in Czechoslovakia, Glauber immigrated to the United States with his parents and grew up in Queens, New York. A graduate of the University of Wisconsin and Harvard Law School, Glauber was in private practice and then became general counsel to the National

Educational Television organization. He started his career as a producer with WNET/Channel 13 in New York. He has produced more than one hundred stories for *60 Minutes* and several one-hour documentaries.

Bob Simon, CBS correspondent, has reported for *60 Minutes,* one of the highest-rated television news programs in history, since 1996. Simon was named CBS Middle Eastern bureau chief in 1987 and since has earned respect as one of the premier broadcast journalists in that part of the world. He was captured by Iraqi forces near the Saudi-Kuwaiti border during the opening days of the Gulf War in January 1991 and spent forty days in Iraqi prisons with the three other members of the CBS News team. Simon wrote about his experience in his book *Forty Days.* Two months after his release, he returned to Iraq to do an hourlong documentary, *Bob Simon: Back to Baghdad,* and he went back again in January 1993 to cover the American bombing of Iraq. Simon has twice won the Overseas Press Club Award, and in 1996 he received the George Foster Peabody Award. He has been honored with numerous Emmys for his international reporting.

CHAPTER ELEVEN: *DIVERSE AND DIVIDED & A TALE OF TWO CULTURES*

Elizabeth Llorente is a senior writer at *The Record of Bergen County,* where for the past eleven years she has specialized in covering immigration and ethnic communities. During that time, Llorente has gained national recognition for her coverage, which includes stories on the abuse of immigrants in federal detention centers and an investigation of a driver's license black market in New Jersey that preyed heavily on immigrants. Llorente has won multiple citations for her work, including the George Polk Award and the Deadline Club Award. She is a two-time winner in the *Let's Do It Better!* program, including the 2004 Outstanding Career Achievement award for her leadership in the field. Her work on Palisades Park was the basis for an ABC *Nightline* feature in which she appeared.

CHAPTER TWELVE: *THE RAPE OF NANKING*

Emerald Yeh is a veteran television journalist in the San Francisco Bay area who has made herself a student of the cultural nuances of that city. A former consumer reporter for KRON-TV—she left in 2002 to become a freelancer—Yeh is a winner of nine Emmys for stories she produced over her twenty-two-year career. Before moving to San Francisco in 1984 to become a weekend anchor and reporter, Yeh worked in Honolulu, Portland, Oregon, and, with CNN, in Atlanta. Most recently she has worked on a documentary dealing with children of alcoholics and developed a companion Website, www.lostchildhood.org.

CHAPTER THIRTEEN: *THE OTHER PRO SOCCER*

Gabriel Escobar is a nationally recognized writer, reporter, and former editor at *The Washington Post.* He started his professional career with the weekly *Queens Tri-*

bune. From there, he headed west but only got as far as the *Dispatch* in Union City, New Jersey. He eventually went to the *Hartford Courant,* where he worked for fifteen months covering the suburbs before moving to the tabloid life of *The Philadelphia Daily News,* where he spent two years. He made the leap to *The Washington Post* in 1990, where he covered police affairs and the local immigrant community; he also did a tour as the paper's bureau chief in South America. Upon his return, he worked on the paper's regional projects team and then joined the national desk, covering immigration. He was named city editor in September 1999. Born in Bogotá, Colombia, Escobar toyed with studying architecture until he realized it involved math. Before entering journalism, he spent ten years at the New York Public Library's main branch on Fifth Avenue, where he learned patience and fortitude. He joined the Pew Hispanic Center as associate director in January 2006.

ABOUT THE EDITORS

Arlene Nortoro Morgan is the associate dean of prizes and programs at the Columbia University Graduate School of Journalism, where she also directs the annual *Let's Do It Better!* Workshop on Journalism, Race, and Ethnicity.

Morgan joined the Columbia staff in August 2000 after a 31-year career at *The Philadelphia Inquirer,* where she served as an assistant managing editor for readership, hiring, and staff development. In addition to her work on issues related to covering and hiring for diversity, Morgan developed an expertise in newspaper credibility when she served as *The Inquirer*'s liaison to the American Society of Newspaper Editors' three-year credibility project. She also is the founding director of the Punch Sulzberger News Management Leadership program, a media management program established in 2005 through a $4 million gift from the Sulzberger sisters to honor their brother, who led *The New York Times* through significant changes during his tenure as publisher.

In 1995, Morgan was honored with the first Knight Ridder Excellence in Diversity Award for her work to diversify *The Inquirer*'s staff and for her leadership in fostering a diverse content and workforce throughout Knight Ridder newspapers, then the corporate owner of *The Inquirer.* A graduate of Temple University in Philadelphia, she was a Fellow in 1996–97 at the Freedom Forum's Media Studies Center, where she started work on the concept for the race workshop and for the textbook project.

Alice Irene Pifer. See page 336 (for Chapter Four: *The Family Secret*).

Keith Woods is Dean of the Faculty at The Poynter Institute, a school for jounalists in St. Petersburg, Florida. He spent sixteen years at the *New Orleans Times-Picayune* as a sportswriter, news reporter, city editor, editorial writer, and columnist. His professional writing won statewide and national awards, including the 1994 National Headliner award he shared with colleagues for the 1993 series

"Together Apart / The Myth of Race." He has served as a committee chair for two Pulitzer Prize juries.

He joined Poynter in 1995 and for seven years led the Institute's teaching on diversity and coverage of race relations as part of the ethics faculty. He is a former editor of *Best Newspaper Writing*, the annual collection of prize-winning stories and photojournalism selected by the American Society of Newspaper Editors. He is the author of four reports for the McCormick Tribune Foundation on diversity issues confronting news executives of color. He has written extensively about how news organizations handle race relations and diversity in the newsroom, boardrooms, newspapers, and broadcasts.

CREDITS

STAFF

Book designers: Brian DiRenzi, Stephanie Gray, and Arlene Notoro Morgan
Book photographers: Stephanie Gray, Yann Nicolas, and Lisa Nipp
Copy editors: Jody Calendar, Barbara Fasciani, and Sarah St. Onge
DVD author: Stuart Math
DVD executive producers: Arlene Notoro Morgan, Alice Irene Pifer, and Keith Woods
DVD producer and writer: Alice Irene Pifer
DVD graphic designer: Ted Glass
Production assistants: Savannah Ashour, David Barillari, Mary Kay Duffy, Stephanie Gray, Philip Herrick, Francisca Hu, Kate Pickert, Laura Reizman, Lisa Smith, and Paul Soto
Project editors: The late John Michel, Juree Sondker, and Ann Young, Columbia University Press
Researchers: Race and Media Forum, The Manship School of Communications, Louisiana State University; Ralph Izard, former associate dean, The Manship School; and Christopher Crafton, Crafton Associates
Teacher's guide authors: Lillian Dunlap and Keith Woods
Videotape editors: David Coffin and Stuart Math
Website designer: Rebecca Leung

FINANCIAL SUPPORT

Financial grants: The Ford Foundation, the W. K. Kellogg Foundation, and the McCormick-Tribune Foundation
In-kind contributions: The Columbia University Graduate School of Journalism, ABC News, CBS News, KRON-TV, NY-1 News, *Lincoln Journal Star*, *Star Tribune*, Minneapolis, and WFLA-TV

NEWS ORGANIZATION SUPPORTERS

ABC News: Tom Bettag, former executive producer, *Nightline*; Tony Brackett, director of rights, clearances, and permissions; Kerry Smith, senior vice president, editorial quality; David Sloan, executive producer, *20/20*; and Emily Stanitz, assistant to Ted Koppel

CBS News: Marcy McGinnis, former senior vice president, hard news; Linda Mason, senior vice president, standards and special projects; and Nathalie Sommer, broadcast associate, *60 Minutes*

KRON-TV, San Francisco: Dan Rosenheim and Stacy Owen, former news directors

NY1 News: Gina Caruso, production manager, and Steve Paulus, senior vice president and general manager

WFLA-TV, Tampa: Forrest Carr, former news director, and Rick McEwen, operations manager

Associated Press: Kathleen Carroll, executive editor; Santos Chaparro, director of events services; and Jack Stokes, director of media relations

Lincoln Journal Star: Kathleen Rutledge, editor

The New York Times: Allan M. Siegal, assistant managing editor

The Record of Bergen County, New Jersey: Frank Scandale, editor

Star Tribune, Minneapolis: Anders Gyllenhaal, editor

The Washington Post: Milton Coleman, deputy managing editor, and Kim Kingsley, assistant director of television and radio projects

EMOTIONAL AND INTELLECTUAL SUPPORT

Erin Biddle Sirop, producer; Callie Crossley, former producer; Alan Esner, editor; Lynn Redmond, producer; Karen Saunders, former producer; Joe Schanzer, editor; and Meredith White, former senior producer, ABC News, *20/20*

Jonnet Abeles, director of the Alfred I. duPont Awards for Broadcast Journalism; Thomas Goldstein, former dean; and David Klatell, vice dean, Columbia University Graduate School of Journalism. Herbert Gans, professor of sociology, Columbia University

Robert Giles and Nancy Hicks Maynard, former directors of the Media Studies Center, The Freedom Forum; and Charles L. Overby, chief executive officer and president, The Freedom Forum

Eugene Roberts, Maxwell King, and Robert J. Rosenthal, former editors, *The Philadelphia Inquirer*

Fanua Borodicz, assistant to the dean; Aly Colón, writing and editing group leader; Karen Dunlap, president; Kenny Irby, visual journalism group leader, The Poynter Institute

Victor Merina, the Institute for Justice and Journalism, University of Southern California, Los Angeles; Carolyn Mungo, managing editor, KRIV-TV, Houston; Philip Martin, editor, and Walterine Swanston, director of diversity, National Public Radio; Patricia Ryan, senior editor, the *St. Petersburg Times*; Sharon Rosenhause, managing editor, the *South Florida Sun-Sentinel*; Ruth Seymour, lecturer, Wayne State University; and Barry Yeoman, freelance writer

SPECIAL RECOGNITION

Jon Funabiki, deputy director, media, arts, & culture, Ford Foundation, for believing in this project

Sig Gissler, founder of the *Let's Do It Better!* Workshop on Journalism, Race, and Ethnicity, and administrator of the Pulitzer Prize

Nicholas Lemann, dean, Columbia University Graduate School of Journalism

C. Patrick Babcock, vice president for programs, health, and Michael P. VanBuren, communication manager, W. K. Kellogg Foundation

Vivian Vahlberg, former director of journalism programs, the McCormick-Tribune Foundation

David Yarnold, former editor, the *Mercury News* in San Jose, California

INDEX

Page numbers for illustrations are in *italic*.

Todd, Neil, 87
Tong, Nancy, 308
"Torn from the Land" (series), 187–96; Alabama investigation of land theft, 197; follow-ups to, 208; interviews for, 205–206; land recovery as outcome of story, 198–99; making of, 201–208; overview, 186; reparations implications in, 208; research for, 201–205
Torres, Juan, 264
Trade and Intercourse Act of 1790, 135, 157
translators: hiring, 248; use of, 227–28
transportation, public: unequal services as racism, 106, 107–108, 111–17
Tribal Land Enterprise program (Sioux), 138
trust: creating in sources, 82, 93–95
"Tug of War" (Shah), 5–15; making of, 17–22; overview, 4
20/20 (TV program): "The Family Secret," 83–100

Umatilla Tribes: land consolidation by, 138
U.S. Department of Interior: as Indian trust fund manager, 134–35. *See also Cobell v. Norton*
Uyeda, Clifford, 300–301, 306

Valdés, Achmed, 53–69, *67*; attitude toward black Cubans, 63–65; friendship with Ruiz, 53–56, *54*, 66–69; Ojito interviews with, 73–74, 76; as white Cuban American, 53, 54, 59–61, *60, 63*
Vassar College: Anita Hemmings as first African American graduate of, 84–85

victimization: African American, 269–71
Villaroman, Rick, 33, *34*, 35–36, 39

Wabnum, Thomas, 157
Walker, David: theft of land of, 189
Waters, Artis, 120
Weathersby, Norman, 189, 190
Welsh, Susan, 96, 99
"What Is Race?" (transcript), 27–32
White, Meredith, 95, 99
Wiggins, Cynthia, *108*; aftermath of death, 117; death in traffic accident as racism, 107–110, 114–15; as teenage mother, 110
Williams, Alicia, 265–66
Williams, Lemon: theft of land of, 189–90, 198–99
Williams, Willie, 198–99, *199*
Wilson, Pete, 26, 27, 33–39, *34*, 47
Winnebago Reservation: fractionated lands on, 136
Wolman, Jon, 207, 208
Wong, Helen, 297–301, *300, 309*
Woo, Charlie, 169
Woods, Keith, 71–77, *243*
World War II: Japanese American internment, 164, 165, 177, 305; Japanese Army atrocities toward Chinese, 297–302, *298*
Wray, Eric, 106, *121*; on making of "The Color Line and the Bus Line," 119–25; on Rashomon reporting, 126

Yeh, Emerald, 296–309, *308*; on making of "The Rape of Nanking," 303–309
Young, Alice, *166*, 167–68

Zia, Hoyt, 170–71, *171*

THIS DVD CONTAINS:

- The **Seven Television Stories** discussed in the book
- **Fourteen Interviews** with the print and broadcast journalists featured in the book
- **Three Discussion Points** for each interview, with links to relevant portions of the interviews
- **Topic Index:** This index cross-references the interviews according to twenty-six categories such as "ethics," "language choices," and "describing people by race and ethnicity" and gives you quick access to dozens of important interview excerpts organized by topic.
- **Journalist Index:** This index is organized according to the people interviewed and contains a listing of each journalist's most relevant comments. (*Note:* Some of the entries within the individual categories may be redundant. This is because the entries are listed in the Topic Index under various headings.)

On the Main Menu, click on one of four sections (IDENTITY, EQUALITY, UNTOLD STORIES, CULTURAL COMPETENCE) to navigate to the track you want to screen.

PART I: IDENTITY

- "Tug of War," *Star Tribune,* Minneapolis: Interview with Allie Shah
- *About Race* Series, KRON-TV: Stories and interviews with Craig Franklin, Karyne Holmes, Pam Moore, and Pete Wilson (two interviews)
- "Best of Friends, Worlds Apart," *The New York Times:* Interview with Mirta Ojito
- "The Family Secret," Story and interview with Alice Irene Pifer and Lynn Sherr

PART II: EQUALITY

- "The Color Line and the Bus Line," ABC News, *Nightline*: Story and interview with Ted Koppel and Eric Wray
- "Broken Trust," Lee Enterprises Newspapers: Interview with Jodi Rave
- "Asian-American," ABC News, *Nightline*: Story and interview with John Donvan

PART III: UNTOLD STORIES

- "Torn from the Land," Associated Press: Interview with Dolores Barclay, Bruce DeSilva, and Todd Lewan
- "Rim of the New World," *The Washington Post:* Interview with Anne Hull
- "The Death of LCpl Gutierrez," CBS News, *60 Minutes II*: Story and interview with Steve Glauber and Bob Simon

PART IV CULTURAL COMPETENCE

- "Diverse and Divided" and "A Tale of Two Cultures," *The Record* of Bergen County, N.J.: Interview with Elizabeth Llorente
- "The Rape of Nanking," KRON-TV: Story and interview with Emerald Yeh
- "The Other Pro Soccer," *The Washington Post:* Interview with Gabriel Escobar